Government Contracting

"This handbook offers much needed guidance for hard pressed practitioners and students of public management alike on the complex choices and managerial challenges posed by the growing governmental reliance on private contractors. The chapters provide clearly written and incisive observations and conclusions on some of the most important and vexing issues that managers and the public face in determining whether to contract and how to ensure that private implementers are accountable for public values and objectives. A book like this should be required reading in public administration courses."

Paul L. Posner, *George Mason University, USA*

Government contracting is one of the most important issues facing federal, state, and local governments. As governments contend with lower tax revenues and a growing belief that smaller government is better government, contracting has become a fundamental means of providing goods and services to citizens. This volume, which is geared toward practitioners as well as students, addresses the broad range of issues that comprise government contracting—from the political, economic philosophy, and value of contracting—to the future of government contracting.

Throughout the volume academic theory provides a foundation to address practical subjects, including the contract process, monitoring and evaluating contracts, ethics, and both federal and state local government contracting. Contributors to this volume are both academicians and practitioners, who together offer their scholarly expertise and practical experience, encouraging readers to ask the very question "What is the role of government in American society?" Through this approach, students will acquire the knowledge needed to understand the various aspects of government contracting, and practitioners will enhance their public procurement skills. *Government Contracting* is ideally suited to MPA students, practitioners in the public sector, and to elected officials looking to enhance their understanding of privatization and contracting in a complex political and economic environment, and to provide public services more effectively.

Robert A. Shick is a Visiting Scholar at Rutgers–Newark School of Public Affairs and Administration (SPAA), and was formerly on the faculty of SPAA and Long Island University. He has extensive experience as a senior administrator in New York City government in contracting-out of government services. Dr. Shick's research is in contracting-out and nonprofit management. He serves on the Editorial Boards of the *Journal for Health and Human Services Administration* and the *Journal of Administrative Services*.

MARC HOLZER, SERIES EDITOR

MUNICIPAL SHARED SERVICES
A Public Solutions Handbook
Alexander C. Henderson, Editor

E-GOVERNMENT AND WEBSITES
A Public Solutions Handbook
Aroon Manoharan, Editor

MANAGING THE NEXT GENERATION OF PUBLIC WORKERS
A Public Solutions Handbook
Madinah F. Hamidullah

PARTNERSHIP GOVERNANCE IN PUBLIC MANAGEMENT
A Public Solutions Handbook
Seth A. Grossman and Marc Holzer

INNOVATIONS IN THE PUBLIC AND NONPROFIT SECTORS
A Public Solutions Handbook
Patria de Lancer Julnes and Ed Gibson, Editors

GOVERNMENT CONTRACTING
A Public Solutions Handbook
Robert A. Shick, Editor

Government Contracting

A PUBLIC SOLUTIONS HANDBOOK

Edited by
Robert A. Shick

NEW YORK AND LONDON

First published 2016
by Routledge
711 Third Avenue, New York, NY 10017

and by Routledge
2 Park Square, Milton Park, Abingdon, Oxon OX14 4RN

Routledge is an imprint of the Taylor & Francis Group, an informa business

© 2016 Taylor & Francis

The right of the editor to be identified as the author of the editorial material, and of the authors for their individual chapters, has been asserted in accordance with sections 77 and 78 of the Copyright, Designs and Patents Act 1988.

All rights reserved. No part of this book may be reprinted or reproduced or utilised in any form or by any electronic, mechanical, or other means, now known or hereafter invented, including photocopying and recording, or in any information storage or retrieval system, without permission in writing from the publishers.

Trademark notice: Product or corporate names may be trademarks or registered trademarks, and are used only for identification and explanation without intent to infringe.

Library of Congress Cataloging in Publication Data
Names: Shick, Robert A.
Title: Government contracting : a public solutions handbook / edited by Robert A. Shick.
Description: New York : Routledge, 2015. | Series: The public solutions handbook series; 6 | Includes bibliographical references and index.
Identifiers: LCCN 2015027172| ISBN 9781138921450 (hardback : alk. paper) | ISBN 9780765642738 (pbk. : alk. paper) | ISBN 9781315686370 (ebook)
Subjects: LCSH: Public contracts—United States. | Letting of contracts—United States. | Contracting out—United States. | Government purchasing—United States.
Classification: LCC HD3861.U6 G6787 2015 | DDC 352.5/30973—dc23
LC record available at http://lccn.loc.gov/2015027172

ISBN: 978-1-138-92145-0 (hbk)
ISBN: 978-0-765-64273-8 (pbk)
ISBN: 978-1-315-68637-0 (ebk)

Typeset in Times New Roman
by Swales & Willis Ltd, Exeter, Devon, UK

Contents

List of Figures — vii
List of Tables — viii
List of Contributors — ix
Series Editor's Introduction, *Marc Holzer* — xiv
Introduction, *Robert A. Shick* — xv

Part I   Government Contracting Theory

1. Political and Economic Philosophy and the Value of Contracting — 3
   Lynne A. Weikart

2. The Contracting Decision — 17
   Olga Victorovna Smirnova and Suzanne Leland

3. The Contracting Process — 38
   William Sims Curry

Part II   Issues in Government Contracting

4. Performance-Based Contracting — 61
   Lawrence L. Martin

5. Contracting with Nonprofit Organizations — 75
   Christopher R. Prentice and Jeffrey L. Brudney

6. Public Private Partnerships: Implications for Public Procurement — 96
   Wendell C. Lawther

7. Monitoring and Evaluating Contracts — 116
   Clifford McCue and Bill Davison

Part III Government Contracting: Ethics, Management and Governance

8. Governance and Contracting 137
   Julia L. Carboni

9. Ethics in Contracting 148
   William Sims Curry

10. Impact of Contracting on Managing Government Organizations 175
    Stephen B. Gordon

11. Contracting in State and Local Governments 203
    Donna T. Ginter

12. Implications for the Future of Government Contracting 226
    Robert A. Shick

About the Editor and Contributors 237
Index 242

Figures

2.1	Initial Production—Public Entity	22
2.2	Initial Production—Private Entity	22
2.3	Bringing Services In-House	23
2.4	Privatization	23
2.5	Competition in the Provision of Services	28
2.6	Intergovernmental Contracts Introduce Competition	29
2.7	Competition between Two Contracts	29
2.8	Monopoly Situation	30
2.9	Partial Contracting Out	30
4.1	The Systems Framework and Government Service Contract Specifications	63
4.2	PBC as a Self-Assessing System	72
10.1	Twenty Problems Created by Government Contracting	177
10.2	The Environment of Governmental Contracting	181

Tables

2.1	Selected Studies on Contracting Out Cost-Savings	26
2.2	Contracting Out Stages	31
2.3	Contracts and Information	32
2.4	Contracts and Trust	33
2.5	Make or Buy Decision and Information	34
3.1	Best Practices Recommended During Contract Planning for Federal, State, and Local Government	39
3.2	Variable Information Table	46
3.3	Underrepresented Contract Provisions	48
3.4	Contrasts between Color, Adjectival, and Numerical Rating Schema	51
3.5	Relative and Numeric Weighting of Proposal Evaluation Criteria	52
3.6	Criteria Types and Formulae	53
4.1	Major Advantages of PBC for Governments and Contractors	64
4.2	Approaches to PBC	67
4.3	The Federal Approach to PBC for Elevator Maintenance Services	68
4.4	Unit Cost/Unit Price Approaches to PBC	70
4.5	Milestone Approach to PBC for Management Consulting Services	71
5.1	Revenue Sources for Reporting Public Charities, 2010	82
5.2	Dollar Amount of Contracts and Grants	84
5.3	2012 Federal Awards to Nonprofit Organizations	85
5.4	2012 Federal Contracts to Nonprofit Organizations	86
5.5	2012 Federal Subcontracts to Nonprofit Organizations	89
6.1	Major Types of P3s	98
7.1	Elements of a Contract Monitoring Plan	118
7.2	Contract Types	120
7.3	Typical Contract Administration Problems	123
7.4	Typical Agenda for a Contract Kick-off Meeting	130
9.1	Actual Coast Guard Proposal Evaluation Results	166
9.2	Adjusted Coast Guard Proposal Evaluation Results	167

List of Contributors

Introduction

Robert A. Shick, Ph.D.
Visiting Scholar
Rutgers University—Newark
School of Pubic Affairs and Administration
111 Washington Street
Newark, NJ 07102
917-273-0663
rshick@newark.rutgers.edu

1. Political and Economic Philosophy and the Value of Contracting

Lynne A. Weikart, Ph.D.
Practitioner-in-Residence
James Madison University
Program in Public Administration
Department of Political Science
2522 Willard Drive, Charlottesville, Virginia 22903
917-494-3231
lweikart@gmail.com

2. The Contracting Decision

Olga Victorovna Smirnova, Ph.D.
Assistant Professor
East Carolina University
Department of Political Science
Brewster A-124
Greenville, NC 27858
252-328-2348
smirnovao@ecu.edu

Suzanne Leland, Ph.D.
Professor
University of North Carolina Charlotte
Ph.D. in Public Policy Program
9201 University City Boulevard
Fretwell 490M
Charlotte, NC 28223-0001
704-687-5937
smleland@uncc.edu

3. The Contract Process

William Sims Curry, MBA, CPCM, Fellow
WSC Consulting, President
17 Northwood Commons Place
Chico, CA 95973-7213
530-899-8436
BCurry@WSC-Consulting.com

4. Performance-based Contracting

Lawrence Martin, Ph.D.
Professor
University of Central Florida
Doctoral Program in Public Affairs
College of Health and Public Affairs
12805 Pegasus Drive
HPA I (Bldg. 80), room 220B
Orlando, FL 32816
407-823-5731
lawrence.martin@ucf.edu

5. Contracting with Nonprofit Organizations

Christopher Prentice, Ph.D.
Assistant Professor
University of North Carolina Wilmington
Department of Public and International Affairs
601 South College Road
Leutze Hall, Room 263
910-962-2135
prenticecr@uncw.edu

Jeffrey Brudney, Ph.D.
Betty and Dan Cameron Family Distinguished Professor of Innovation
in the Nonprofit Sector
University of North Carolina Wilmington
Department of Public and International Affairs
601 South College Road
Leutze Hall, Room 255 A
Wilmington, NC 28403
910-962-3920
brudneyj@uncw.edu

6. Public Private Partnerships: Implications for Public Procurement

Wendell Lawther, Ph.D.
Associate Professor
University of Central Florida
School of Public Administration
HPA II Room: 238L
12805 Pegasus Drive
Orlando, FL 32816
407-823-5361
wendell.lawther@ucf.edu

7. Monitoring and Evaluating Contracts

Clifford McCue, Ph.D.
Associate Professor
School of Public Administration
Florida Atlantic University
P.O. Box 450892
Sunrise, FL 33345
954-444-9321
Cmccue143@gmail.com

Bill Davison, CPPO
Director of Purchasing
Stearns County, Minnesota
705 Courthouse Square, Room 47
St. Cloud MN 56303
320-291-4069
billdavison1@gmail.com

8. Governance and Contracting

Julia L. Carboni, PhD
Assistant Professor
Indiana University School of Public and Environmental Affairs
Indiana University Lilly Family School of Philanthropy
Indiana University-Purdue University Indianapolis
801 West Michigan Street, BS 4066
Indianapolis, IN 46202
317-274-8705
jcarboni@iupui.edu

9. Ethics in Contracting

William Sims Curry, CPCM, Fellow
WSC Consulting, President
17 Northwood Commons Place
Chico, CA 95973-7213
530-899-8436
william.s.curry@gmail.com

10. Impact of Contracting on Managing Government Organizations

Stephen B. Gordon, PhD, FNIGP, CPPO
Professor of Practice
Program Director, Graduate Certificate in Public Procurement and Contract Management
Old Dominion University
Strome College of Business
School of Public Service
2084 Constant Hall on 49th Street
Norfolk, VA 23529
757-683-6049
sbgordon@odu.edu

11. Contracting in State and Local Governments

Donna Ginter, Ph.D.
C.P.M., CPPO, CPPB
Executive Director, Procurement and Travel Services
The George Washington University
45155 Research Place, Ste. 205D
Ashburn, VA 20147
571-553-4276
dginter@gwu.edu

12. Implications for the Future of Government Contracting

Robert A. Shick, Ph.D.
Visiting Scholar
Rutgers University—Newark
School of Pubic Affairs and Administration
111 Washington Street
Newark, NJ 07102
917-273-0663
rshick@newark.rutgers.edu

Series Editor's Introduction

I am proud to introduce the fifth volume in the *Public Solutions Handbook Series: Government Contracting*, edited by Robert A. Shick. This volume addresses government contracting, one of the most important issues facing federal, state, and local governments. As governments face lower tax revenues due to the downturn in the economy and an increasing philosophical and value-based belief that a smaller government is a better government, contracting has grown to become an important method of providing government services. The chapters in this volume cover the full range of issues that comprise the field of government contracting. The authors provide valuable analyses and insights into the broad conceptual and theoretical issues in economic and political theory that form the foundation for government contracting. In addition, the volume addresses application-focused subjects, such as the contract process, monitoring and evaluating contracts, and ethics. The authors of the chapters are both academicians and practitioners, who together contribute their scholarly expertise and practical experience in the field.

The authors highlight key issues that practitioners should take into account when considering contracting as the means to delivering government services, how to effectively address these issues, and the processes that will enhance the success of these efforts. For instance, the volume discusses the elements and benefits of performance contracting and when and how public/private partnerships should be employed. The chapters form the bases for students of government contracting to become grounded in the essential issues in the field, and prepare them to assume public sector positions, where there is currently a shortage of contracting professionals. Academics will benefit from seeing a detailed and discerning presentation of components of the field, and how these elements relate to one another to comprise an integrated whole. Shick's analysis reveals that successful contracting is dependent on three aspects of government contracting: the effectiveness of the decision on whether or not to contract, the management of the contract, and the monitoring and evaluation of the contract. Overall, the volume addresses the means for government contracting to achieve its intended goals of lower costs and improved quality.

Introduction

Robert A. Shick

Currently, every level of government is confronting some very difficult issues and choices. These questions include the role of government in American society, which services should government provide, and whether these services should be provided by the public or private sectors. These issues have largely been driven by the financial strains the country has faced in the last two major fiscal crises, one in 1990 and the other in 2008. This is accompanied by political and value considerations about these issues.

Government contracting, a field in public administration whose importance and impact has grown over the last thirty-five years, has been one of the major focuses of these issues. This stems from two different perspectives, views on the role of government in society and the cost of government services. The cost of government has garnered interest in the role of government and the appropriate provision of these services by the public or the private sectors. There are also value and philosophical concerns about the role of government, which drive interest in government contracting.

This volume, which is geared to practitioners as well as students, addresses the broad range of issues that comprise government contracting, from the political, economic philosophy and value of contracting to the future of government contracting. Academic theory provides the basis for the topics covered, and is used in developing the material in each of the chapters. There is also a *Key Points* section at the end of each chapter. The term "contracting" may be referred to as "procurement" in some of the chapters. The authors who have contributed to this volume are both academics and practitioners; they provide an integrated base of knowledge to understand the subject of government contracting. Through this approach, students will acquire the knowledge needed to understand the various aspects of government contracting and practitioners will enhance their competencies to perform in their positions more effectively.

Part I covers the theoretical underpinnings of government contracting and the initial steps in the contracting process.

In Chapter 1, Lynne Weikart provides a comprehensive review of the political and economic ideas that form the basis of government contracting, the history of government contracting in the United States, and the approach to contracting, including transparency, equity, human capital, accountability, and quality, which establishes the context to examine this important government function.

In Chapter 2, Olga Smirnova and Suzanne Leland move the discussion forward into the application of contracting by addressing whether government should contract-out or provide services through internal resources, including the relationship of contracting to the New Public Management movement, decision-making theories, and empirical evidence on the results of government contracting. Different costs of contracting, such as conversion costs, transaction costs, mixed provision of services, and the results of contracting efforts are also covered.

In Chapter 3, William Curry covers best practices in implementing the different steps in the contract process once the decision is made to contract-out, including: contract planning, issuance of solicitation and preparation of contractor responses, selection of the successful contractor, negotiation, contract preparation, review and clearance, contract award, contract administration, and contract closeout and audit.

Part II of the volume covers different types of contracts and contracting issues that warrant specific focus, such as performance contracting, contracting with nonprofit organizations, public/private partnerships, and monitoring and evaluating contracts.

In Chapter 4, Lawrence Martin examines performance based contracting, which has become the standard for government contracts to attain accountability from delivering services by contract. Martin provides an in-depth view of the different aspects of performance based contracting, including the design and performance specifications of performance based contracts, the advantages of performance based contracts, performance based contracts and government performance, accountability, and performance measurement, the use of performance based contracting, approaches to performance based contracting, and an assessment of the effectiveness of performance based contracting.

In Chapter 5, Christopher Prentice and Jeffrey Brudney review contracting with nonprofit organizations, which have become an important partner of government to deliver human services. Prentice and Brudney review the scope of government contracting with nonprofit organizations, characteristics of nonprofit organizations, theoretical background to government contracting with the nonprofit sector, third party government, scope of government contracting with nonprofit organizations, benefits and drawbacks to government contracting with nonprofit organizations, and the results of government contracting with nonprofit organizations.

In Chapter 6, Wendell Lawther examines a form of government contracting, public/private partnerships, a more complex arrangement than traditional contracting, which has been used extensively for infrastructure projects, but could also be employed in other areas, such as economic development. Lawther reviews the difference between public/private partnerships and contracting, the types of public/private partnerships, the public/private partnership creation process, which includes planning, the selection of a public/private partnership as the desired method to complete a project, the award steps, and the post-contract public and private award relationships.

In Chapter 7, Clifford McCue and Bill Davison cover the concepts and steps in monitoring and evaluating government contracts, an element of the contracting process in which insufficient attention and resources have been devoted. McCue and Davison provide a comprehensive process to accomplish this, comprised of developing a contract monitoring and evaluation plan to identify, document, and specify each contract deliverable, method of evaluation, timeframe, budget, and performance criteria. The plan is also designed to maintain information that is accessible and tracks deliverables, require on-going progress reports, both from the contractor and the government contract administrator, identify the level of surveillance needed to minimize problems, conduct a "kick off" or post award meeting with the contractor and establish a regular meeting schedule, and contain an internal plan to resolve performance issues, and establish a contract resolution and corrective action plan.

Part III of the volume covers a number of generic issues in contracting, governance and contracting, ethics in contracting, the impact of contracting on managing government organizations, and contracting in state and local government.

In Chapter 8, Julia Carboni examines the issues in governance and contracting in order to untangle some of the complexity associated with managing contracts for complex services. Carboni covers the government contract literature, characteristics of the contract services, characteristics of the contractors, and characteristics of the market.

In Chapter 9, William Curry reviews the issues in ethics in contracting and the resulting corruption, which has become all to commonplace. Curry covers contract corruption in U.S. history, modern day contract corruption, corruption versus incompetence, corruption during different steps in the contracting process, including procurement planning, Request for Proposals, preparation of the contract proposal, evaluation of contract proposals, misleading negotiations, contract award, contract administration, and recommendations to alleviate corruption.

In Chapter 10, Stephen Gordon covers the impact of contracting on managing government organizations. Contracting has brought new challenges to management, with new skills and approaches being required for the government sector to manage effectively. Gordon surveys the meaning and scope of public contracting, the history and environment of contracting in the public sector, and the potential for public contracting to become a strategic tool by employing a more relationship-based approach that is focused on the goals of what contracting is trying to accomplish.

In Chapter 11, Donna Ginter reviews contracting in state and local government. Contracting at the state and local level is the focus of many reform efforts and the entry point for public policy implementation in the areas of economic development, sustainability, and social responsibility. Ginter examines the history of state and local procurement, the American Bar Association Model Procurement Code for state and local governments, goals and objectives of state and local procurement, competition requirements, small dollar procurements, best practices in procurement, cooperatives and group purchasing organizations, environment in which public procurement functions, political considerations in state and local procurement, sustainability at the state and local level of procurement, role of states and local governments in creating markets, public institutions of higher education, procurement ethics in state and local government, and public procurement as a profession.

The volume concludes with Robert A. Shick's perspectives on the future of government contracting. Shick reviews the current state of government contracting and employs the contents of each of the chapters in this volume to form a view of government contracting in the future.

Contracting will continue to play an important role in the functioning of federal, state, and local governments, as will the discussion of the role of government in American society. This volume provides valuable information to better understand government contracting in a complex political and economic environment, to provide public services more effectively.

Part I

Government Contracting Theory

1

Political and Economic Philosophy and the Value of Contracting

Lynne A. Weikart

INTRODUCTION

Contracting out is extremely controversial in America. Contracting out usually involves "competition among private companies in a bidding system to perform traditional government activities, such as sanitation and highway maintenance."[1] The rationale for using another sector (private or nonprofit) to provide government goods and services is that competition will reduce costs and improve quality. It helps to understand the development of contracting out in this country because our political and economic institutions shape the process of contracting out. These institutions are comprised of the formal and informal rules of the game, and the rules have changed at critical times throughout our history.

Three major events in history helped change the rules of the contracting game. The first change began in 1776, when Americans challenged the British to think differently—that all mankind had inalienable rights. These ideas, taken from prominent political and economic theorists such as John Locke and Adam Smith, set the stage for a new kind of government: one of consent. The second change occurred with the near collapse of capitalism and the subsequent election of Franklin Delano Roosevelt (FDR) in the midst of the Great Depression with the people saying, "Do something, do anything." And FDR proceeded, with the help of the economist, John Keynes, to put into place the 20th-century federal model of a quasi-safety net for Americans. The third change started with the election of President Ronald Reagan (RR), a follower of economist Milton Friedman. Ronald Reagan argued that government was not the solution; it was the problem, and he proceeded to devolve some federal government services to the state and local level.

These historic events carried the seeds of turmoil; in each era, a transformation began that changed the relationship between citizens and their government. Contracting out is an essential part of that relationship. Although contracting out for goods and services by government officials has existed since America's inception, our views about contracting out have shifted dramatically over time, just as our economic views have changed throughout our history. This chapter examines the ideas behind contracting out and explains why Americans, throughout much of their history, have held the belief that contracting out is much more effective and efficient than government services.

POLITICAL IDEAS

America's founding fathers were students of the enlightenment. In fact, the portraits of three philosophers from the enlightenment—John Locke, Francis Bacon, and Isaac Newton—hang in Monticello, the home of revolutionary Thomas Jefferson. John Locke wrote about the social contract, the relationship between society and government in which men consented to be governed. Jefferson used Locke's theories to justify his opinion that Americans had a natural right to rebel against the British and form a new nation. Francis Bacon, the father of the scientific method, informed Jefferson's study of agriculture on his plantation. At the same time, Bacon's thesis of religious tolerance had an enormous influence on Jefferson. Jefferson used Newton's mathematical interpretation of the physical world to understand the non-physical world. Jefferson believed that scientific principles could help create an ordered, predictable, law-governed political world that followed scientific principles.

John Locke (1632–1704), in his theory of the social contract, advocated religious tolerance and man's reason and tolerance. Locke referenced a specific value system. He believed that the state of mankind's nature was good, and he argued that the social contract made between government and citizens meant that every man had a right to defend his life, health, liberty, or possessions.[2] In effect, man could learn to govern himself. And he believed that the government's duty was to protect the rights of the individual. At the same time, Locke advocated revolution if government became a tyrannical force against its citizens.

Political philosopher Thomas Hobbes (1588–1679) outlined his own contradictory view of the social contract. Hobbes theorized that humans are exclusively self-interested, that people act only their own best interests as they perceive them. Unlike Locke, Hobbes believed that human beings could be rational, that they pursued their desires as efficiently and maximally as possible. Hobbes had a set of values he applied to his writing—the state of nature was brutal and mankind could only survive through a strong monarchy.[3]

Although Hobbes had his admirers, most Americans turned to Locke's ideas during the revolution. Distrust in a powerful government and the belief in human progress were influenced by Locke. The American revolution of 1776 was about getting the British government off the backs of a people, a people who wanted to form their own small government. And it stayed small for a reason. Americans believed in laissez-faire, a product of the enlightenment, which called for freedom from government restrictions, and the form of government, which caused them to come to America.

In the 19th century, adding to the laissez-faire approach was the concept of Social Darwinism. Charles Darwin's *On the Origin of Species*, published in 1859, created the idea of "survival of the fittest" even though Darwin never used those words. Social Darwinism fit easily into Hobbes' theory of a brutal society. It did not take long for Darwin's theory to be extended so that people could rationalize their wealth. After all, if one believed in Darwin's theory of natural selection, then the strong should see their wealth and power increase while the weak should see their wealth and power decrease. People had to create their own pathways to survival. Social Darwinism fit nicely with the philosophy of Adam Smith—allowing the market to determine success and failure in the business world. In order to survive in the business world, a business leader had to defeat their competitors.

In the 20th century, a different kind of revolution took place in America. President Franklin Delano Roosevelt (1882–1945) took control of the federal government (1933–1945) in the midst of the greatest depression America had ever experienced. Roosevelt (FDR) delivered government intervention in a big way—controlling prices and hiring a large number of the unemployed to work in federal work programs. "Enlightened business is learning that competition ought not to cause bad social consequences which inevitably react upon the profits of business itself. All but the hopelessly reactionary will agree that to conserve our primary resources of manpower, government must have some control over maximum hours, minimum wages, the evil of child labor and the exploitation of unorganized labor."[4] He instituted the New Deal and changed the country from a laissez-faire approach to an interdependent one—federal government working with the states and local governments to deliver desperately needed services to the millions of Americans who had been left without work. FDR led the expansion of government. The size and number of government agencies increased enormously for the next 50 years. Large regulatory agencies were created that oversaw corporate impact on banking, environment, and a host of other arenas.

Views about government contracting shifted again during the Reagan era. President Reagan characterized government as the problem. From his presidency (1981–1989) came a renewed cry to eliminate fraud and inefficiencies in government services by contracting out more not less because the business community was believed to be more efficient and less corrupt. The idea behind contracting out in the Reagan revolution was that a "contractual relationship would give the public sector all the advantages of the market without undermining the level of public service."[5]

ECONOMIC THEORIES

The classic political ideas that underlined a traditional economic model of free enterprise held sway in America until the Great Depression. The free market advocated by Adam Smith (1723–1790) has long held Americans in awe. Adam Smith, the founder of capitalism, held that mankind's self-interest could lead to better outcomes: "beneficial outcomes are achieved not by an appeal to the benevolence of individuals, but by the direction of the self-interested actions of individuals by an invisible hand" (of the market place).[6] "It was the inherently selfish and competing interests of individuals that can never be reconciled by an interfering government except through the free allocation of resources and rewards in the marketplace." Businesses could become quite ruthless in the pursuit of survival. Of course, Adam Smith warned that a business-dominated political system would allow a conspiracy of businesses and industry against consumers, with the former scheming to influence politics and legislation "in any particular branch of trade or manufactures, is always in some respects different from, and even opposite to, that of the public ... The proposal of any new law or regulation of commerce which comes from this order, ought always to be listened to with great precaution, and ought never be adopted till after having been long and carefully examined, not only with the most scrupulous, but with the most suspicious attention."[7] But Americans paid little attention to Smith's warning. They were much more interested in Smith's "invisible hand of the marketplace." This free-market orthodoxy existed until John Maynard Keynes published *The General Theory of Employment, Interest, and Money* in 1936.

Keynes wrote at a time of the need to control concentrated private economic power, powers that dominated government and permitted enormous suffering of working people. Keynes' *General Theory* introduced that idea that full employment could only be maintained with the help of government spending. Keynes advocated for deficit spending during economic hard times to maintain full employment. Government was a tool to be used to aid the private sector. Keynes emphasized "the role of governmental fiscal intervention in stabilizing the business cycle, thereby improving the economic outcomes."[8] Keynes was the economist whom Roosevelt relied upon to use government as a tool to boost the American economy in the midst of the Great Depression, and his theories laid the groundwork for the American quasi-welfare state. Keynes' view of a prominent role for government may have been revolutionary but it was not to last. In the life of the nation, Keynes economic ideas were very much in a minority. What we need to understand is that Keynes' theory of government intervention has been the exception not the rule in America's history. Keynesian theories continued through Presidents Truman, Eisenhower, Johnson, Nixon, and Carter. President Johnson's Great Society had the same goals as Roosevelt—to use government services to end poverty. And after 50 years those ideas were replaced with classical economics once more.

A number of economists played important roles in the great revival of classical economics between 1950 and 2000, but none was as influential as Milton Friedman, whose views toward Roosevelt's government intervention were quite stark: "When everybody owns something, nobody owns it, and nobody has a direct interest in maintaining or improving its condition. That is why buildings in the Soviet Union—like public housing in the United States—look decrepit within a year or two of their construction."[9] Milton Friedman was reacting to the rise of communism, which advocated for state control of production. He and President Reagan were in complete agreement, and it was Reagan's election in 1980 that signaled the dominance of Friedman's ideas and the decline of Keynesian theories. Similar to Keynes, Friedman was very much a product of the times. As leader of the University of the Chicago School, Friedman saw government services as a monopoly, while the private sector used competition to drive down prices. Friedman stood for the belief in the efficiency of the private sector and was skeptical about government intervention in the private sector. Milton Friedman had an enormous influence on the training of future economists; he spearheaded a broad, but incomplete rollback of Keynesian theories. Friedman advocated using the private sector to keep a check on government: "If economic power is joined to political power, concentration seems almost inevitable. On the other hand, if economic power is kept in separate hands from political power, it can serve as a check and a counter to political power."[10] By the end of the 20th century, classical economics had regained its place in American politics, and Friedman deserved much of the credit.

Friedman's students continued his logic. From the premises of Hobbes' "rational man," and Friedman's endorsement of classical capitalism, public choice theory was born. James Buchanan, one of the founders of public choice theory, defined individuals as furthering their own self-interests and believed that collective action is modeled with individual decision-makers using the political process to further their self-interests. This, combined with the Hobbesian view of the inefficiency of bureaucracy, led to the rise of public choice theory. After all, without competition, government bureaucracy will continue to grow, taking needed resources from the people. Buchanan advocated for market-based solutions to social and economic problems. Public-choice theory is now at the heart of mainstream economics in America today and, consequently, dominates the public debate over the role of government.

The New Public Management (NPM) movement fits nicely into the new theories of market competition in service delivery and private sector superiority. The New Public Management theories were first discussed in 1982, when Peters and Waterman published *In Search of Excellence*. Peters and Waterman advocated for humanistic strategies and cultural changes in organizations to lead employees to more productivity instead of a rational management style. "*In Search of Excellence* provoked an intense public discussion and helped turn business towards a more humanistic management style—and soon this movement began to spread to public management as well. More and more scholars asked whether it might be possible to make public organizations excellent by adapting Peters and Waterman's ideas."[11] David Osborne and Ted Gaebler added to Peters and Waterman's theory with the concept of public entrepreneurship. They developed an elaborate case for completely transforming bureaucratic government into entrepreneurial government, arguing not that government should be abolished but that it should be reinvented.[12] Government in the era of instant communication and niche marketing must become adaptable and efficient, borrowing such concepts from the private sector. Although NPM originated in Great Britain and America, it has now spread to other capitalist countries such as Australia, Canada, Denmark, New Zealand, etc. Former Vice-President Al Gore endorsed the market-oriented NPM model during the 1990s.

An accompanying theory involves the libertarians who read the works of Ayn Rand and thoroughly endorsed her views. Libertarianism is a philosophy that calls for maximizing individual rights and keeping government rules and regulations to a minimum. In a recent essay, Paul Krugman explained the difficulties with the liberatarians' thinking:

> Well, think about global warming from the point of view of someone who grew up taking Ayn Rand seriously, believing that the untrammeled pursuit of self-interest is always good and that government is always the problem, never the solution. Along come some scientists declaring that unrestricted pursuit of self-interest will destroy the world, and that government intervention is the only answer. It doesn't matter how market-friendly you make the proposed intervention; this is a direct challenge to the libertarian worldview.[13]

A SHORT HISTORY OF GOVERNMENT CONTRACTING OUT

Throughout our history, the federal government has contracted out. During the American Revolution, George Washington depended on private contractors to supply guns, bullets, and uniforms. He complained about the slow and unpredictable production of private arms and munitions producers. Washington despaired over the quality of the uniforms he obtained from a private contractor.[14] When the New York legislature asked the federal government for help in building the Erie Canal in 1817 to connect the Great Lakes to the Atlantic Ocean, Congress turned them down; it was not a federal matter. New York State built it. During Abraham Lincoln's administration, the secret service to guard the president was born and immediately contracted out to Pinkerton's Detective Agency. During the reconstruction era (1865–1976), convict leases were made to private landowners to lease prisoners to work in factories and on farmland.[15] In 19th-century New York, the City Charter itself mandated contracting out for all city construction work.[16] Until the Great Depression, before Keynes' theories briefly took center stage, the federal government had only a small role to play in American life.

Contracting out has certainly been the norm in our nation's history. Yet, there were always attempts to control contracting out. Slowly, law and regulation began to form around it, and, as might be expected, increased regulation resulted in increased disputes. Early on, the first Secretary of Finance (called Superintendent), Robert Morris (1734–1806), overhauled the contract system. "He put in place a system that would be very recognizable to today's contract professionals. Invitations for bids would be made available to "respected business people" ("Construction Contracting," 1–2), remaining open until a specific date. The bids would then be opened, negotiated, and awarded. Morris had two evaluation criteria: the bidders must be "men of substance and talents," and the terms must be "most beneficial to the public."[17] Before the 1850s, a contractor's rights were limited by the principle of sovereign immunity: that is, a legal doctrine in which government cannot commit a legal wrong and thus cannot be sued. The Tucker Act of 1855 changed this law, so that contractors could sue. The Tucker Act established the Court of Claims to "render judgment upon any claim against the United States founded either upon the Constitution, or any act of Congress or any regulation of an executive department, or upon any express or implied contract with the United States" (28 USC §1491(a)(1)), thereby waiving sovereign immunity in these instances. The act has been revised by Congress and clarified by case law (in particular, *Cooke v. United States* in 1875), but is still current today.[18]

At the start of the Civil War, Congress passed the Pacific Telegraph Act of 1860 to facilitate transcontinental communication. It required the Secretary of the Treasury to solicit contract bids publicly and mandated that contracts be awarded only to the lowest bidder.[19] During the Civil War, President Abraham Lincoln, fed up with rifles that didn't work and blankets that were worn through, signed the Federal False Claims Act (FCA) into law in 1863 to combat defense contractor fraud during the Civil War. The law allows private individuals with knowledge of past or present fraud committed against the federal government to sue on the government's behalf. Private citizens who file FCA whistleblower lawsuits are commonly referred to as qui tam plaintiffs, relators, or just whistleblowers. Defense contractor fraud is the oldest type of whistleblower claim.[20]

In the late 19th century, Americans faced a concentration of economic power that threatened to diminish any resemblance of independent national political power. America was in the midst of turmoil transitioning from a "proprietary-competitive stage of capitalism to a corporate-administered stage of capitalism—one dominated by large corporations."[21] This concentration of economic power in the nation is similar to that at the beginning of the 21st century. The reaction of Americans to the "robber barons" of the late 19th century ushered in the Progressive Era. The Progressive Era represented that period (1880s–1920s) when reformers sought to limit corruption in government and increase regulation and antitrust legislation against the largest American corporations.

Theodore Roosevelt (1858–1919) became president (1901–1909) during the Progressive Era of the early 20th century. He sought to regulate business and bust the large corporate trusts that had developed. He brought 40 anti-trust suits and passed legislation, such as the Meat Inspections Act and the Pure Food and Drug Act. Theodore Roosevelt's term of office marked the beginning of a progressive shift in the federal government, towards actively monitoring the private sector. During this time, the number of government employees grew. Theodore's distant cousin, Franklin Delano Roosevelt, reinforced this trend.

President Franklin Roosevelt took office in March of 1933 in the midst of the Great Depression, and the government role in providing public services expanded. Although contracting out was ever present, America turned to government for the solution. President

Roosevelt embraced Keynes' theories through the influence of his advisors, Harry Hopkins and Henry Wallace. He linked Keynes' idea of deficit spending to economic security—each deserving citizen would be guaranteed a basic level of economic security. President Franklin Roosevelt upset fiscal conservatives with his deficit spending. Such spending brought protests from fiscal conservatives, which FDR answered in 1936 at a campaign speech in Pittsburgh:

> To balance our budget in 1933 or 1934 or 1935 would have been a crime against the American people. To do so we should either have had to make a capital levy that would have been confiscatory, or we should have had to set our face against human suffering with callous indifference. When Americans suffered, we refused to pass by on the other side. Humanity came first.[22]

Roosevelt believed government was a mechanism that would do good if given enough resources. He spoke most eloquently in his Economic Bill of Rights speech on January 11, 1944: "We have come to a clear realization of the fact that true individual freedom cannot exist without economic security and independence. Necessitous men are not free men. People who are hungry and out of a job are the stuff of which dictatorships are made."[23]

President Truman continued Roosevelt's legacy. Harry Truman won fame as a senator when he chaired the Senate Special Committee to Investigate the National Defense Program (1941–1944) to deal with problems of waste and corruption during World War II. These are but a few of the countless examples in which presidents dealt with corruption in contracting. In our history, ways to combat corruption within contracting were ever present.

President Dwight Eisenhower (1890–1969), a progressive Republican, continued FDR's New Deal. He used the federal government to create the Interstate Highway System. In addition, he had an enormous interest in the federal promoting science. He expanded government by creating the Defense Advanced Research Projects Agency that helped create the internet and the National Aeronautics and Space Administration, and the National Defense Education Act which helped establish the next generation of scientists. In civil rights, he sent in federal troops to Little Rock to force the state and local officials to desegregate the public schools. He pushed for further signed civil rights legislation in 1957 and 1960 to protect the right to vote. And lastly he desegregated the armed forces and, for the first time in America's history, black and white men served together. One of his most famous speeches was at the end of his presidency when he warned against the military-industrial complex: "In the councils of government, we must guard against the acquisition of unwarranted influence, whether sought or unsought, by the military-industrial complex. The potential for the disastrous rise of misplaced power exists and will persist."[24] President Eisenhower, in dissent with Milton Friedman, warned against private power gaining too much influence. It was in this postwar period that nonprofit organizations began to provide human services through government contracting. The growth of the nonprofit arena was encouraged by the foundation world that sought to alleviate problems of capitalism such as poverty and lack of opportunity.

For fifty years Keynes' theories held sway through Republican and Democratic terms, and then in 1980 President Ronald Reagan rejected Keynesian economics in favor of Milton Friedman: "Government's first duty is to protect the people, not run their lives."[25] President Reagan returned America to the dominance of the private sector and, as such, returned contracting out to prominence. Reagan's speeches constantly denigrated the public sector: "What are the most frightening nine words in the English language: I'm from the government and I'm here to help." He appointed government officials at every level who supported his ideas. E.S. Savas, one of the founders of privatization, got his start as the Assistant Secretary of U.S. Department of Housing and Urban Development under Reagan.[26] "Far too many government services—federal, state and local—are provided as monopolies when they need not be, and it is very difficult to tame monopolies and make them work in the public interest. So the introduction of competition is appropriate whether the competition comes about from the use of vouchers, competitive bidding, franchising or volunteer efforts. It is the introduction of competition that makes them different."[27] As Reagan's views gained currency, many state and local officials took an interest in contracting out.

After President Reagan, President Clinton accepted the need to reinvent government. In 1993, for example, the Clinton administration, under Vice-President Al Gore's direction, developed the National Performance Review, reforming and reinventing public procurement and contracting on the federal level.[28] Reagan's views continued into the presidency of Barack Obama. An example of this is that President Obama placed high-ranking officials in government who supported contracting out, such as Ted Mitchell, Undersecretary of Education. He sought to privatize the Tennessee Valley Authority in his 2015 budget proposal. The TVA is one of Roosevelt's classic achievements of government intervention and government operated institutions.

THE APPROACH

The contracting out of the provision of government services has become a major method by which a national conservative movement seeks to reduce the size and scope of government by expanding the private sector. Using reasoning from Milton Friedman, contracting-out will reduce the cost of government, and, at the same time, increase quality of the goods and services purchased. Contracting out has thus become a tool to promote the reduction in the size of government and the corresponding promotion of the private sector. It is a movement begun by President Reagan to encourage the private sector to participate in areas traditionally reserved for the public sector. But it is also a movement that has deep roots in America. What changed in the last half of the 20th century is the tremendous growth of privatization of government services, which has resulted in governments at every level being far more involved in contracting out public goods and services.

While stemming from different political and economic approaches, the use of contracting can be viewed as an option to provide government services—one mechanism being government and the other being the private or nonprofit sectors. The determination of which sector to use, in this methodology, is which sector will better fulfill the needs of citizens in terms of cost and quality.

There are consequences to reducing the size of government and increasing contracting out of needed public services. Shick and Weikart discussed several of these consequences.[29] First, Congress and the President may not set public policy; rather, it must be set by private individuals (McConnell 1967). President Obama has turned to philanthropy to finance projects that the federal government can no longer afford to do. "For better or worse," said Steven A. Edwards, a policy analyst at the American Association for the Advancement of Science, "the practice of science in the 21st century is becoming shaped less by national priorities or by peer-review groups and more by the particular preferences of individuals with huge amounts of money."[30]

Second, the prevalent idea of making government smaller ignores that smaller units is a prevailing "orthodoxy of private power."[31] As international corporations have grown to dominate American economic life, Americans have no sector strong enough to balance that power. The result, for example, is that large corporations that pay minimum wages bid for government work in what used to be seen as traditional government services, such as prisons and welfare systems.

Third, workers lose out when contracting out is implemented. When government agencies embrace contracting out over delivering in-house services, the private sector almost always decreases the wages and benefits. Government workers are either out of a job or must take lower wages during the same job for a private company. In effect, contracting out leads to a race to the bottom in terms of salaries and benefits.

Fourth, implementation of contracting out is key. The steps in the contracting process, including the decision to contract, the Request for Proposals, the contract document, selection of contractors and monitoring of contractors are critical to getting a good deal for the public. If these functions are not performed by an adequate number of staff trained in contracting out, government will not attain the very goals they are trying to achieve through contracting—lower costs and improved quality.

For all these reasons contracting out remains a challenge. For students and practitioners of government services, the path is cloudy. Are we to encourage contracting out and continue the march to the reduction of the public sector? Are we to reject contracting out and fight to build the public sector? There is a third path—a difficult one. We must return to Locke and his discussion of values. He distrusted power and he had enormous faith in progress. What kind of society do we wish to become? The capitalism in our history had serious problems, as demonstrated by the percentage of our population that is still poor and the recent near collapse of our financial markets. We do not need to return to the era of robber barons. At the same time, capitalism has had incredible beneficial outcomes—the creation of vast wealth has meant a rising standard of living up to a point until capitalism has captured so much power that it has forced a reduction in wages. And we are at that point.

Our approach to government contracting out, then, becomes part of a larger argument concerning our economic system and the return of government spending to average citizens. This means we must be willing to talk about common public values when we talk about contracting out. We need to build a consensus. When we are thinking about letting out contracts for a profit or a nonprofit to administer our services, we need to weigh the consequences by creating a set of public values on which we can all agree.

- Transparency: The first public value is transparency. The private sector operates with proprietary information; that is, information is private, while government information is owned by the public and is public. If contracting out is to work, then we must find a way to extend transparency to the private sector.
- Equity: We need to think about the equity issues; that is, we need to insure that all services are provided with similar resources and not just a prize few. A good example is the neglect of neighborhood parks during the Bloomberg administration (2002–2014). In New York City, Mayor Michael R. Bloomberg had invested "years of huge capital expenditures on parks, with almost $1 billion going to a small number of parks, like Brooklyn Bridge Park, Governors Island and the High Line."[32] These capital expenditures were often connected to private sector companies and nonprofits that oversaw the implementation of renovated parks. Yet a vast number of neighborhood parks remained neglected.
- Protecting human capital: We also need to think about the value of human capital. We need to weigh the consequences for the workers. If workers are to be transferred to the private sector, we need to insure that the workers get a living wage and benefits.
- Accountability: Another value is that of protecting the public from bad deals through increased vigilance on contracting decisions and the contract process. For example, a private company paid the city of Chicago $1.15 billion for the right to collect all parking fee revenues for 75 years. "The economist Roger Skurski calculated the current value of the deal. . . . his conservative estimate was that "the city could have earned about $670 million more by keeping the asset."[33] These kinds of inequities and lost revenues are the result of contracting gone very wrong.
- Quality: On a state level, when elected officials discover that contracting out prison services are "cheaper," we need to think about the quality of the service and the basic humane treatment of the prisoners. We need to insure that prisoners are treated properly in private sector facilities; we need to insure that the guards have decent wages.

- Unintended consequences: We need to protect against unintended consequences—we need to insure that the private sector does not become the "town crier" for more increased provision of a government service, so that they can make more money.

At any one time all of these public values are involved in major issues of contracting out. Consider the current controversy over the long wait lines at the Veterans Administration (VA). This is a classic case in which those who advocate privatization claim that the answer is obvious—privatize the VA. Yet, those patients served by the VA are convinced that their level of service is excellent. If we can agree on common public values, then when Congress people say they wish to privatize the Veterans Administration, we need to insure that accessibility and quality of care is actually available in the private sector. Many times it is not. In rural areas of this country, veterans would find it very difficult to get high quality health care. On the other hand, if the VA is doing excellent work caring for our returning veterans, then we must insure that we provide sufficient resources to the VA to continue that work.

If we viewed contracting out as a tool to be used in the right circumstances within a common value system that protects human capital and the recipients of the services, then indeed contracting out can be a valuable tool. However, if we base contracting decisions on political and economic philosophy, looking only at a faster and cheaper service that would give an immediate financial reward regardless of long-term costs, then the public will be resentful and the consequences for our country quite severe. It is clearly preferable to pursue the former approach with a watchful eye of the consequences of these decisions.

KEY POINTS

1. For much of American history, our government sector was small and citizens did not look to government to solve their problems.
2. This viewpoint changed with the progressive era beginning with the 20th century. FDR and Theodore Roosevelt both challenged the view that the private sector was sufficient for citizens' needs. Keyesian economics became the norm for the next 50 years.
3. However, with the advent of a conservative president, Ronald Reagan, in 1980, a new economist dominated—Milton Friedman. His theories resulted in a return to privatization and endorsement of widespread contracting out.
4. However, without a common set of public values underlining contracting out, there is no agreement among Americans about the size and scope of this form of privatization. These public values—transparency, equity, protecting human capital, accountability, quality and the recognition of unintended consequences—are crucial. If these public values can be included in the public debate and can be framed as necessary for further contracting out, then Americans can have some assurance that service, whether delivered by government or by the private sector, would be adequate and of high quality.

NOTES

1. Merrell, Seth & Phelps, Richard P. 1994. *A Primer on Privatization for Educators*. Available at www.richardphelps.net/Privatization.doc. Accessed February 19, 2015.
2. Locke, J. (1690), *Second Treatise of Government* (10th ed.), Project Gutenberg.
3. Hobbes, T. "What Is Moral and Political Philosophy?" Available at http://www.iep.utm.edu/hobmoral/.
4. Roosevelt, F. D. 1937. "Message to Congress on Establishing Minimum Wages and Maximum Hours," May 24, 1937. "The American Presidency Project." Available at http://en.wiliquote/wiki/Franklin_D._Roosevelt.
5. Sclar, E. (2000). The Urge to Privatize in *You Don't Always Get What You Pay For,* page 5.
6. Broad, William J. 2014 March 15. "Billionaires with Big Ideas are Privatizing American Science." *The New York Times*. Accessed May 20, 2015. Available at http://www.nytimes.com/2014/03/16/science/billionaires-with-big-ideas-are-privatizing-american-science.html?_r=0.
7. Gopnik, A. "Market Man." *The New Yorker* (18 October 2010): 82.
8. Kaplan-Lyman, J. (2012). *15 Yale Human Rights and Developmental Law Journal*, 177.
9. Friedman, M. (2012). "Free to Choose—a Personal Statement." http://www.businessinsider.com/milton-friedman-quotes-2012-7.
10. Friedman, M. (1962). *Capitalism and Freedom*. Chicago: University of Chicago Press, page 16.
11. Keraudren, P. & van Mierlo, H. "Theories of Public Management Reform and Their Practical Implications." Available at http://arnop.unimaas.nl/show.cgi?fid=11875.
12. Ibid.
13. Krugman, P. (2014, June 17). "Interests, Ideology and Climate." *The New York Times*. Available at http://www.nytimes.com/2014/06/09/opinion/krugman-interests-ideology-and-climate.html?src=me&module=Ribbon&version=origin&region=Header&action=click&contentCollection=Most%20Emailed&pgtype=article.
14. Stanton, A. T. "Contracting Out the Presidency: New Challenges in Executive Branch Management." Available at http://www.onedayonejob.com/jobs/center-for-the-study-of-the-presidency-and-congress/.
15. xiii Alex Lichtenstein, *Twice the Work of Free Labor: The Political Economy of Convict Labor in the New South*, Verso Press, 1996, p. 3.
16. Adler, M. (1999 Spring/Summer). "Been There, Done That! The Privatization of Street Cleaning in 19th Century." New York, New Labor Forum.
17. Keeney, S. 2007 Summer. "The Foundations of Government Contracting." *Journal of Contract Management*, Summer 2007, 5/1, 7–19.
18. Keeney, S. 2007 Summer. "The Foundations of Government Contracting." *Journal of Contract Management*, Summer 2007, 5/1, 7–19.
19. Stanton. Available at http://www.onedayonejob.com/jobs/center-for-the-study-of-the-presidency-and-congress/.
20. http://www.hornsbylaw.com/defense-contractor-fraud-attorneys.
21. Sclar, M. J. (1988). *Corporate Reconstruction of American Capitalism 1890–1916*. London: Cambridge University Press, page 33.
22. Roosevelt, Presidential Library, IBID.
23. Roosevelt, Franklin. Presidential Library. http://www.fdrlibrary.marist.edu/aboutfdr/budget.html.
24. Smith, J. E. (2012). *Eisenhower in War and Peace*. New York: Random House, page 760.
25. Quote by Ronald Reagan at the National Conference of the Building and Construction Trades, AFL-CIO (March 30, 1981).
26. Savas, bio. Available at http://www.baruch.cuny.edu/spa/facultystaff/facultydirectory/bio_savas.php.

27. Savea, E. S. (1985). "The Efficiency of the Private Sector," in *The Privatization Option: A Strategy to Shrink the Size of Government,* edited by S. M. Butler, pages 15–31. Washington DC: The Heritage Foundation.

28. National Performance Review 1993.

29. Shick, R. & Weikart, L. (2010), "Public organizations undergoing change: A study in Urban Contracting," *Public Affairs Quarterly 33/1.*

30. Broad, W. J. (2014 March 15). "Billionaires with Big Ideas are Privatizing American Science," *The New York Times.* Available at http://www.nytimes.com/2014/03/16/science/billionaires-with-big-ideas-are-privatizing-american-science.html.

31. Ibid.

32. Foderado, L. W. (2014, May 6). "Focusing on Lesser-Known Open Spaces in New York." *The New York Times.* Available at http://www.nytimes.com/2014/05/07/nyregion/focusing-on-lesser-known-open-spaces-in-new-york.html?module=Search&mabReward=relbias%3Ar.

33. Mihalopoulos, D. (2009) November 19. "Company Piles UP Profits from City's Parking Meter Deal." *The New York Times.* Available at http://www.nytimes.com/2009/11/20/us/20cncmeters.html?pagewanted=all&module=Search&mabReward=relbias%3Ar.

REFERENCES

Adler, M. (1999). *Been There, Done That! The Privatization of Street Cleaning in 19th Century New York.* New York, NY: New Labor Forum.

Broad, W. J. (2014 March 15). *Billionaires with Big Ideas are Privatizing American Science,* The New York Times. Retrieved from http://www.nytimes.com/2014/03/16/science/billionaires-with-big-ideas-are-privatizing-american-science.html?_r=0

Friedman, M. (1962). *Capitalism and Freedom.* Chicago, IL: University of Chicago Press.

Friedman, M (1980). Free to Choose—a Personal Statement. Retrieved from http://www.businessinsider.com/milton-friedman-quotes-2012-7.

Gopnik, A. (2010). The Market Man. *The New Yorker.* Retrieved from http://www.newyorker.com/magazine/2010/10/18/market-man.

Keeney, S. (2007). The Foundations of Government Contracting. *Journal of Contract Management,* Summer 2007, 5/1, 7–19.

Lichtenstein, A. (1996). *Twice the Work of Free Labor: The Political Economy of Convict Labor in the New South.* New York, NY: Verso Press.

Locke, J. (1690), *Second Treatise of Government* (10th ed.), Project Gutenberg.

McConnell, G. (1967). *Private Power and American Democracy.* New York, NY: Alfred A. Knopf.

National Performance Review (1993). Roosevelt, Franklin D. Presidential Library. Retrieved from http://www.fdrlibrary.marist.edu/aboutfdr/budget.html.

Saves, E. S. 1985. The Efficiency of the Private Sector, in *The Privatization Option: A Strategy to Shrink the Size of Government,* edited by S. M. Butler, pages 15–31. Washington DC: The Heritage Foundation.

Shick, Robert & Weikart, Lynne. 2010. Public Organizations Undergoing Change: A Study in Urban Contracting. *Public Affairs Quarterly,* 33/1.

Sclar, Elliot D. 2000. *The Urge to Privatize in You don't always get what you pay for.* Ithaca & London: Cornell University Press.

Sklar, Martin J. 1988. *Corporate Reconstruction of American Capitalism 1890–1916.* London: Cambridge University Press.

Smith, Jean Edward. 2012. *Eisenhower in War and Peace.* New York: Random House.

2

The Contracting Decision

Olga Victorovna Smirnova and Suzanne Leland

INTRODUCTION: WHY CONTRACT?

Governments not only select which services to provide, but also who produces them (Brown & Potoski, 2003). In the past, most governments typically produced services in-house, but the rise of New Public Management coupled with fiscal stress has led government contracting to be more frequent and widespread in the United States than before. Since the 1980s, governments at the federal, state and local levels began to commonly engage in contracting out with a third party to deliver services. The third party in the relationship can be defined as a private, nonprofit or even another government that is capable of producing and providing the service. In many cases, the government is still responsible for the services from a legal perspective. The government usually provides the financial incentives for the contractors to perform the services.

The general philosophy underlying the New Public Management movement is that government should consider privatization if a private or nonprofit vendor produces a good or service. Contracting out a form of privatization provides an opportunity to improve production efficiency because of its potential to create competition among possible vendors. Likewise competition can improve service quality (Savas, 1987; 2000, 2005; Brown, Potoski & Van Slyke, 2006). Keeping services in-house does not provide the same opportunity because, without competition, public employees have weak incentives to improve production efficiency (Levin & Tadelis, 2010). However, efficiency is not the only value considered by decision-makers; there are multiple values that public officials must weigh, including equity, access, accountability, reliability, and service quality. And a growing body of literature indicates that contracting out may not produce desired savings (Miranda & Lener, 1995; Brown, Potoski & Van Slyke, 2006).

In the provision of services and goods, the government has different competing goals such as equity and effectiveness, while for private companies the main goal is profit. Quite often, public entities are legislatively prohibited from turning down or price discriminating[1] against various customers. Also, the government entity is responsible for the financing of the services in front of a broader range of stakeholders than a private entity (in this case, the private entity is responsible for profits in front of their stakeholders, usually shareholders or owners).

In many cases, the services provided by local governments actually fail the "yellow pages test" where there are not any private firms delivering these types of services in their local area. If competition is present, the organization may not have the internal capacity to take advantage of it. Since each economic exchange involves transaction costs (e.g. the costs of drafting the contracts, monitoring services, finding qualified bidders, etc.), the transaction costs of contracting out to an entity with conflicting goals may outweigh any of the market benefits (Williamson, 1981). For example, if there are potential cost-savings from private provision of local transit services, these cost-savings should outweigh the costs of entering and successfully monitoring such a contract. Thus, to have costs savings and improved services requires the government to be a "smart buyer" and know who to award the contract to and how to actually monitor the contract (Kettl, 1993). Governments must be skillful purchasing and monitoring agents (Van Slyke, 2003; Savas, 1987).

There are also other considerations for public officials that determine whether to make or buy a service besides efficiency and cost-savings. These include equity, access, accountability, reliability, and quality of services provided. For example, providing equitable service to certain areas may be legislatively mandated. Ensuring that all citizens have equal access to the services may add to overall costs. The necessity of a local government to stay accountable and provide full information to customers may run contrary to the private contractor's need for privacy and protection of business secrets. Avoiding disruptions or changes may also factor into the decision of how to provide services. In other words, the government may prefer the reliability of in-house operations to the potential cost-savings of contracting out. If an initial contract does not provide savings, the government agency may continue to use the same provider because of established external political relationships and service quality. They may also have their capacity to actually deliver the service themselves and may have sold key assets, making the switch back to in-house cost prohibitive in the short term. Finally, public officials may have political incentives to either contract out or operate services fully in-house that override any other concerns.

For these reasons, it is important to understand the dynamics of decision-making in general and then apply them specifically to contracting out. In this chapter, we begin by introducing the different decision-making theories and how they explain government officials' decisions to contract out. Our goal is to distinguish between different models of decision-making and how they would relate to a government's perspective on contracting out. Next, we will discuss the empirical findings to date. Finally, we will offer some practical advice on contracting out.

DIFFERENT DECISION-MAKING THEORIES AS APPLIED TO CONTRACTING DECISIONS

There are several prominent decision-making theories used to explain the contracting out of services. These are the rational-comprehensive model (emphasizing the values of efficiency and effectiveness), incremental theory or incrementalism (emphasizing the importance of politics and responsiveness), and mixed scanning, which has emerged as a combination of the two based on the organization's goals and circumstances (Etzioni, 1967).

The rational-comprehensive model is viewed as normative by many public administration scholars, and posits that people have a high degree of control over the decision-making process. Under this theory, public officials can first identify the problem, set their goals, select the criteria, weigh the alternatives, and then select among them according to their merit. In the case of the decision to contract out services or keep them in-house, this decision-making theory assumes that governments are "smart buyers" and would be able to conduct a cost-benefit analysis to determine if contracting out is the best alternative. This approach assumes that individuals have full information about outcomes, benefits, and costs of various alternatives. However, in the public sector, the benefits (and sometimes costs) cannot be always fully measured and anticipated. Some goals can conflict (e.g. equity and efficiency) with each other at various times.

The rational approach to contracting out requires an exhaustive analysis of all of the different options for providing the services and substantial organizational capacity. However, there are significant costs to incorporating all of the relevant information. One would have to ensure that government resources would be spent on both creating and keeping adequate competition and oversight of the execution stage of the contract. The transactions costs of such decision-making can outweigh any cost-savings. Brown, Potoski, and Van Slyke (2008) indicate that the initial choice of service provision significantly affects subsequently considered alternatives. That is, an agency that has contracted in the past is more likely to consider similar alternatives (or pulling services in-house) compared to the agency that has never contracted out (or has never operated services in-house).

Conversely, the incremental approach to decision making (incrementalism) posits that the public administrator has a much lower degree of control over the decision-making process. Information is often imperfect; there is never enough time to collect all of it, and public administrators may not always calculate the full costs and benefits of contracting out a service versus keeping that service in house. In this decision-making model, maintaining the status quo is preferred to making any dramatic changes.

The incremental approach assumes that people will forsake any potential cost-savings in order to maintain stability in service delivery and avoid potential political conflict. Small reversible steps are preferred to drastic changes. Thus, this theory does not explain when radical changes occur. There have been modifications to this theory, mainly punctuated equilibrium, which does explain how an abrupt change occurs.

But the "punctuation" is rare, and stability still remains the primary driving force in decision-making. Incrementalism means considering fewer options and ignoring important components that might lead to problems and inefficiencies in service delivery.

The mixed scanning model combines the elements of both the incremental and rational–comprehensive models (Etzioni, 1967). This model provides for a particular procedure for the collection of information and a strategy for allocating resources in the decision-making process. A mixed scanning approach focuses on the development of criteria for considering contracting out a particular service. This could include modifying existing arrangements and awarding contracts. The agency may start with projecting the costs of in-house provision and then compare these costs with the potential contractor's price. The latter can be determined through the research of the nation-wide market or benchmarking against the other local contracts for similar services.

The difference between the mixed scanning approach and incrementalism is the potential for a change in service provision arrangements; ultimately, the government considers the conversion from in-house services, changing the status quo dramatically. What separates this approach from the rational decision-making path is the fact that not all alternatives can possibly be considered, and not all relevant information can be taken into consideration. For example, under the rational approach, the government would need to list all the alternatives for the services that they could contract, identify all the criteria, calculate all benefits and costs, and select the alternative with the highest benefits. Under incrementalism, the decision would be described as the choice between a limited set of alternatives (e.g. previously familiar to the local government), and compared on the political acceptability of the alternatives by various stakeholders. Under the mixed-scanning approach, the contracting out decision incorporates the use of systematic criteria for assessment within the time and resources constraints of the local governments.

Both the incremental and mixed scanning models predict path-dependency and inertia. Inertia in service provision stems from the capacity issues inherent in the conversion between different types of service provision. That is, when a city contracts out, it may lose the capacity to operate services in-house. For example, when a contractor does not operate in accordance with the agreement, even if this agreement allows for early termination by the city, such a contract may not be terminated due to the difficulties of finding quickly who else can perform the same services. Thus, Bel and Fageda (2010) and Miranda and Lerner (1995) argue for partial contracting as a solution to this dilemma. For example, if a city were to consider contracting out for trash collection, they may divide the city into four zones. Each zone would be bid on if the current in-house exceeded a specific amount per service or a number of complaints were filed. The city could require that they keep one zone in-house to retain their capacity. The system would help foster competition but would not necessarily set arrangements indefinitely.

The following section discusses the empirical evidence on contracting out savings to this date.

EMPIRICAL EVIDENCE ON CONTRACTING OUT SAVINGS

Early studies on contracting out typically find cost-savings in US urban transit (Talley and Anderson, 1986), US municipal expenditures (ICMA data used by Miranda & Lerner, 1995; Miranda, 1994), Canadian and UK waste collections (Domberger & Jensen, 1997), and a variety of services in the US (Savas, 2000). But these studies have quite often been based either on the evaluation of one company (Talley & Anderson, 1986), or utilization of cross-sectional data (Miranda, 1994). As more empirical studies have been conducted, the results have revealed fewer instances of empirical cost-savings (Warner, 2012). Earlier studies emphasized the potential of cost-savings from competition and assumed that contracting out would allow local governments to capitalize on those savings. The later literature has unmasked a more complex picture of contracting markets.

Sclar (2015) stresses the conflict of the long-term social goals with the short-term private returns in the public infrastructure financing. Also, in line with the mixed scanning model, the institutional knowledge of the services, and the tacit knowledge needed to provide a good quality of service, may be lost in contracts (Sclar, 2000). Cohen and Eimicke (2008) provide a toolset for responsible contract management, which emphasizes the unique circumstances of public management, including the accountability required for public entities. The majority of recent research underscores the importance of transaction, conversion, and other costs that public agencies encounter in the contracting out process.

Conversion Costs

Essentially, deciding whether or not to contract out becomes the decision between providing or buying services. Hefetz and Warner (2004) discuss starting positions that influence contracting out. It is not a one-directional street. A service can start in-house, become outsourced to a private entity, and then be brought back in-house. Alternatively, the government may start contracting out and find that they have lost the capacity to bring services back in-house. The following set of figures represents varying starting positions.

Each point where the production changes hands represents a potential point for conversion costs or one-time costs associated with change from in-house to contracts or from contracts back to in-house operations. These costs do not include the transaction costs or the costs associated with the contract itself, and that may involve drafting contracts, monitoring contracts, and other things.

Since we are looking at the contracting process as a separation of production (financing) and provision of services, we can start with the situation where a public entity contracts out for services. In this situation (depicted in the figure below), there may be an underlining reason why the services were not provided by the private entities in the first place, such as lack of potential profits.

Figure 2.1 **Initial Production—Public Entity**

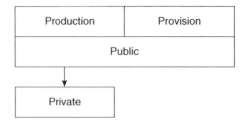

Another starting point can be with the private financing and provision of services (common for public transit in the early 1900s), transitioning to public financing of services with private provision (contracting out). For example, in public transit, where this situation can be often found, the transit used to be provided by private companies in many places. However, with the changes of American cities and lower population densities,[2] the profitability of transit declined substantially and cities had to step in to continue transit services. In such situations, the contracts are often with the original company that used to provide the services from the very beginning, and the public sector brings in financing and oversight (Figure 2.2).

The situation becomes more complex as municipalities change service provisions again and bring services in-house, as shown in Figure 2.3. The difficulty of bringing services in-house can differ based on starting positions (e.g. initial public or initial private production and provision). But, in both cases, underlining problems with contracts (e.g. loss of quality, increase in prices, etc.) are similar.

Finally, there is also a potential for complete privatization, which includes the sale of all assets, and full private production and provision of services. For example, in 2009 the city of Chicago "sold" the city's parking meters to private companies. Chicago handed over full control of the asset to a private company for 75 years and lost control over how the meters were operated and maintained. The danger is, of course, that the city may be

Figure 2.2 **Initial Production—Private Entity**

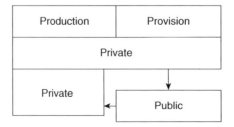

Figure 2.3 **Bringing Services In-House**

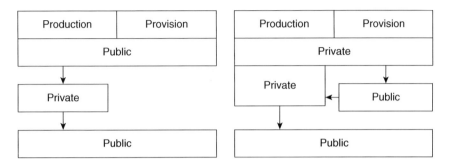

desperate for one-time-only cash and may sell the asset that they could eventually earn much more revenue over time. Since this type of deal entails expensive assets, they often have long contract lengths (such as 75 years in this case).

Notice that the following figure depicts this situation with the intermediate step of contracting out, but privatization can occur as direct sales of public assets without any contracting out in-between.

Local governments may also stop providing functions altogether or provide totally new functions through contracting (Hefetz & Warner, 2004). For example, a local government may choose to add new services through contracts. At the same time, since contracting out involves the conversion of service provision, public agencies may lose the capacity to provide these services. Faced with an opportunistic contractor and lack of competition, the local government may choose to stop providing services all together due to legal liabilities.

From a standpoint of incrementalism, the multiple changes of service production should not necessarily happen, as they represent a break from the previous path. From the standpoint of rational decision-making, the situations where government may lose

Figure 2.4 **Privatization**

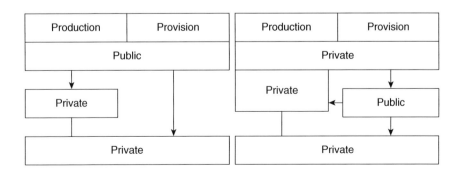

capacity or fail to realize cost-savings should not happen due to all the collected information. However, the mix-scanning model allows for both changes and mistakes. There is also empirical evidence that explains various contracting out components.

Additional Costs to Consider When Deciding if Contracting Out Is Right for Your Organization

The literature highlights the importance of both efficiency concerns and politics. Levin and Tadelis (2010) find that contracting is inversely related to the high transaction costs and citizen sensitivity to quality. This may be due to certain interactions between those functions that are very difficult to measure and higher responsiveness to citizens' complaints.

The pitfalls of contracting out include the need for specific technical knowledge (e.g. at bidding and drafting of the contracts) (Rehfus, 1990). After the contract has been awarded, the agencies must monitor contracts for compliance. Therefore, contracts should specify the costs, including transaction costs, the outcomes, and monitoring from the onset. Monitoring may include inspections, reports, complaints, benchmarking, and accountability and performance standards. In reality, however, not all monitoring opportunities are always included, and public agencies should be aware that, without including certain monitoring practices, they may not be legally allowed to conduct monitoring operations such as official inspections.

The Government Accountability Office (GAO) has identified different problems with contracting at both the federal and local level since the 1980s. One of the latest reports in this series highlighted the use of contracting in public transit (GAO, 2013), which found both opportunities and challenges to contracting out public transit. Opportunities for contracting out most services include the expansion of existing services or the addition of new services. Contractors can also implement new technologies or innovations. At the same time, challenges to contracting out services involve the short-term nature of potential cost-savings, especially if they are predicated on the sale of a major asset. Also, the majority of long-term cost savings come from lower wages and reduced benefits for workers.

Miranda and Lerner (1995) argue for mixing in-house and contracting out provision of services because it creates competition in the provision of services. This is a counterintuitive finding (usually duplication is viewed as inefficient), but it is supported by subsequent studies (Bel & Fageda, 2010). Hefetz and Warner (2004) and Brown and Potoski (2006) argue for similar mechanisms to increase cost-savings from contracting out by mixing the provision of services by contractors and in-house employees. The duplication of service provisions (e.g. through contracting and in-house provisions) leads to higher resiliency in the cases of service disruptions. It also creates the competition in the provision of services. At the same time, Zullo (2007) finds contracting an "all or nothing" situation in the US transit, with more efficient agencies either fully contracting out or keeping all of their services in-house. There is also evidence from the private sector that mixed or even selective contracting, for example in IT services, may provide more benefits than the outsourcing of all IT services (Lacity et al., 1996).

This brings us to the key question of how cost-savings are generated by contracting out. Even though contracting out has been an on-going practice in public agencies for over 30 years, there are limited large-scale empirical findings of cost-savings. The following table summarizes important academic articles published on contracting out with the focus on cost-savings for local governments. The functions excluded from the table include, for example, education because schools are usually privatized or chartered. Also, liquor stores are excluded as these services are usually provided and controlled by the state-level government. Highways are usually financed and produced through public-private partnerships that also represent a separate type of privatization. Table 2.1 lists selected studies on cost-savings from contracting out in chronological order.

Blom-Hansen (2003), studying one-cross-section (n=270) of Denmark's public road provision by municipalities, finds savings from contracting out. This article also underscores the importance of politics (party affiliations) for contracting decisions. Another set of services provided at the state level is social services. GAO (1997) found problems with accountability in contracting out social services at the state level.

The majority of the most recent studies in various functional areas have mixed findings with regard to cost-savings. There are multiple studies that focus on the city services in general and not specific functions. Among the specific functions studied for contracting out savings, the most frequently studied functions include transit and water/sewer. One of the reasons for this is the availability of the data, such as ICMA's data on cities.

The studies that have found cost-savings from contracting out were published earlier and usually have a very limited scope (e.g. the case-studies (Talley & Anderson, 1986) or cross-section (Miranda, 1994). A similar observation has been made by Warner (2012). When more data is examined, the results become more complicated and are less likely to indicate cost-savings. Some of the later studies are also based on case-studies as these studies allow collecting contextual information.

The problem in collecting empirical studies is that there are not enough data in various areas. Austin and Coventry (2001) compare the results of the 1995 Census of State and Federal correction facilities and the 1997 results of the National Survey of State Prison populations. Their findings indicate that private prisons operate mostly as public facilities. The very modest findings found in cost-savings are results of mostly labor cost-savings, but these costs reductions are not always commensurable with increased risk.

Table 2.1

Selected Studies on Contracting Out Cost-Savings

Author (date)	Function	Data source and n	Statistical analysis	Cost-savings	Results
Talley and Anderson (1986)	Paratransit	One company	Case-study	Yes	Contracting also influences unions to cut their costs
Miranda (1994)	City-functions	82 ICMA	Cross-sectional study	Yes	Political factors also influence contracting out decisions
Austin and Coventry (2001)	Prisons	Comparisons of 1995 and 1997 findings	Comparative	Yes, but risks are high	Cost-savings are modest, if existing, and there are persistent management and safety problems
Brown et al (2007)	Social services and refuse collection	Individual case studies	Case-studies	Mixed	More uncertainty is related to less competition, and fewer savings
Zullo (2007)	Transit	NTD 1993–2004, 392–456 agencies per year	Panel, HLM	No	Contracting does not generating savings due to lack of competition
Bel, Fageda, and Warner (2010)	Water delivery and solid waste	1965–2010 all published studies	Meta-regression analysis	No	Meta-regression analysis of all published studies between 1965 and 2010 found no cost-savings
Milward (2010)	Network-based public services	Case studies	Historical analysis by function of 20th century	No	Comprehensive overview of empirical studies on network-based services (such as water, transit, and telecommunications) finds no cost-savings
GAO (2011)	Transit	All NTD over 600	Survey of contracting opinions, over 600	Mixed	Mixed findings: the report highlights both challenges and opportunities
Girth and Johnson (2012)	City services	2195 city officials, 2009	Cross-sectional survey, self-reporting	Mixed	Only 55% report that contracting produces savings

Brown et al. (2007), studying individual case studies of social services and refuse collection, find mixed results. Zullo (2007) studying the universe of transit agencies over a 12 year period finds no savings. Bel, Fageda, and Warner (2010) conduct a meta-regression analysis of all studies since 1965 and find no cost-savings from contracting out. Milward (2010) conducts an in-depth historical analysis of contracting out, and also finds no cost-savings even though the historical analysis (Milward, 2010) focuses on network-based services. Network based services such as water or transit are among those that should be easiest to measure. Finally, the GAO (2011) and Girth and Johnson (2012) provide survey results where managers themselves report the cost-savings, and their findings are mixed. Some governments report cost-savings, while others do not.

There are several reasons why contracting out may not generate cost-savings that we will explore in the next section.

WHY CONTRACTING OUT GETS MIXED REVIEWS

There are several reasons why contracting out may not generate the anticipated savings. Since the earliest empirical and theoretical studies, competition is highlighted as the most important factor of how contracting out savings can be realized (Savas, 2000; Miranda & Lener, 1995; Smirnova & Leland, 2013). Thus, the lack of competition leads to a situation where a government monopoly is substituted by a private monopoly with limited government oversight. Also, the competition may exist at different stages of the contracting process while being absent in others.

There are three major stages of contracting that require different technical skills: the make or buy decision, bidding, and contracting itself. The very first stage is the decision on whether to provide services in-house or contract out. This is the stage where cost-benefit analysis and other important fiscal and legal considerations should be thoroughly analyzed. It is at this stage that the agency should decide whether there is enough competition at both bidding and provision of services. Both transaction and conversion costs should be taken into consideration at this stage.

In some instances, there may be adequate competition in the bidding process (e.g. from large national companies), but none of the firms are local. In rare situations, there may be limited bidding, but some competition in the provision of services. It is the competition in the provision of services that affects the cost-savings from contracting out (Smirnova & Leland, 2013).

The bidding stage requires specific technical knowledge of what goes into the contract, expectations of outcomes, and monitoring specifications. Both legal and fiscal concerns should be addressed at this stage. For some areas, the recruiting of vendors may occur at this stage requiring additional time commitment. Finally, the contracting out stage requires time and staff to perform contract monitoring.

Competition

Competition in the provision of services is represented in Figure 2.5 below. In this situation, there is only one contract, but there are multiple private companies providing the same services, which creates competition in the provision of services or some form of benchmarking for the public agency.

This situation has several benefits due to the competition among the vendors. The agency has an easier time finding the qualifying vendor (no need for recruiting). During the contract duration, the monitoring can be done by comparing the performance of the contract to comparable services of the competitors. Besides, the competition keeps the company under the contract in check. Even in such situations there may be room for contracting opportunism (from either side under the contract) due to incomplete information.

The situation with multiple vendors in the same area is a rare occasion for public services. However, there are may be multiple public entities performing similar services, and in this situation, depicted in Figure 2.6, the competition can be established by signing contracts with other public agencies and private vendors. Both intergovernmental and private contracts can be compared. Quite often, intergovernmental arrangements include police functions, for which there may not be direct equivalent in the private market. Brown et al. (2006) and Sclar (2015) highlight the importance of values in the public service provision and how intergovernmental contracts or contracts with non-profit organizations can be more in line with the public values. As we move along the line of competition, we also see larger vendors, but fewer of them.

What happens when there are not many vendors in the area? An agency may recruit separate vendors for multiple contracts. When a public agency has multiple (e.g. two in Figure 2.7) contracts for similar functions (e.g. transit in different geographical areas of the city), these contracts can be compared to each other. Notice that, in this situation, without any vendors in the local area, the public agencies have to be actively recruiting outside vendors for bids. The competition for bids, however, does not guarantee the competition in the production of services. Sometimes if vendors are from a different state, they are used to following a separate set of regulations in the provision of the

Figure 2.5 **Competition in the Provision of Services**

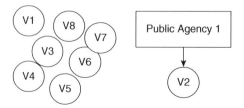

Figure 2.6 **Intergovernmental Contracts Introduce Competition**

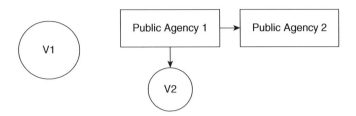

service. For example, a specific garbage truck may be legal in one state but not another, due to different environmental requirements, and, therefore, these companies may not be true competitors in certain markets.

Figure 2.8 is an example of a situation where there is only one available vendor in an area, which leads to a monopoly. This can become complicated in cases where the vendor has more bargaining power (e.g. by having multiple contracts with different public agencies) compared to a local government. Assuming that both the public agency and the vendor have only one contract for specific public functions (e.g. transit operations), there is room for both sides not to deliver on the contract. In this situation, opportunism may arise from the lack of comparison and knowledge about the desired outcomes. This is the problem of incomplete information that the mixed-scanning model incorporates into the contracting decision.

In this case, the potential scenario recommended by the literature (Brown et al., 2006; Hefetz & Warner, 2004) is to maintain a portion of services in-house, as shown by Figure 2.8, which indicates that both a vendor and a department within the public agency provide similar services. The advantage of this approach is that it creates a comparison base and may allow a public entity to bring services back in-house relatively quickly if there are problems with the contract. For example, a city could designate four different zones for trash pick-up. One of the zones would always be kept in house so that there is a comparison and the city still retains the capacity to deliver the service.

Figure 2.7 **Competition Between Two Contracts**

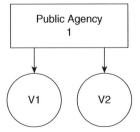

Figure 2.8 **Monopoly Situation**

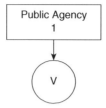

Competition not only allows agencies to benchmark the performance of contracts, but also pushes companies to innovate and be more efficient than their competitors. And in the case of public contracts, there is an additional advantage of generating the necessary information about the outcomes.

Incomplete Information

Contracts invariably raise the questions of complete and incomplete information. Even though there is a very well developed game theory approach to incomplete contracts (Guriev and Kvasov, 2005; Baker et al., 2002), in reality the consequences of incomplete contracts are not fully incorporated into the contracting out decision-making in public entities. What do we mean by complete information? This includes the information necessary for decision-making at every stage of the contract. In essence, this is the assumption that rational decision-making theory makes: individuals have complete information. Both incrementalism and mixed-scanning theories emphasize the lack of complete information.

In order to understand the nature of information, we have summarized some of the things to consider for contracting out in Table 2.2.

Monitoring may require specific technical knowledge and even legal requirements entered in the contract itself. In some areas, unless the monitoring is specifically discussed in the contract, it may not be legally allowed. Even though we have mentioned

Figure 2.9 **Partial Contracting Out**

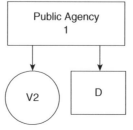

Table 2.2
Contracting Out Stages

Stage	Things to consider
Make or buy decision	Is there competition in the area?
	How service production is defined
	Where would cost-savings originate?
Bidding	Design outcome
	Draft the bid and the contract
	Recruit vendors if necessary
	Select best choice
Contracting out	Maintain performance through monitoring (how?)
	Manage contract

Notes: Based on Brown et al. (2006).

that the opportunistic actions can come from both sides of the contract, the public entity in the majority of cases retains the legal responsibility for the services (and has its reputation at stake) creating more opportunities for the opportunistic behavior from the vendors. The reputation is an example of asset specificity.

Asset specificity refers to the extent certain assets can be used or redeployed outside of a given market transaction (see Table 2.3). Different types of asset specificity were identified by Williamson (1990). For example, a public entity might have a very specific site for the library, and it may be difficult to use that site for anything else (or to use that site during the contract period for anything else). There can also be physical asset specificity, for example special transportation vehicles, which cannot be used for anything else. Brand names and reputations also represent examples of asset specificity. And it is the public agency that is usually publically accountable for the operations. There can also be a specific temporal specificity, for example, concessions during municipal celebrations. And finally, there can be dedicated assets to the specific contract or transaction when, for example, a company has to buy additional equipment to win the contract. In each of these situations, the agency, with highly specific assets, is the party most invested in the transaction and, thus, the party that stands to lose the most.

In the case of high asset specificity, the companies may prefer to enter long-term contracts or contracts with fewer details to encourage innovation and mutual growth (Guriev & Kvasov, 2005). The complete information contracts (or contracts that spell out all the details of service production) are usually low in asset specificity and include such examples as payroll, landscaping, street cleaning, and building security. Incompleteness of contracts and how it influences contract specifications is summarized in the following table. On one side of the spectrum is a "complete" contract where all outcomes, time schedules, etc., can be fully detailed. Such contracts will have certain duration and specified outcomes. In this case, a shorter contract allows for the fuller investment.

In the case of highly specific assets such as the operation of an airport, a prison, ambulance service, fire prevention/suppression or toxic waste disposal, long-term or even "ever-green" (Guriev & Kvasov, 2005) contracts with advance termination notice become the best contract specifications. Such contracts allow parties to fully invest in the transaction, but still be held accountable (hence advance termination notice).

One of the ways to deal with incomplete contracts is through relational contracts and establishing trust, but trust requires time (Brown et al., 2007). In the situations with incomplete contracts, relational, long-term, and undetermined contracts may allow parties to meet opportunities and challenges of the future. But such long-term contracts run contrary to the often-rebid full information contracts that create cost-savings according to New Public Management.

Another important aspect of contracting out due to incomplete information is the first-mover advantage. That is, the first contractor receives certain advantages through experiential learning that may not necessarily be replicated by other vendors. The incomplete information discussed here implies not only uncertainty about outcomes, but also ambiguity.

The difference between uncertainty and ambiguity is the difference between not knowing the probability of outcome "A" happening vs. not knowing what outcome "A" could actually be.[3] The long-term relational contract allows both parties to learn to work with each, and also lets public entities to get fuller information about potential outcomes. The private company gets to become more introduced to public values. That is why competition or trust is so important in contracting relationships. In the cases where the full outcomes are not understood or known before the transaction takes place, either competition or trust can help to develop that knowledge.

However, such contracts preclude any competition that may arise from rebidding the contracts. The lack of competition may be the ultimate answer to why there are still not any definitive studies on cost-savings from contracting out. Brown et al. (2007) study the key components of contracting success: completeness of information and trust. As

Table 2.3
Contracts and Information

Information about outcomes	Asset specificity	Time limits	Nature of the contract
Complete information contracts	Low	Short, easy to define end terms	Legalistic contract that may mitigate conflict, but miss arising opportunities
Incomplete contract	High	Indefinite contract with advance notice termination clause	Relational contract that allows experiential learning, but may incentivize opportunistic behavior

Note: Based on Guriev and Kvasov (2005), Brown et al. (2006) and Brown et al. (2007).

Table 2.4
Contracts and Trust

	Trust low	Trust high
Complete contract	Complete contract lowers the risk	Complete contract creates higher transaction costs and can limit creativity
Incomplete contract	Potential for opportunism	More creativity and flexibility

relationships between vendors and agencies deteriorated, the parties resolved to more "complete" contracts that may remove flexibility but introduce more certainty. At the same time as trust between parties has been increased, so the contracts become less complete.

The contracts with low trust and incomplete information provide the most room for opportunism. The contracts with highest trust and complete specifications can actually stifle the parties from meeting future opportunities. In both cases, the opportunity cost of the transaction is very high. In the situations of incomplete contracts, the public entities have to strive to develop trust with their vendors. In the situations with complete information, the public entities may rely more on the legalistic contracts. The problem here is that sometimes the nature of public services does not necessarily land to a complete contract. Table 2.4 summarizes the relationships between trust and contract specification (complete vs. incomplete contracts).

The politics of contracts may also reduce cost-saving. The vendor contributions to political campaigns of elected officials may also influence the contracting decision-making (Miranda, 1994). This may push public entities to contract out even in the situations where the cost-savings are not warranted. There are also political factors pushing public agencies away from contracting such as union opposition to contracting out. Since, in many cases (Austin & Coventry, 2001), the contracting out savings have been found due to the labor factor, the union opposition may provide concessions in order to make in-house operations more efficient and effective in the light of contracting out threats.

This political nature of public policy is best captured by mixed-scanning models of decision-making as they allow for management to strive for more rational decisions amidst all the constraints. In the final section, we provide additional advice for the public administration professionals who may face production and provision choices.

CONCLUSIONS

Greve (2001) called contracting out a "rubber duck in a tub" (p. 282) because, no matter how much savings are found or not realized, the concept of contracting out is here to stay. For some agencies, contracting out could offer an opportunity for greater flexibility. But in other cases it may be the only way to provide local services. Contracting out for public goods creates a situation requiring local governments to be involved in active management of contracts and creation of competition.

The government that plans to contract out for a service that requires highly specific assets is usually more invested in the contract and more vulnerable to the opportunism than a company with fewer specific assets in the contract. In such situations, long-term contracts are preferred even though they may undermine competition. From a mixed-scanning model decision-making standpoint, this may be a good option as long as the information is continuously updated and monitored.

A lot of the literature (Miranda, 1994; Warner, 2012; Austin & Coventry, 2001; Sclar, 2000) has discussed the importance of political factors influencing the decision to contract out. Campaign contributions from vendors, opposition from unions, and other political forces may shape and influence how the contracts take place, including the belief that contracting out reduces the size of government. Another important factor is path-dependency. Once certain decisions are made (e.g. contracting out for sewer services), reversing this decision may also involve transaction and conversion costs. Both incrementalism and mixed-scanning theories emphasize the significance of previous decisions on the currently considered alternatives. However, it is the mixed scanning model that proposes the systematic selection of provision and production options.

Based on the literature findings to date, Table 2.5 summarizes important elements to consider in decision-making regarding contracting out.

If there is strong competition among vendors, full information about outcomes, and high potential savings from contracting out, then the public agency should buy the services. The agency may also opt to contract out if there is limited in-house capacity to provide the services, but the provision of these services is highly desirable or even legislatively mandated. Such cases may arise when a local government is mandated by either state or federal governments or public to provide the services. However, the cost-savings are not likely to materialize in this special case.

If there is greater uncertainty about outcomes, no local competition, and little information about the outcomes (e.g. the measurements need to be defined), and little potential

Table 2.5

Make or Buy Decision and Information

	Buy	Make
High/Full	Competition among vendors	
	Information about outcomes	
	Potential savings from contracting out	
		Uncertainty
Low/Incomplete	Limited capacity	
		No competition
		Information about outcomes
	Uncertainty	
		Potential savings from contracting out

savings from contracting out, then the public entity is better to make the products/services in-house. Situations with limited information create the potential for high transaction costs that may eat up any minimal cost-savings from contracting out.

KEY POINTS

- Contracting out represents a public management dilemma between make (in-house provision) and buy (contract out) decisions.
- Transaction costs (including the costs of drafting contracts, administering bids, conducting monitoring, resolving disputes) should be included alongside conversion costs (one-time expenditures of getting expertise and needed capacity to change the service provision) when making the decision to contract out services.
- An adequate analysis of the costs and benefits should be conducted when making a decision to contract out a service.
- There are mixed results regarding the benefits of contracting out in terms of costs and quality.
- Both efficiency considerations and politics influence contracting out decisions.
- To maximize cost-savings from contracting out, public managers should become efficient contract managers and focus either on a legislative approach (if services are easy to measure) or a trust approach (if services are difficult to measure) to contracting.
- Ultimately, there is a greater likelihood of achieving cost-savings when the competition among vendors is present in the provision of services and the goals of the agency and vendors are aligned.

NOTES

1. Some prices may be set by legislation, while some may be set through the public and board meetings. However, the private companies' price-setting mechanism may work less formally. That is, private companies can address market changes more frequently adjusting for supply and demand fluctuations.

2. Low population density makes planning transit stops and routes more complicated. For example, in places with higher population densities, a larger number of passengers may be collected at any given stop compared to areas that are less dense.

3. We employ the concept of ambiguity here as discussed by Multiple-streams theory (Zahariadis 2007).

REFERENCES

Austin, J., & Coventry, G. (2001). *Emerging issues on privatized prisons*. NCJ 181249. Bureau of Justice Assistance, National Council on Crime and Delinquency. Retrieved from https://www.ncjrs.gov/pdffiles1/bja/181249.pdf.

Baker, G., Gibbons, R., & Murphy, K. (2002). Relational contracts and the theory of the firm, *The Quarterly Journal Economics*, *117*(1), 39–84.

Bel, G., & Fageda, X. (2010). Partial privatisation in local services delivery: An empirical analysis of the choice of mixed firms, *Local Government Studies, 36*(1), 129–149.

Bel, G., Fageda, X., & Warner, M. (2010). Is private production of public services cheaper than public production? A meta-regression analysis of solid waste and water services, *Journal of Policy Analysis and Management, 29*(3), 553–577.

Blom-Hansen, J. (2003). Is private delivery of public services really cheaper? Evidence from public road maintanance in Denmark, *Public Choice, 115*(3/4), 419–438.

Brown, T. L., & Potoski, M. (2003). Managing contract performance: A transaction costs approach. *Journal of Policy Analysis and Management, 22*(2), 275–297.

Brown, T. L., Potoski, M., & Van Slyke, D. M. (2006). Managing public service contracts: Aligning values, institutions, and markets. *Public Administration Review, 66*(3), 323–331.

Brown, T., Potoski, M., & Van Slyke, D. (2007). Trust and contract completeness in the public sector, *Local Government Studies, 33*(4), 607–623.

Brown, T. L., Potoski, M., & Van Slyke, D. (2008). Changing modes of service delivery: How past choices structure future choices. *Environment and Planning C: Government and Policy, 26*, 127–43.

Cohen, S. & Eimicke, W. (2008). *The responsible contract manager: Protecting the Public Interest in an Outsourced World*, Georgetown University Press.

Domberger, S., & Jensen, P. (1997). Contracting out by the public sector: Theory, evidence, prospects, *Oxford Review of Economic Policy, 13*(4), 67–78.

Etzioni, A. (1967). Mixed-scanning: A"third" approach to decision-making. *Public Administration Review*, 385–392.

GAO (Government Accountability Office) (1997). Social service privatization. Expansion poses challenges in ensuring accountability for program results, Retrieved from http://www.gao.gov/archive/1998/he98006.pdf.

GAO (2011). Public transit: Transit agencies use of contracting to provide services, Retrieved from http://www.gao.gov/assets/660/658171.pdf.

GAO (2013). Public transit: Transit agencies' use of contracting to provide service. Retrieved from http://www.gao.gov/products/GAO-13-782.

Girth, A. & Johnson, J. (2012). Saving money by contracting for public services. In R. Kemp (Ed.) *Municipal Budget Crunch: A Handbook for Professional* (pp. 22–24). Jefferson, NC: McFarland and Company Inc.

Greve, C. (2001). New avenue for contracting out and implications for a theoretical framework, *Public Performance and Management Review, 24*(3), 207–284.

Guriev, S. & Kvasov, D. (2005). Contracting on time, *The American Economic Review, 95*(5), 1369–1385.

Hefetz, A. & Warner, M. (2004). Privatization and its reverse: Explaining the dynamics of the government contracting process. *Journal of Public Administration Research and Theory, 14*(2), 171–190.

Kettl, D. F. (1993). *Sharing power: Public governance and private markets*. Washington, DC: Brookings Institution Press.

Lacity, M. Willcocks, L., & Feeny, D. (1996). The Value of Selective IT Sourcing, *MIT Sloan Management Review*. Retrieved from http://sloanreview.mit.edu/article/the-value-of-selective-it-sourcing/.

Levin, J., & Tadelis, S. (2010). Contracting for government services: Theory and evidence from US cities. *The Journal of Industrial Economics, 58*(3), 507–541.

Milward, R. (2011). Public enterprise in the modern western world: An historical analysis. *Annals of Public and Cooperative Economics, 82*(4), 375–398.

Miranda, R. (1994). Privatization and the budget-maximizing bureaucrat. *Public Productivity and Management Review, 17*(4), 355–369.

Miranda, R., & Lerner, A. (1995). Bureaucracy, organizational redundancy, and the privatization of public services. *Public Administration Review*, 193–200.

Rehfus, J. (1990). Contracting out and accountability in state and local governments: The importance of contract monitoring. *State and Local Government Review*, 22(1), 44–48.

Savas, Emanuel S., (1987). *Privatization: The key to better government*. Vol. 35. Chatham, NJ: Chatham House Publishers.

Savas, E. S. (2000). *Privatization and public-private partnerships*. New York, NY: Chatham House Publishers.

Savas, E. S. (2005). *Privatization in the city: Successes, failures, lessons*. Washington, DC: CQ Press.

Sclar, E. (2000). You don't always get what you pay for: The economics of privatization. Series: A Century Foundation Book. Ithaca, NY: Cornell University Press.

Sclar, E. (2015). The political economics of investment utopia: Public-private partnerships for urban infrastructure finance. *Journal of Economic Policy Reform*, 18(1), 1–15.

Smirnova, O. & Leland, S. (2013). The role of power and competition in contracting out: An analysis of public transportation markets. *Administration and Society*, 46(6), 1–23.

Talley, W. & Anderson, E. (1986). An urban transit firm providing transit, paratransit and contracted-out services: A cost analysis," *Journal of Transport Economics and Politics*, 20(3), 353–368.

Warner, M. (2012). Privatization and urban governance: The continuing challenges of efficiency, voice and integration. *Cities*, 29(Supplement 2), s38–s43.

Williamson, O. (1981). The economics of organization: The transaction cost approach. *American Journal of Sociology*, 87(3), 548–577.

Williamson, O. (1990). A comparison of alternative economic approaches to economic organization. *Journal of Institutional and Theoretical Economics*, 146(1), 61–71.

Van Slyke, D. (2003). The mythology of privatization in contracting for social services, *Public Administration Review*, 63(3), 296–315.

Zahariadis, N. (2007). Multiple streams theory. In P. Sabatier (Ed.), *Theories of the policy process*, Boulder, CO: Westview Press.

Zullo, R. (2007). Transit contracting reexamined: Determined of cost efficiency and resource relocation. *Journal of Public Administration Research and Theory*, 33(4), 517—534.

3

The Contracting Process

William Sims Curry

The objectives of this chapter on the contract process are to present and discuss the general steps in the contracting process and describe best practices associated with each process step.

THE CONTRACTING PROCESS

Milestones in the contracting process in this book begin with procurement planning and terminate with contract closeout and audit. The contracting process milestones, depicted below, were gleaned from a review of best practices in federal, state, and local agency contracting:

- Contract planning
- Issuance of solicitation and preparation of contractor responses
- Selection of the successful contractor
- Negotiations
- Contract preparation, review and clearance
- Contract award
- Contract Administration
- Contract closeout and audit.

The discussion of each of these processes in the contracting process and associated best practices comprise the remainder of this chapter.

Contract Planning

Contract planning, frequently referred to as advance contract planning, is initiated upon recognition of the need to acquire goods or services and terminates upon release of the solicitation to private sector firms. When the needed goods or services are low in value and complexity, the contract planning process may be informal. As the value and complexity of the goods and services increase, however, the need for a more formalized approach to contract planning is necessary. Careful planning in advance of releasing the solicitation will help limit the extent and severity of future adverse outcomes from deficient contractor selection and contract administration efforts. Informal contract planning for low value, low complexity acquisitions can likely be accomplished by a single individual. An ad hoc committee, however, might be the preferred option, or prescribed method, for planning high value, highly complex acquisitions.

The large number of issues to be addressed in planning for a large, complex acquisition is best met through development of an advance contract plan. The elements that are recommended for inclusion in the advance contract plan are listed in Table 3.1, Best Practices Recommended During Contract Planning for Federal, State and Local Government.

Table 3.1
Best Practices Recommended During Contract Planning For Federal, State, and Local Government

Best Practice	Recommended for Federal*	Recommended for State & Local
Establish agency website for communication management prior to contractor selection	√	√
Identify prospective contractors and determine whether sole source justification is required	√	√
Determine if preference will be given, or not given, to local contractors		√
Determine type of solicitation	√	√
The terms "proposal" and "bid" are not used Interchangeably		√
Determine type of contract	√	√
Use word that best compels contractors to perform tasks in all contract documents	√	√
Describe specifically weighted proposal evaluation criteria, including price, in solicitation	√	√
Establish proposal evaluation criteria and proposal scoring method	√	√
Describe potential contractor presentation in solicitation	√	√
Specify proposal format and page limit in solicitations	√	√
Include model contract, statement of work, and all contract documents in solicitations		√
Bids opened publically while proposals and quotations are opened in confidence		√
One page contract format containing variable data		√
Cost plus a percentage of costs (CPPC) contracts prohibited		√
Unallowable costs specified		√
Standard terms and conditions		√
Define responsibility and responsiveness in solicitation	√	√
Describe debriefing and protest options in solicitation		√
Management of contractor performance	√	√

* All of the best practices in Table 3.1 are recommended for federal, state & local government. Checkmarks are not indicated for federal government agencies if current regulations presently require compliance or the best practices are otherwise not applicable.

*Establish Agency Website for Communication Management
Prior to Contractor Selection*

Federal, state, and local government agencies are occasionally beset by instances where one or more prospective contractors receive differing, more, or more timely information concerning a particular acquisition than competing contractors. A best practice to avoid this problem is to establish an agency website where all questions from prospective contractors and agency response are posted. The recommended approach to managing pre-proposal communications through such a website is to describe the website in the solicitation, instruct contractors to direct all inquiries to one agency contact person, ensure that the agency's contact person develops the agency response, and that the contractor questions and agency responses are posted to the website where all prospective contractors will simultaneously have access to all the pre-proposal questions and agency responses. A description of the operation of the process for managing communications through implementation of a website is more fully explained subsequently in the section entitled "Issuance of solicitation and preparation of contractor responses."

Obtaining adequate competition is essential to obtaining optimal price, quality, and on-time delivery as well as ensuring that acquisitions are not tarnished by corrupt, inappropriate, non-competitive procurements. The development of a list of prospective contractors is best begun early in the procurement process to avoid ill-conceived sole source contracts. If there is truly just one contractor that can provide the needed product or service, it is appropriate to develop the sole source justification at this point in the contracting process.

*Determine Price Threshold Where Written Sole Source
Justification Is Required*

Guidelines for determining the dollar threshold where sole source justification is required are clearly defined in the FAR. The threshold for state and local governments, however, vary greatly. The terms and conditions published in The American Bar Association's (ABA's) 2000 Model Procurement Code for State and Local Governments (ABA Model Procurement Code), §3-204, Small Purchases and §3-205, Sole Source Procurement, recommend the establishment of price thresholds for awarding contracts according to simplified small purchase procedures and the establishment of a threshold wherein a designated agency official executes a written authorization to award contracts on a sole source basis.

*Determine if Preference Will Be Given, or Not Given, to Local
or Domestic Contractors*

When the selection of contractors that will receive solicitations is based on their geographical location, it is necessary to ensure that there is no illegitimate restraint of trade.

Federal government agencies may be restrained by trading treaties from limiting participation in acquisition to domestic companies. State and local governments may also be challenged by their decisions to restrict competition to local suppliers. State and local governments using federal grant monies may be restrained or encouraged to restrict competition to local firms. When expending funds received through grants, it is essential to study the grant provisions to ensure compliance with restrictions against or encouragement for local contracting policies.

Determine Type of Solicitation

Determining the type of solicitation for federal contracting professionals is well defined in the FAR. Two relevant FAR subparts are 14.2, Solicitation of Bids, and 15.2, Solicitation and Receipt of Proposals and Information. Similar guidance for state and local governments is provided in the ABA Model Procurement Code. Differentiation between bids and proposals can be discerned through the reading of §3-202, Competitive Sealed Bidding, and §3-203, Competitive Sealed Proposals. Certain state and local governments have begun using requests for bids (RFBs) for solicitation documents. The use of RFBs is discussed in the following section.

The Terms "Proposal" and "Bid" Are Not Used Interchangeably

Distinct differences in treating proposals received in response to RFPs and between bids received in response to IFBs could cause protests from prospective contractors claiming that their bids or proposals were handled improperly. Protests have the potential for resulting in delays in awarding contracts, lawsuits, and excess work on the part of procurement professionals who fail to use the proper terminology in their solicitation documents.

Federal contracting offices, because they are required to follow FAR provisions, are not normally confronted by the use of inappropriate solicitation terminology. On rare occasions, however, federal agencies have improperly referred to bids rather than proposals when using an RFP as their solicitation document.

Review of state and local government solicitations revealed not only incorrect terminology for contractors' responses to solicitations, but also use of the terms "proposal," and "bid" synonymously within a single solicitation document. The treatment of bids and proposals in the ABA Model Procurement Code §3-202 and §3-203 should make it clear that the terms "bid" and "proposal" have distinctly differing definitions and should not be used interchangeably.

Certain state and local government agencies have fairly recently begun using solicitation documents referred to as requests for bids (RFBs). The review of numerous RFB texts revealed that they closely parallel the provisions of IFBs. Other than discouraging the use of RFBs, however, this type of solicitation document is not discussed further here.

Determine Type Of Contract

Cost reimbursement contracts are more predominant in federal contracting than in state and local government contracting. Small local government agencies that do not acquire large-scale complex projects where it is difficult to determine costs in advance may have little or no need to use anything but fixed price contracts. Should state and local governments find it necessary to award cost reimbursement contracts, they can find an excellent discussion of the selection of contract types in FAR part 16, Types of Contracts, and subpart 16–104, Factors in selecting contract types where federal contracting professionals are afforded excellent guidance. State and local employees who may be novices with respect to cost reimbursement contracts will find that FAR contract clauses for cost reimbursement contracts serve as excellent models to consider when developing their own cost reimbursement contracts.

Use Word That Best Compels Contractors to Perform Tasks in All Contract Documents

State and local government contracting professionals do not enjoy the standard solicitation and contract language provided in the FAR. To impose an absolute responsibility for federal contractors to perform contractual tasks, FAR uses the word "shall" as the imperative. It is noteworthy that FAR definitions at §2.101 define "shall" as the imperative and for the definition of "must" readers are referred to "shall."

The DoD Federal Acquisition Regulation Drafting Guide indicates for following guidance for use of the words shall, must, should, will, and may:

(a) Use the term "shall" to indicate an obligation to act. In the FAR, "shall" and "must" have the same meaning. "Shall" is the preferred term to use. In provisions and clauses, do not state an obligation for the Government to act. State that the Government "will."
(b) Use the term "should" to indicate an expected course of action or policy to be followed unless inappropriate for a particular circumstance.
(c) Use "will" to indicate an anticipated future action or result.
(d) Use "may" to indicate a discretionary action.

The ABA Model Procurement Code[1] advises state and local governments that "shall denotes the imperative."

Federal workers, therefore, have sufficient guidance for using the word that best compels contractors to perform specific tasks when using boilerplate solicitation and contract provisions. State and local workers are advised to follow ABA Model Procurement Code guidance. Federal, state, and local government acquisition personnel, however, are advised to use caution while using locally produced documents such as statements of work, specifications, and other documents associated with solicitations and contracts regarding terminology intended to compel contractors to perform specific tasks. Although statements of work and specifications are prepared by engineers or other technically trained professionals, the best practice recommended here is for contracting professionals to review all such technical documents to ensure that "shall" is used to compel contractors to perform, and "will" is used to indicate anticipated future government actions or results.

Government contracting professionals, while performing this review of technical documents prior to incorporation into contractual instruments, are advised to ensure that there are no tasks that fail to identify the party of the contract designated to perform said tasks. Past reviews of statements of work have revealed instances where there is typically a section where the contractor "shall" perform certain tasks, another section where the agency "will" perform anticipated future actions or results, and, unfortunately, sometimes a section of tasks to be performed without designating which party to the contract bears responsibility for performing such tasks. When a document is vague with respect to what party will perform specific tasks, the burden is normally placed on the party responsible for preparing the document. Since the government prepares its contractual documents, the government is likely to be held responsible for accomplishing tasks in the statement of work when the responsible party is not designated. In cases where such tasks without a designated party are found in contractual documents, government procurement officials are encouraged to coordinate with the responsible technical personnel to ensure that ambiguities are removed from these documents.

Describe Specifically Weighted Proposal Evaluation Criteria, Including Price, in Solicitation

FAR §15.304, Evaluation Factors and Significant Sub factors, requires, at minimum, inclusion of the following information on evaluation factors (criteria) in federal government solicitations:

(d) All factors and significant subfactors that will affect contract award and their relative importance shall be stated clearly in the solicitation (10 U.S.C. 2305(a)(2)(A)(i) and 41 U.S.C. 253a (b)(1)(A)) (see 15.204-5(c)). The rating method need not be disclosed in the solicitation. The general approach for evaluating past performance information shall be described.

(e) The solicitation shall also state, at a minimum, whether all evaluation factors other than cost or price, when combined, are—

  (1) Significantly more important than cost or price;
  (2) Approximately equal to cost or price; or
  (3) Significantly less important than cost or price (10 U.S.C. 2305(a)(3)(A)(iii) and 41 U.S.C. 253a(c)(1)(C)).

Adherence to these minimal requirements for stating the importance of evaluation criteria in relevant terms, however, renders federal procurements subject to corruption. Should proposal evaluators have a favored contractor, the flexibility offered in the level of importance permitted by stating criteria importance in relative terms permits the placement of greater importance on the criteria where the favored contractor is strongest and lesser importance on the criteria where the favored contractor is weakest. If the contracting agency assigns specific numeric values to the evaluation criteria and reflects those numeric values in the solicitation, proposal evaluators are restrained from adjusting the importance of criteria to benefit favored contractors. The absence of standardized contracting practices for state and local governments results in wide disparities with respect to statements regarding the importance of evaluation criteria in their solicitations. The best practice for state and local governments, however, is consistent with federal contracting in that greater transparency into the proposal evaluation process lessens opportunities for favoritism in the award of contracts. Another benefit of numeric values (see Table 3.4 for an example) is increased transparency for prospective contractors. Prospective contractors are able to determine the specific importance of each criterion rather than merely relying on relative values. Knowing the specific importance for each criterion permits contractors to place greater emphasis on developing solutions for the more important criteria. Prospective contractors are also better able to determine if the government placed the proper emphasis on the criteria when identifying the proposal offering the best value to the agency.

The government benefits through numerical weighting of evaluation criteria by obtaining the capability to weigh criteria ratings through formulae that generate weighed ratings that reflect not only the proposal evaluators' ratings but a numerical value that also includes the importance the government assigned to each criterion. The benefits to numerical weighting assigned to evaluation criteria are more fully developed and apparent to readers in the discussion of the recommended process for rating proposals during the "evaluation of proposals" phase of the contracting process.

Establish Proposal Evaluation Criteria and Proposal Scoring Method

The FAR clearly requires consideration of price or cost when selecting contractors. The ABA Model Procurement Code includes §3-203(7), Award, indicating that award shall be made on the basis of "price and the evaluation factors set forth in the Request for Proposals." Despite this requirement, however, a review of state and local government solicitation documents revealed the identity of evaluation criteria but frequently failed to name price or cost as an evaluation criterion. It appeared, however, that failure to list price or cost was an oversight. It is believed that state and local government agencies routinely consider price or cost when selecting contractors. The best practice recommended here is to include price or cost as a selection criterion in solicitations to avoid complications that might arise should there be any inconsistency between the selection criteria reflected in solicitation and the criteria used in the evaluation of proposals. The recommended best practice for selecting the best value proposal is described in the contracting process referred to as "Selection of the best value proposal."

Describe Potential Contractor Presentation in Solicitation

When planning for a procurement action, the procurement planning team might wish to consider inviting companies that submitted proposals to make presentations to the proposal evaluation team. Since proposals may be self explanatory, however, it is recommended that contractor presentations be made at the discretion of the agency, and that the option for contractor presentations be described in the solicitation. If one or more contractors are offered the opportunity to make presentations, all contractors in the competitive range should be offered the same opportunity.

Specify Proposal Format and Page Limit in Solicitation

Specifying the format for proposals submitted by competing contractors will simplify the evaluation process of multiple proposals that are required to be prepared in an identical format. Requiring proposal sections mirroring the evaluation criteria further simplifies the proposal evaluation effort and helps ensure that material relating to evaluation criteria in each contractor's proposal is not overlooked. Establishing a page limit will ensure that extraneous materials need not be considered by members of the proposal evaluation team. Page limits for each section of the proposals that also mirror the evaluation criteria will result in homogenous proposals, thus greatly simplifying the contractor selection process.

Include Model Contract, Statement of Work, and All Attachments in Solicitations

Federal contracting offices, as well as most state and local agencies, consistently follow the best practice of including a model contract, statement of work, and all contract related attachments in their solicitations. This best practice streamlines the contracting process by providing prospective contractors with all contractual documents for their review early in the contracting process to avoid untimely surprises in contractor responsibilities that could potentially delay contract award.

Bids Opened Publically While Proposals and Quotations Are Opened in Confidence

FAR provisions ensure that federal solicitations state that bids in response to IFBs are opened publically and that proposals in response to RFPs are opened in confidence.

Although most state and local governments also conform to this practice, a review of solicitations released by certain state and local government agencies revealed advice in RFPs that proposals would be publically opened. The ABA Model Procurement Code states, in §3-203(4), Receipt of Proposals, that proposals are to be opened so as to avoid disclosure of the contents and not made available for public disclosure until the contract has been awarded.

One Page Contract Format Containing Variable Data

This is yet another best practice wherein federal contracting offices benefit through standard regulations and forms that generally separate variable contract data from boilerplate information. State and local government agencies that imbed variable data within verbiage more suited for inclusion in boilerplate risk errors committed by including information from previous contracts in more recent contracts. An example of an area for entering variable information is provided as Table 3.2, Variable Information Table.

Table 3.2
Variable Information Table

VARIABLE INFORMATION TABLE						
					Contract Number	
Term of This Contract (Complete Dates in Just One of the Following Three Shaded Rows)							
√ Below	Term Begins			Term Completion Date			
	On Following Date			On Following Date		
	Receipt of Notice to Proceed			Calendar Days Following Notice to Proceed		
	Upon Execution by Agency			Calendar Days Following Agency Contract Execution		
Agency Department				FOB Point		
Terms			Basis of Price (Do Not √ More Than One of the Following Four Blocks)				
Price		Fixed Price		Annual Price		Monthly Price	Hourly Rate
Not-to-Exceed Price			√ if Reasonable Expenses authorized in addition to Hourly Rate			
Contractor Contact Information			Agency Contact Information			
Contractor			Project Manager			
Address			Address			
City, State & ZIP			City, State & ZIP			
Telephone			Telephone			
Email			Email			

Cost Plus a Percentage of Costs (CPPC) Contracts Prohibited

FAR Subpart 16.1, Selecting Contract Types, prohibits use of cost plus a percentage of costs contracts. This type of contract rewards the contractor for incurring excess costs. Whatever allowable costs the contractor incurs are reimbursed at cost plus the percentage of the incurred costs. The cost reimbursement percentage is normally established at the inception of the contract. The more the contractor spends, the higher its profits. The ABA Model Procurement Code §3-501, Types of Contracts, also includes a prohibition against the use of CPPC contracts. Despite FAR restrictions against CPPC contracting and the recommended prohibition against CPPC contracting in the ABA's Mod Procurement Code, solicitations and model contracts continue, although rarely, to provide for reimbursement of costs plus a percentage of costs.

Unallowable Costs Specified

An entire section on unallowable costs is included in FAR. The FAR section contains a list of and definitions for unallowable costs. ABA's Model Procurement Code §7-101, Cost Principles Regulations Required, fails to explicitly prohibit payment of unallowable costs, but does recommend exclusion of costs such as fines, entertainment, advertising, and other costs that most government employees and taxpayers may not consider appropriate for reimbursement by government agencies. The best practice recommended here, naturally, is to include a prohibition against paying defined unallowable costs in the model contract attached to the solicitation and the final version of the contract that is awarded. State and local government agencies seeking advice on developing internal guidance for specifying unallowable costs might start by reviewing guidance provided in the FAR.

Standard Terms and Conditions

FAR provides a list of contract provisions and detailed instructions for including such provisions in solicitations and contracts. The provisions and instructions for use of standard terms and conditions for state and local governments are not nearly as comprehensive. A review of contract provisions for states and local governments participating in a research project revealed that certain states and local governments' standard terms and conditions failed to include provisions for the contract clauses listed in Table 3.3, Underrepresented Contract Provisions.

The best practice recommended for state and local government contracting activities with respect to standard terms and conditions is to periodically request their legal counsel to review the standard terms and conditions to determine whether any of Table 3.3, or other relevant contract provisions should be incorporated in their standard terms and conditions.

Table 3.3
Underrepresented Contract Provisions

Amendments	Insurance
Americans with Disabilities Act	Nondiscrimination
Applicable law and forum	Notices
Assignment of antitrust claims	Officials not to prosper
Audit and employee interviews	Ownership
Budget contingency	Payment of taxes
Compliance with laws	Performance evaluation
Confidentiality	Political contribution disclosure
Conflict of interest	Remedies not exclusive
Copyrights	Subcontracting
Document retention	Successors and assigns
Drug free workplace	Survival of provisions beyond the contract term
Entire agreement	Termination for default or convenience
Health Insurance Portability and Accountability Act	Unallowable costs
Indemnification	Workers' compensation
Independent contractor	

The absence of provisions for termination of contracts for default or convenience will likely complicate termination of the contract either for the convenience of the government or default on the part of the contractor. This topic is explored in greater detail during the discussion of the contract administration process.

Define Responsibility and Responsiveness in Solicitation

Solicitations oftentimes contain, and are recommended to include, a requirement for contractors to be responsible as a prerequisite for contract award. If the solicitations do not define responsible and responsive (when applicable), contractors disqualified on the basis of failing to be meet these requirements are more likely than not to dispute or protest their disqualification. FAR §9.1, Responsible Prospective Contractors, includes an extensive discussion of responsibility for prospective contractors. Insight into the development of a definition of responsive can be found in FAR §§14.202-6, Final review of invitations for bids; 14.404-4, Restrictions on disclosure of descriptive literature; and 14.408-4, Economic price adjustment.

Describe Debriefing and Protest Options in Solicitation

Government contractors are generally afforded the opportunity to protest solicitation provisions or the selection of a contractor for award of a contract. Protests of federal government agencies' contracting actions may be filed before or after contract award. Protests may be filed directly with the agency, the Government Accountability Office (GAO), or the U.S. Court of Federal Claims.

State and local government offices have agency unique procedures for filing protests. Generally, however, protests are to be filed with the agency's office having overall responsibility for contracting matters. General Services offices commonly have such overall contracting responsibility for state and local government agencies. Describing protest procedures in the solicitation ensures that protests are filed properly. Protests that are improperly filed may prove more problematic than properly filed protests.

Management of Contractor Performance

Consideration of how the agency will manage contractor performance needs to be undertaken during the contract-planning phase of the contracting process to ensure that the solicitation specifies, the contract requires, and the contractor understands the processes for:

- Submission of contractor reports and the scheduling of meetings needed to properly manage contractor performance.
- Billings and progress payment requests are made in the correct format and timeframe.
- Agency has rights to visit the contractor's facility and hold discussions with contractor personnel.
- Processing of contract changes according to the agency's practices.
- Agency has authority to take appropriate actions to deal with substandard contractor performance.
- Contractor's requirement for maintaining contractual records for the designated time period.

ISSUANCE OF SOLICITATION AND PREPARATION OF CONTRACTOR RESPONSES

Solicitation documents include primarily requests for proposals (RFPs), invitations for bids (IFBs), and requests for quotes (RFQs). Due to their complexity and the extended timeframe from issuance of solicitations to award of contracts, RFPs appear most prone to developing provisions that differ between various government agencies. All types of solicitations, however, must conform to the rule that solicitations are provided concurrently to all prospective contractors.

Following the issuance of solicitations, the primary activity being conducted is preparation of contractor responses to the solicitation. Although the discussion of activities conducted following release of solicitations and receipt of contractor responses is not discussed in the FAR version of the acquisition cycle, government has significant responsibilities during this timeframe. While the government may appear to merely be awaiting contractor responses to its solicitation, there are challenges to federal (Federal Acquisition Regulation, Subpart 1.6) as well as state and local[2] governments' responsibility for complying with the key procurement tenet for treating all contractors equally.

Although the contracting officer may have ensured that solicitations and addenda thereto sent to prospective contractors were identical and transmitted at the same time, one or more contractors may innocently, or not so innocently, pose a question to a member of the government's proposal evaluation team and receive a direct reply that is not communicated to the competing contractors. Such a reply to fewer than all prospective contractors likely constitutes the failure to treat all contractors equally and introduces an opportunity for corruption of the procurement process. One example of just such a breach occurred during the acquisition of permanent canal closures and pumps for Lake Pontchartrain in the greater New Orleans metropolitan area. The US Army Corps of Engineers stated in its RFP that the budgeted amount was $700 million. The RFP also advised prospective contractors that proposals should utilize the full budgeted amount and that lower priced solutions may be determined non-competitive and eliminated. A Corps of Engineers official, however, informed one company representative that it would be to its advantage to propose a price less than the budgeted amount. All the companies but one proposed the full budgeted amount. The company that was advised to propose a lower price came in $25 million under budget and was selected for contract award based on a determination that the strengths and weaknesses of the competing contractors did not support a $25 million premium. A best practice to avoid providing a competitive advantage, such as the one described above, is to manage communications between the agency and prospective contractors. This can be accomplished by implementing a communications management plan that designates, in the solicitation, one government representative to whom all questions regarding the solicitation are to be directed. To ensure that questions are in writing, so as to avoid misinterpretations, and timely, it is recommended that all questions be posed via e-mail to the agency representative designated in the solicitation. To ensure that questions receive identical government responses and are made available to all contractors at the same time, it is recommended that no direct response be made to the contractor posing the question, but that all questions and government responses be posted on an agency website. It is also recommended that the government website where contractor questions and agency responses are posted be identified in the solicitation.

SELECTION OF THE SUCCESSFUL CONTRACTOR

This phase of the contracting process begins upon receipt of the contractors' responses to the government's solicitation and concludes when the contract is awarded. The evaluation of proposals is decidedly the most challenging aspect of the contractor selection process. The evaluation of bids consists primarily of the determination of the contractors' responsiveness and responsibility, and then selecting the lowest price responsive bid from a responsible contractor. Responses to solicitations for information and quotes are not significant with respect to the topic of this chapter and, therefore, are not included in this discussion. The balance of this section, therefore, will be dedicated to the evaluation of proposals. The objective of proposal evaluation is to select the contractor proposing the best value to the government. Identification of the contractor offering the best value is most effective when evaluation criteria are assigned numerical weights and proposals are scored numerically. State and local governments follow this practice fairly consistently. Federal agencies, however, normally assign relative weights to evaluation criteria and use adjectival or color codes to score proposals. The FAR, as indicated in the following quoted passage does permit numerical scoring of proposals:

> (a) Evaluations may be conducted using any rating method or combination of methods, including color or adjectival ratings, numerical weights, and ordinal rankings.

Despite this flexibility in FAR, however, DoD restricts rating methods to color or adjectival ratings. A review of protests of federal contractor selections sustained by the Government Accountability Office (GAO) reveals that the practice of limiting of rating methods to color or adjectival ratings frequently results in ambiguous decision matrices prepared by DoD proposal evaluation teams. Other federal agencies, in fact, follow DoD's lead in relying solely on color or adjectival ratings. Therefore, this unfortunate practice is widespread throughout the federal government. An illustration of the ambiguity resulting from this practice is provided in Chapter 9, Ethics in Contracting, in the section on "Avoidance of Contracting Practices That Contribute to Procurement Fraud." Determinations made by the GAO regarding the propriety of contractor selection pertain solely to federal contracting and are not directly related to federal subcontracting or to federal and state contracting. Despite ample differences between scoring practices of state and local government agencies, as well as federal government prime contractors,

Table 3.4

Contrasts between Color, Adjectival, and Numerical Rating Schema

Color	Adjectival	Numeric	Description
Blue	Outstanding	90–100	Proposal reflects an exceptional approach and understanding of the requirements. The proposal contains multiple strengths and no deficiencies.
Green	Excellent	80–89	Proposal reflects an exhaustive approach and understanding of the requirements. The proposal contains at least three strengths and no deficiencies.
Yellow	Good	70–79	Proposal reflects a favorable approach and understanding of the requirements. Proposal contains at least two strengths and no deficiencies.

the need to implement proposal-scoring techniques that explicitly identify the contractor offering the best value is fundamental throughout all levels of government contracting.

The recommended process for selecting the contractor offering the best value is to use a scale of 70–100 to score subjectively rated criteria and to use contractors' proposed values (or values recalculated for reasonableness if applicable) for objectively rated criteria.

Table 3.4, Contrasts between Color, Adjectival, and Numerical Rating Schema, depicts the scheme for the scale of 70–100 for subjectively rated criteria. This table also demonstrates how proposal evaluation team members restricted to color and adjectival ratings are forced to assign tied scores to certain criteria despite determining differences in the merits of prospective contractors' proposals.

The evaluation of a criterion for two or more proposals may meet the description associated with the blue or outstanding rating in Table 3.4, and, therefore, must be assigned identical scores despite proposal evaluation team members discerning differences in the quality between competing proposals. When using numeric ratings, however, it is possible to assign any scores in the range from 90 to 100 to criteria meeting the description for blue or outstanding ratings. This capability to assign differing scores to proposals meeting the description of blue or outstanding ratings permits proposal evaluators to reflect discerned differences in the qualities of competing proposals.

Another distinct advantage to using numeric scores is that they can be weighed to reflect the importance to the government of the various criteria. Table 3.5 provides a contrast between relative and numeric rating schemes. When all criteria ratings are numeric, they can be combined to obtain a single number with the highest combined number designating the proposal offering the best value. State and local governments routinely assign numeric weights to evaluation criteria. Most federal agencies, however, follow DoD's lead in restricting criteria weighting to relative terms.

Obtaining a single combined score is complicated by the fact that certain objective criteria, such as price, are more favorable to the government when values are low. This challenge, however, can be met by using a formula that weighs both subjectively and objectively rated criteria while converting low scores to high values when low values benefit the government. Use of similar formulae was implemented by at least seven

Table 3.5

Relative and Numeric Weighting of Proposal Evaluation Criteria

Relative weighting of criteria	Numeric weighting of criteria	
The evaluation criteria are management approach, corporate experience, personnel, past performance, and price. The non-price criteria are of equal importance to each other and, when combined, are significantly more important than price.	Management Approach	18
	Corporate Experience	18
	Personnel	18
	Past Performance	18
	Price	28
	TOTAL	100

Table 3.6
Criteria Types and Formulae

Criteria rating description	Formulae
Subjective criteria – high numbers favorable	S = R(W/HR)
Objective criteria – high numbers favorable	S = V/(HO/W)
Objective criteria – low numbers favorable	S = HO-(V-L)/(HO/W)
Objective criteria with an optimal value	
(Ascending section of line)	S = V/(OV/W)
(Descending section of line)	S = (OV—(V—OV))/(OV/W)
Objective criteria with a suboptimal value	
(Descending section of line)	S = SV—(V—LVL)/(SV/W)
(Ascending section of line)	S = SV—(HVL—V)/(SV/W)

states, two large cities, and one large university. The formulae for the criteria rated subjectively and objectively when either high or low values are favorable to the government are reflected in Table 3.6 Criteria Types and Formulae.

Where: HO =   Highest observed value
HR =   Highest assigned subjective rating
HVL =   High value limit
L =   Lowest observed value
LVL =   Low value limit
OV =   Optimal value
R =   Actual subjective rating
S =   Weighed score
SV =   Suboptimal value
V =   Observed value
W =   Criterion weight.

Examples of cryptic proposal evaluations abound in GAO determinations made in response to protests of the selection of companies for award of federal contracts. Although GAO determinations apply solely to federal government contracting, the contractor selection deficiencies noted in the following examples apply equally to state and local contracting as well as to subcontracting by federal prime contractors.

Ensure That Government Does Not Afford One, or More, Contractors.
A Competitive Advantage Over Other Contractors

The earlier discussion of the best practice of establishing a website to help manage communications prior to contractor selection explained how this practice contributes to equal treatment of contractors. Although agencies have established such a website, close attention is required to ensure that contractors are treated equally. One example wherein the GAO determined that government provided two contractors an unfair advantage over their competitors during the evaluation of proposals occurred when the U.S. Department of State (DOS) failed to establish a common cutoff date for filing final proposal revisions (FPRs). In this case DOS originally determined that three proposals were in the competitive range and that two proposals were excluded from the competitive range. Following discussions with the two excluded companies, their proposals were reinstated in the competitive range and they were permitted to submit FPRs. The DOS failed, however, to provide the original three contractors in the competitive range the opportunity to submit FPRs. A protest followed, and in sustaining the protest the GAO determined that "the agency failed to provide a common cutoff date for FPR submission."

Proposals Are Evaluated Stringently According to the Contractor Selection Criteria[3], Stated in the Solicitation

A best practice to ensure that proposals are evaluated according to the selection criteria in the solicitation is to prepare proposal evaluation forms with evaluation criteria, exactly as they appear in the solicitation, for use by the proposal evaluation team members. Agencies that use information technology (IT) systems to prepare solicitations have the relevant information available to develop computer prepared proposal evaluation forms that duplicate the selection criteria exactly as reflected in the solicitation. Having the proposal evaluation criteria printed directly on the forms used to evaluate proposals provides assurances that proposals will be evaluated strictly according to the criteria in the solicitation.

Proposals Are Scored in Conformance to the Methodology Described in the Solicitation

The third and final best practice relevant to the evaluation of proposals is to prepare proposal evaluation forms that duplicate the scoring methodology reflected in the solicitation. Just as with selection criteria, IT systems contain sufficient information to duplicate the proposal scoring methodology on the proposal evaluation forms exactly as they appear in the solicitation.

NEGOTIATIONS

When government includes a model contract, scope of work, specifications, and deliverables in the solicitation and the successful contractor does not take exception to any contract provisions, there may be few if any issues to negotiate. Negotiations with the apparent successful contractor during this phase of the contract process could involve provisions of the contract that is to be awarded. Changes in provisions to the model contract included in the solicitation that are not provided for all competing contractors could be considered as favoritism toward the contractor that obtained changes to the contract provisions. Discussions with contractors during this phase of the contracting process, therefore, present challenges to maintaining uniform solicitation provisions. When changes are made to provisions of the model contract, which was an integral part of the solicitation, for fewer than all the competing contractors, the results may appear to be more serious than a simple administrative error.

A more blatant form of nefarious actions during negotiations is the act of misleading of contractors. Although the following case is based on a GAO determination, the need to prohibit the misleading of contractors during negotiations is obviously applicable throughout all levels of government contracting. One notable case where the GAO determined that the agency mislead a contractor during negotiations involves agency advice to a contractor that it increase its proposed number of full-time employees (FTEs) for a particular task. After the contractor increased its proposed FTE's for that task by 40 percent, the agency selected a competing contractor based on the competitor's proposed lower price. The contractor claimed that the agency asked for the increase due to budgetary reasons, but the agency denied that charge. The agency's documentation of the proposal evaluation, however, indicated that the contractor's staffing was adequate. The agency assigned that contractor 461 out of a possible 500 points on its criterion for managerial and operational approach. It is difficult to determine if this act of misleading the contractor was the result of incompetence or for more nefarious reasons. The question regarding the motivation for actions by public officials is discussed in greater detail in Chapter 9, Ethics in Contracting.

Best practices for conducting negotiations are to present the agency's rationale for all offers and counteroffers, present a written description of detailed offers to ensure complete understanding of the complexities, and to treat all competing contractors equally. Making offers to contractors without presenting the government's rationale is tantamount to horse-trading. The reasoning for treating contractors equally is the same as discussed earlier in this chapter.

CONTRACT PREPARATION, REVIEW, AND CLEARANCE

Preparation of the contract document can normally be accomplished by modifying the model contract from the solicitation by incorporating the successful contractor's information and any changes to the provisions agreed to between the agency and the successful contractor. Care should be taken, however, to ensure that provisions more favorable than those in the model contract are not included in the final contract document unless the competing contractors had an opportunity to submit their proposals, or submit an FPR, based on the provisions of the final contract. Final review and clearance of contract documents vary from agency-to-agency, but routinely include review or clearance by procurement staff, finance, and legal counsel.

CONTRACT AWARD

Government agencies are oftentimes required to announce their intention to award contracts to permit competing contractors the opportunity to file a protest prior to contract award. Once all the preceding actions have been taken, and any protests have been addressed, the contract may be awarded to the successful contractor. Depending on the contracting agency's procedures, distribution of contractual documents may be accomplished as an administrative exercise or the agency may hold a formal post-award briefing to ensure that the agency and the contractor have a complete understanding of one another's roles and responsibilities.

CONTRACT ADMINISTRATION

The contract administration phase of the contracting process involves the contractor fulfilling its responsibilities according to the provisions of the contract. The government's activities during this phase on the contracting process includes monitoring the contractor's progress, evaluating invoices and approving payment when warranted, advising the contractor of agency initiated changes to the contract, evaluating contractor initiated changes to the contract, negotiating contract changes when deemed appropriate, and amending the contract to reflect negotiated changes.

A best practice during this phase of the contract process involves scrutiny of the contractor's performance to ensure compliance with contractual requirements. Cost reimbursement or large, complex fixed price contracts likely require the contractor to prepare earned value data submitted periodically to the agency for evaluation and to identify contract requirements that require added scrutiny. A key recommendation offered here is for the government to assign at least one person to monitor the contractor's activities and be prepared to approve or provide guidance on the approval of the contractor's tasks, evaluate validity of earned value reports, and sign-off on contract payments. The government's efforts to bring a noncompliant contractor into compliance should be thoroughly documented in the contract file.

The government may wish to terminate a contract after it has been awarded. If termination is due to the contractor's default, the government will use the default termination provisions of the contract. If the government wishes to terminate the contract due to no fault of the contractor, the government will use the convenience termination provisions. For government agencies that fail to include termination provisions in their contracts, this process is likely to be considerably more difficult. A significant difference between the convenience and default termination provisions is that the contractor receives more generous settlement provisions through the termination for convenience. Prior to terminating a contract for default, the contractor is normally given a show cause notice to permit the contractor to demonstrate why the contract should not be terminated for default. The government's contract file should contain evidence of its efforts to bring the contractor into compliance prior to issuance of the show cause notice. Should the government determine, after reviewing the contractor's response to the show cause notice, that it does not have a firm basis for a default termination, it may still wish to terminate the contract. In this instance, the government may discontinue the pursuit of a default termination and initiate a termination for convenience.

CONTRACT CLOSEOUT AND AUDIT

The contract closeout and audit phase of the contracting process begins upon contract completion or termination and concludes when contract files are transferred to records staging where they will be stored and eventually destroyed on or soon after the required retention period. Agency tasks during this phase of the contract process typically include reporting of contract completion, removal of excess funding, and preparation of a contractor performance report.

Certain completed contracts are normally selected for audit. Contract audits typically include an evaluation of the source selection process, full and open competition requirements, adequacy of the sole source recommendation if applicable, effectiveness of socioeconomic contracting obligations, adequacy of the contractor's performance, propriety of contractor payments, identification of problems encountered, and preparation of lessons learned if appropriate.

KEY POINTS

- Although contracts vary greatly regarding goods and services being procured, the contract process is well defined and includes government and contractor responsibilities throughout.
- Contrasts between commercial and government contracting necessitate the assignment of staff specifically trained in government contracts prior to their participation in the contracting process.
- All phases of the contract process are important, but contract planning is especially critical and, when well executed, contributes immensely to the success of the entire contracting effort.
- Implementation of an effective contractor selection process provides the best assurances for selection of the contractor that will provide the best value to the government and to taxpayers.
- A source selection process that clearly identifies the proposal offering the best value helps protect the government and taxpayers from the possibility of procurement fraud.

- Best practices in contracting have been sought since the beginning of commerce, but revised procedures developed through continuous improvement are applicable in the contract management field and should be vigorously pursued.

NOTES

1. The American Bar Association (ABA) 2000 Model Procurement Code for State and Local Governments is not mandatory for any state or local government unless adopted by that state or local government.

2. The American Bar Association (ABA) 1979 Model Procurement Code for State and Local Governments includes eleven basic principles; the fifth basic principle is "Equal Treatment of Bidders/Offerors." Issuance of the ABA's 2000 Model Procurement Code for State and Local Governments did not suspend provisions of the original 1979 provisions.

3. The federal government refers to proposal evaluation criteria as "factors" The ABA's 2000 Model Procurement Code for State and Local Governments refers to both "factors" and "criteria" In this book, however, the term "proposal evaluation criteria" or "criteria" will be used unless referring to FAR or Model Procurement Code passages.

REFERENCES

Curry, W. S., (2014). *Government abuse: Fraud, waste, and incompetence in awarding contracts in the United States*, London: Transaction Publishers.

Federal Acquisition Regulation, Subpart 1.6—Career Development, Contracting Authority, and Responsibilities, §1.602 Responsibilities.

Federal Acquisition Regulations, 15.305, Proposal evaluation.

U.S. Department of Defense, Defense Federal Acquisition Regulation Supplement (DFARS) §215.300.

U.S. Department of Defense, "Federal Acquisition Regulation Drafting Guide," Version 5, April 30, 2011.

U.S. Government Accountability Office, "PCCP Contractors, JV; Bechtel Infrastructure Corporation;" File number B-405036; B-405036.2; B-405036.3; B-405036.4; B-405036.5; and B-405036.6; August 4, 2011.

U.S. Government Accountability Office, "Raytheon Technical Services Company LLC," File number B-404655.4, B-404655.5, and B-404655.6, October 11, 2011.

U.S. Government Accountability Office, "SeKON Enterprise, Inc.; Signature Consulting Group," File number B-405921 and B-405921.2, January 17, 2012.

Part II

Issues in Government Contracting

4

Performance-Based Contracting

Lawrence L. Martin

INTRODUCTION

Perhaps no other development in recent years has had a greater impact on government procurement than performance-based contracting (PBC) (Martin, 2005; 2002). Beginning at the federal level and spreading to states and local governments, PBC has become the standard when contracting for services. For example, the *Federal Acquisition Regulation* (*FAR*), the rules that govern federal procurement and contracting, states that PBC is the "preferred method" for acquiring services (*FAR*, 2014). It is also estimated that PBC is utilized by about 40 percent of state and local governments (Martin et al., 2010). PBC is also the preferred state approach when contracting for social services, particularly child welfare services (Never & DeLeon, 2014; Lu, 2013; Collins-Camargo, McBeath & Ensigh, 2011).

Today, some government somewhere is utilizing PBC for just about every conceivable service imaginable, including consulting, research and development, prisoner reentry, housing, building maintenance, public health, parks and recreation, fleet management, job training, lottery operations, marketing, social services, elevator maintenance, and the list goes on and on (Martin & Miller, 2006). It should be noted that PBC methods are also used for other types of contracting including construction and infrastructure (Lawther & Martin, 2014; Lawther & Adler, 2008). However, the discussion here focuses on PBC for services.

WHAT IS PBC?

No universally agreed upon definition of PBC exists. However, several definitions have been proposed. The National Association of State Procurement Officials (NASPO, 2008, p. 3) defines PBC as "a request for proposal on a negotiated procurement where . . . Proposers/Contractors are encouraged to offer solution based proposals that focus on the outcomes rather than prescriptive specifications. Price is usually a minor factor in the award criteria." Unfortunately, the NASPO definition focuses only on the *procurement* (acquisition) aspects of PBC while essentially ignoring the contractual aspects.

Consequently, the NASPO definition does not really illuminate the differences between PBC and more traditional forms of government service contracting. Additionally, the contention that price is a minor consideration in PBC is highly questionable and not universally accepted. The *Federal Acquisition Regulation* (*FAR,* Subpart 37.6) proposes a different and more complex definition of PBC:

> Performance-based contacting methods are intended to ensure that required performance quality levels are achieved and that total payment is related to the degree that services are performed or outcomes achieved meet contract standards. Performance-based contracts use measurable performance standards (i.e., in terms of quality, timeliness, quantity, etc.) and specify procedures for reductions of fee or for reductions to the price of a fixed-price contract when services are not performed or do not meet contractual requirements.

The *FAR* definition gets closer to the essence of PBC by focusing on the *contracting* aspects (e.g., measurable contract performance standards and fee/price reductions when contractor performance is unsatisfactory). However, the *FAR* definition applies only to federal departments and agencies and has not been embraced by state and local governments. Similar to the FAR, but more generalizable to state and local governments, is the PBC definition proposed by the National Institute of Governmental Purchasing (NIGP). NIGP, like NASPO, is a professional organization of government procurement and contracting individuals. Unlike NASPO, however, the membership of NIGP is comprised disproportionally of local government (municipal and county) officials.

The NIGP defines PBC as "a results oriented contracting method that focuses on the outputs, quality and outcomes of service provision and may tie a portion or all of a contractor's compensation as well as contract extensions or renewals to their accomplishment" (NIGP, 2012). The NIGP definition focuses on the actual work to be performed by contractors as described in contract work statements, the measurement of contractor performance (in terms of outputs, quality and outcomes) and the tying of payments as well as contract extensions and renewals to their accomplishment. As such, the NIGP definition is concerned with the differences between design and performance specifications and promoting greater use of the latter.

These three deferring definitions highlight some of the major conceptual and experiential differences in how PBC is understood by federal, state and local government procurement and contracting work forces. For the purposes of this chapter, the NIGP definition will be adopted. The rationale is that the NIGP definition comes closest to promoting a conceptual understanding of the major differences between PBC and more traditional approaches to government services contracting. The NIGP definition also has the added advantage of having been adopted by the Chartered Institute of Purchasing and Supply of the United Kingdom, which means the definition also travels reasonably well internationally (NIGP, 2012).

DESIGN AND PERFORMANCE SPECIFICATIONS

The outputs, quality and outcomes referenced in the NIGP definition of PBC refer to a class of government contract requirements called performance specifications. The actual work to be performed by contractors, as opposed to the myriad "boiler plate" clauses (e.g., equal employment opportunity, prevailing wage, environmental protections, etc.) generally found in most government contracts, can be classified as either *design* specifications or *performance* specifications (NASPO, 2008). At its core, PBC, following the NIGP definition, involves the utilization of performance specifications, while simultaneously attempting to minimize the use of design specifications.

Design Specifications

Design specifications are concerned with how a service is conceptualized and delivered. Utilizing the systems approach as a conceptual framework (Figure 4.1), design specifications can be thought of as input and process activities.

Design specifications essentially tell contractors "how to do the work." The purpose of design specifications is to reduce, or to remove entirely, contractor discretion over how a service is designed and delivered. Consider, for example, a contract for parks maintenance services that primarily utilizes design specifications. A contract of this nature might contain literally dozens of design specifications that tell the contractor the minimum number of staff that must be employed (input), the type of equipment that must be used (input), how often trash cans must be emptied (process), how frequently the grass must be cut (process), how often trees, shrubs and plants must be fertilized (process), and a myriad other input and process activities.

Performance Specifications

Performance specifications, on the other hand, are concerned with the results of service provision in terms of outputs, quality and outcomes. Outputs refer to how much service is provided. The ratio of outputs to inputs is the classic definition of efficiency. Quality

Figure 4.1 **The Systems Framework and Government Service Contract Specifications**

Inputs →	Process →	Outputs →	Quality →	Outcome
[Design	Specifications]	[Performance	....	Specifications]
- staff	- methodologies	- service volume	- timeliness	- results
- facilities	- approaches	- units of service	- reliability	
- equipment	- strategies		- conformity	
- supplies				
- material				

refers to the quality of the outputs provided in terms of timeliness, reliability, conformity and other considerations. Outcomes refer to the results, accomplishments or impacts (the effectiveness) of services.

Performance specifications do not tell contractors how to do the work. Instead, performance specifications tell contractors the results that are expected and leave the "how to" up to them. Contractors are free to choose their own methods (inputs and process) of delivering the service and accomplishing the expected performance. Continuing with the example of a parks maintenance contract, performance specifications might state that facilities are to be maintained in good operating condition (quality/outcome); grass is to be neatly trimmed (outcome); courts and ball fields are to be visibly free of trash and weeds (outcome), etc.

ADVANTAGES OF PBC

In a very real sense, PBC attempts to overcome the historic disconnect between the motivation for governments to contract and how they actually go about contracting. One of the primary motivations for government contracting, and indeed one of the primary motivations for all forms of privatization, is the assumption that the private sector is more efficient and more innovative than government (Savas, 2001). However, the preference of governments for the use of design specifications has actually worked to reduce the discretion of private sector contractors, which in turn reduces their ability to be more efficient and innovative, thereby negating the primary motivation for governments to contract in the first place. PBC, with its preference for performance specifications over design specifications, overcomes the historical contracting disconnect and offers several advantages to both governments and contractors (Table 4.1).

PBC AND GOVERNMENT PERFORMANCE ACCOUNTABILITY AND PERFORMANCE MEASUREMENT

The increasing use of PBC is also, partially, a reflection of government's adoption of performance accountability and performance measurement. For the last 20 plus years, governments at all levels (federal, state and local) have been moving towards greater use of

Table 4.1
Major Advantages of PBC for Governments and Contractors

- Contractors can utilize new and innovative service delivery approaches.
- Contractors can focus on the results to be achieved rather than the process of service delivery.
- Governments can reduce transaction costs (monitoring and supervision) by focusing on observable measures of performance (outputs, quality and outcomes).
- Governments can reduce service delivery costs by paying only for the performance achieved.

Source: Adapted from: Martin & Miller, 2006; Martin et al., 2010

performance accountability and performance measurement. The two major drivers of the government performance accountability and performance measurement movement are the *Government Performance & Results Act*, and the "service efforts and accomplishments" (SEA) reporting initiative of the Governmental Accounting Standards Board (GASB).

GOVERNMENT PERFORMANCE AND RESULTS ACT

The Government Performance & Results Act of 1993 (Public Law 103–62) requires all federal departments and agencies to annually report to the President and Congress on the performance of their programs, services and activities. GPRA, as the act is generally known, requires federal departments and agencies to "establish performance indicators to be used in measuring or assessing the relevant outputs, service levels, and outcomes of each program activity." The act further states that, "an outcome measure means as assessment of the results of a program activity . . . while an output measure means the tabulation, calculation, or recording of activity or effort" (GPRA, Section 1115). Congress renewed its commitment to performance accountability and performance measurement when it passed the *GPRA Modernization Act of 2010*. As part of the act, Congress stressed the need to make greater use of performance information in strategic decision-making (including budgeting) and in the use of networks and networking tools (e.g., contracts and grants) (Moynihan, 2013).

SERVICE EFFORTS AND ACCOMPLISHMENTS (SEA) REPORTING

The Governmental Accounting Standards Board (GASB) is the organization that establishes "generally accepted accounting principles" for state and local governments. In keeping with the direction of the federal government, GASB recommends that state and local governments also adopt performance accountability and performance measurement. GASB has put forth an approach that it calls "service efforts and accomplishments" (SEA) reporting (GASB, 1994). Like GPRA, GASB's SEA reporting encourages state and local government programs, services and activities to collect and report information on their performance, including outputs, quality and outcomes. Given its accounting and financial management perspective, GASB's SEA reporting also advocates for the greater use of unit costs (e.g., cost per output, cost per quality output and cost per outcome). From time-to-time, GASB has reconfirmed its commitment to performance accountability and performance measurement, and, in 2010, issued voluntary guidelines (GASB, 2010).

Public policy today is quite clear in calling for government programs, services and activities to embrace performance accountability and performance measurement. PBC can be thought of as a method of translating performance accountability and performance measurement into performance specifications for use in government contracting.

USE OF PBC

It is estimated that more than 50 percent of federal service contracts today utilize PBC (Newell, 2008). Similar data on the use of PBC by state and local governments is not available. However, some speculations on the use of PBC by state and local governments can be made based on a 2009 national survey conducted by the National Institute of Governmental Purchasing (Martin, 2010; Martin et al., 2009). Some 600 NIGP members responded to the self-selection convenience survey. When asked about PBC use in their governments, 40 percent indicated that they made at least some us of PBC approaches.

In a follow up question respondents identified three major factors mitigating against the greater use of PBC: (1) lack of staff trained in the use of PBC, (2) lack of PBC knowledge on the part of top administrators, and (3) lack of PBC knowledge on the part of contractors. These findings underscore the point that to make greater use of PBC, governments must first insure that their procurement and contracting work forces are well grounded in its principles and practices. Both the Government Accountability Office (GAO, 2002) and the Office of Federal Procurement Policy (OFPP, 2007) reached this same conclusion. They have noted the lack of familiarity with PBC principles and practices on the part of significant segments of the federal procurement and contracting work force and have advocated for more training on PBC.

In another follow up question contained in the NIGP survey, respondents were asked if they thought the use of PBC by their governments would increase, decrease or stay the same. Half (48.4 percent) of the respondents said they believed the use of PBC would increase, while the other half (47.3 percent) said they believed the use of PBC would stay about the same. Only a small proportion (4.6 percent) said they thought the use of PBC would decrease.

In summary, it would appear that PBC is here to stay, but its principles and practices still remain unclear to a large segment of the government procurement and contracting work force. Consequently, it can be said that interest in PBC remains high, but its actual use has yet to become a standard operating practice.

PBC APPROACHES

There are numerous approaches to the implementation of PBC (Table 4.2). However, all of the PBC approaches identified in Table 4.2 share a common objective: encouraging contractors to focus more on performance. It should be noted that Table 4.2 is not meant to be an exhaustive treatment of PBC approaches. New PBC approaches are being invented all the time. The number and variety of PBC approaches are limited only by the creativity of government procurement and contracting work forces.

Table 4.2
Approaches to PBC

- Federal Approach
- Award Fee
- Award Term
- Benchmarking
- Share-in-Savings
- Revenue Sharing
- Hold Back
- Unit Cost/Unit Price (output, quality or outcome)
- Milestone.

THE FEDERAL APPROACH TO PBC

The federal government has its own unique approach to PBC. According to the *Federal Acquisition Regulation* (*FAR*), for federal contracts to be considered "performance based," they must contain four critical elements: (1) performance requirements, (2) performance standards, (3) a quality assurance plan, and (4) positive and negative incentives. Any federal contract that does not include all four elements is not considered to constitute PBC.

Performance requirements are the identified performance measures used in the contract. *Performance standards* define the allowable deviation, if any, from the performance requirements. The performance standards are also referred to as the "acceptable quality level" (AQL). The *quality assurance plan* (QA plan), also referred to as a "surveillance plan" or a "monitoring plan," specifies how the government will determine contractor performance using at least one of the following: 100 percent inspection, random sampling, periodic inspection or customer input. *Positive and negative incentives* are included and tied to the QA plan. In the case of the federal approach, a picture is worth 1,000 words of description. Table 4.3 is a hypothetical example of federal performance based contract for elevator maintenance services.

STATE AND LOCAL GOVERNMENT APPROACHES TO PBC

The federal approach to PBC is considered by many state and local governments to be overly complex, particularly for less experienced government procurement and contracting staff. Additionally, because state and local governments are not bound by the requirements of the *Federal Acquisition Regulation*, they are free to develop their own individual approaches to PBC. Some of the more common state and local government approaches to

Table 4.3

The Federal Approach to PBC for Elevator Maintenance Services

Specifications of Tasks/Statement of Objectives	Performance Measures/ Performance Requirements	Performance Standards Acceptable Quality Level	Incentives and Penalties	Monitoring/ Quality Assurance Plan
to maintain building elevators in working order	all four elevators are function at all times	95%	- achievement of standard = none - above standard = incentive - below standard = penalty	- periodic inspection by government - customer input
to perform preventive maintenance	all preventive maintenance performed as scheduled	95%	- achievement of standard = none - above standard = incentive - below standard = penalty	periodic inspection by government
to respond to emergency calls	All emergency calls responded to within 2 hours	95%	- achievement of standard = none - above standard = incentive - below standard = penalty	100% inspection by government
to satisfy government building employees	All government building employees satisfied with elevator operations	85%	- below standard = loss of contract	customer input
to submit elevator maintenance repair records	all reports submitted on time	95%	- achievement of standard = none - above standard = incentive	third party certification (city department of business regulation)

Source: Adapted from Martin & Miller (2006), p. 116

PBC include: award fee, award term, benchmarking, share-in-savings, revenue sharing, holdbacks, unit cost/unit price (output, quality and outcome) and milestone.

Award Fee Approaches

Award fee approaches to PBC are essentially "lump sum" bonus systems. A specified amount of money (the bonus) is identified that contractors can earn upon completion of their contracts provided specified levels of performance are achieved. Performance can be operationalized in terms of output, quality or outcome performance measures, as well as any other performance objectives mutually agreed upon. Because award fee approaches represent bonuses, and not decreases in any agreed upon compensation, no economic downside exists from the perspective of contractors.

Award Term Approaches

Award term approaches to PBC constitute non-monetary bonus systems. Under award term approaches, contractors can earn extensions to existing contracts or the award of new contracts for achieving specified levels of performance. Again, there is no economic downside for contractors, but there is considerable upside benefit. Contractors are guaranteed additional work while avoiding the costs and risks associated with competing in another procurement.

Benchmarking Approaches

Benchmarking approaches to PBC are, likewise, bonus systems. Benchmarking approaches are sometimes referred to as "hurdles" (GAO, 2006). Benchmarks, or hurdles, are identified in terms of performance standards. If contractors achieve the identified performance standards, they qualify for bonus payments. Unlike award fee approaches, benchmarking approaches are not restricted to "lump sum" payments made at the end of contract terms, but may also include payments for the achievement of specific levels of performance during the contract. One variation of this approach to PBC is to tie specific bonus payments to the accomplishment of specific benchmarks in terms of outputs, quality or outcomes. A second method is to tie bonus payments to the relative performance achieved by contractors providing the same or similar services. For example, a contractor's performance would need to exceed the performance of other contractors (a best in class approach) in order to qualify for a bonus payment. Again, because benchmarking approaches are essentially bonus systems, there is no economic downside for contractors.

Share-in-Savings Approaches

Share-in-savings approaches to PBC are also called "gain sharing" (GAO, 2003). As the name implies, in share-in-savings approaches, contractors share in any surplus contract funds not expended during the term of the contract. Share-in-savings approaches are most applicable in cost reimbursement type contracts where a specific amount of funding is budgeted. If contractors manage their costs judiciously, they share in any fund balances remaining at the end of the contract term. The cost sharing arrangements (e.g., 90/10, 80/20, 75/25, 50/50, etc.) are negotiated as part of the contract.

Revenue Sharing Approaches

Revenue sharing approaches are yet another form of gains sharing. Like share-in-savings, the name "revenue sharing" pretty much sums up these approaches to PBC. Contractors are expected to generate some amount of revenue. In one variation of this approach, contractors' operating costs are covered under the terms of their contracts, consequently the amount of revenue generated and the contractors' share of that revenue represent a bonus. In other variations, contractors are expected to generate revenue sufficient to cover some percentage of their operating costs. The revenue expectation range can vary significantly (5 percent, 10 percent, up to 100 percent) of operating costs. This approach, of course, presupposes that the services in question are ones in which user fees can be charged or some other type of revenue stream identified. Revenue sharing approaches do have potential negative implications for contractors if they are required to recover a portion of their operating costs.

Hold Back Approaches

Under hold back approaches to PBC, a portion (e.g., 2 percent, 5 percent, 10 percent, etc.) of contractors' compensation is held back and is payable at the end of the contract terms provided the contractors achieve specified levels of performance. Operationally, contractors could be required to meet all performance requirements or some percentage (75 percent, 80 percent, etc.). Hold back approaches can have a negative economic effect on contractors. Under hold back approaches, revenue that contractors expect to earn, and upon which they may have based their contract pricing are placed in jeopardy. If contractors do not meet their performance requirements, they can lose money.

Table 4.4

Unit Cost/Unit Price Approaches to PBC

Service	Service Unit	Type of Unit	Cost/Price Per Unit
Ambulance Services	One Trip	Output	X$ Per Trip
Job Training Services	One Person Placed in a Job	Outcome	X$ Per Person Placed
Traffic Management Services	One Traffic Light Fixed	Output	X$ Per Traffic Light Fixed
Economic Development Services	Number of New Companies Relocating to the Area	Outcome	X$ Per Company Relocating to the Area
Street Repair Services	Number of Pot Holes Repaired	(Output)	X$ Per Pot Hole Repaired
Sidewalk Repair Services	Number of Linear Feet of Sidewalk Replaced	(Output)	X$ Per Number of Linear Feet of Sidewalk Replaced

Table 4.5
Milestone Approach to PBC for Management Consulting Services

Milestone	Due Date	% of Fee
Contract Award	July 1	10%
Submission & Acceptance of Management Study Plan (output/quality)	August 15	10%
Submission & Acceptance of Interim Progress Report (output/quality)	December 1	20%
Submission and Acceptance of Draft Final Report	March 1	20%
Submission & Acceptance of Final Report (Outcome/quality)	May 1	40%

Unit Cost/Unit Price Approaches

Unit cost/unit price approaches are the first of what can be truly called complete "pay-for-performance" approaches to PBC. Contractors are paid an agreed upon amount of money for each unit of service provided. The units of service are generally of the output or outcome type (see Table 4.4).

Milestone Approaches

Milestone approaches to PBC are appropriate when the service can be conceptualized as a project with identifiable start and stop points and major milestones along the way. In such situations, milestone approaches to PBC represent a form of project management. This approach is similar to the progress payments approach used in construction contracting (Lawther & Adler, 2008). Two variations of milestone approaches to PBC are: (1) tying specific payments to accomplishment of specific milestones and (2) tying a proportion or percentage of a fixed-fee/fixed-price contract to the accomplishment of specific milestones. A milestone approach to PBC tying a proportion or percentage of a fixed-price/fixed-fee contract for management consulting services might look something like Table 4.5.

ASSESSING THE PERFORMANCE OF PBC

A question frequently asked is: does PBC produce better results than more traditional approaches to government services contracting? While the desire to frame the question thusly is understandable, it really misses the whole point of PBC. When a government and a contractor enter into PBC and agree upon a set of contract performance measures and payments, and the contractor meets those expectations and is compensated appropriately, then, by definition, the PBC contract is a success. When contract performance expectations are not achieved, the government withholds compensation and may decide

Figure 4.2 **PBC as a Self-Assessing System**

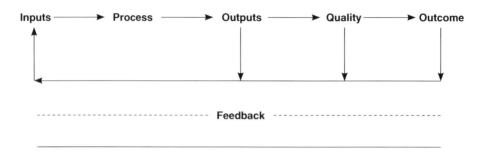

not to do business with that contractor in the future. Success and failure, then, is determined on a case-by-case (contract-by-contract) basis according to assessment (evaluation) criteria mutually agreed upon by the contracting parties. PBC is, in a very real sense, a self-evaluating system (Figure 4.2) that does not require a comparison or control group.

When data on the outputs, quality and outcomes of PBC are collected, reported and utilized to monitor and assess contractor performance, the result is a self-evaluating system (Kettner, Moroney & Martin, 2013).

The social science and evaluation communities view the idea that PBC is essentially a self-evaluating system with some suspicion. This suspicion goes to the heart of the difference between government performance accountability and performance measurement and what can be called more formal program evaluation techniques (McDavid, Huse & Hawthorn, 2013; Kettner, Moroney & Martin, 2013; Rossi, Lipsey & Freeman, 2004).

KEY POINTS

- There is no universally agreed upon definition of PBC.
- PBC is an umbrella term that includes many approaches that attempt to alter contractor behaviors to focus more on performance.
- PBC focuses on the use of performance specifications (output, quality and outcome), while attempting to minimize the use of design specifications.
- PBC can include monetary and non-monetary approaches as well as incentives and penalties.
- PBC is a self-evaluating system that is accomplished on a case-by-case (contract-by-contract) basis.

REFERENCES

Collins-Camargo, C. McBeath, C., B. & Ensign, K. (2011). Privatization and performance-based contracting in child welfare: recent trends and implications for social service administrators. *Administration in Social Work, 35.* (2007): 494–516.

Federal Acquisition Regulation (FAR). (2014). Subpart 37.6—Performance-Based Contracting. Retrieved from http://www.acquisition.gov/far/05-05/html/Subpart%2037_6.html.
Government Accountability Office (GAO) (2002). *Contract management: Guidance needed for using performance based service contracting.* Washington, DC: GAO.
Government Accountability Office (GAO) (2003). *Contract management: Commercial use of share-in-savings contracting.* Washington, DC: GAO.
Government Accountability Office (GAO) (2006). *Grants management: Enhancing performance accountability provisions could lead to better results.* Washington, DC: GAO.
Governmental Accounting Standards Board (GASB) (2010). New suggested guidelines will help governments provide a more complete picture of their performance. Retrieved from http://gasb.org/resources/ccurl/708/389/SEA%20SG%20PLA%20Final.pdf.
Kettner, P., Moroney, R. & Lawrence. M. (2013). *Designing and managing programs: An effectiveness-based approach.* Thousand Oaks, TA: Sage Publications.
Lawther, W. & Adler, J. (2008). *Contracting for construction services.* Herndon, VA: National Institute of Governmental Purchasing.
Lawther, W., & Lawrence L. M. (2014). Availability payments and key performance indicators: Challenges for effective implementation of performance management systems in transportation public private partnerships. *Public Works Management & Policy, 19*, 219–234.
Lu, J. (2013). *The performance of performance-based contracting in human services.* Paper presented at the 11th Public Management Research Conference, Madison, Wisconsin, June 20–22.
Martin, L. L. (2002). *Making performance based contracting perform: What the federal government can learn from state & local governments.* Washington, DC: IBM Center for the Business of Government.
Martin, L. L. (2005). Performance-based contracting for human services: Does it work? *Administration in Social Work, 29*, 63–77.
Martin, L. L. (2010). Performance based contracting for services: a survey of NIGP members. Presentation made to participants at the 2010 General Services Administration Forum in Orlando, Florida (2010). Retrieved from http://www.google.com/url?sa=t&rct=j&q=&esrc=s&frm=1&source=web&cd=4&ved=0CDgQFjAD&url=http%3A%2F%2F208.112.78.139%2FgsaSchedule2010%2Ftraining%2Fppt%2FPerformanceBasedContractingForNIGP.ppt&ei=NU6tVJeYKuPjywOA14HgAQ&usg=AFQjCNHWGzxia2iotoeYGUDvrJSDS6ODUA&bvm=bv.83134100,d.bGQ.
Martin, L.L., & Miller, J. (2006). *Contracting for public sector service.* Herndon, VA: National Institute of Governmental Purchasing.
Martin, L. L., McCue, C., Allaf, M., & Borger, T. (2010). *Performance-based contracting for services: A survey of NIGP members.* Retrieved from http://www.uky.edu/SocialWork/qicpcw/documents/PBC-NIGP%20survey.pdf.
McDavid, J., Huse, I. & Hawthorn, L. (2013). *Program evaluation & performance measurement: An introduction to practice.* Thousand Oaks, CA: Sage Publications.
Moynihan, D. (2013). *The new federal performance system: Implementing the GPRA modernization act.* New York, NY: IBM Center for the Business of Government. Retrieved from http://www.businessofgovernment.org/report/new-federal-performance-system-implementing-gpra-modernization-act.
National Association of State Purchasing Officials (NASPO) (2008), *State and local government procurement: A practical guide.* Lexington, KY: NASPO.
National Institute of Governmental Purchasing (NIGP) (2012). Public procurement practice: Performance based contracting. Retrieved from http://principlesandpractices.org/wp-content/uploads/2013/04/PerformanceBased.pdf.
Newell, E. (2008). Performance-based contracting. *Government executive.* Retrieved from http://www.govexec.com/magazine/features/2008/02/performance-procurement/26214/.

Never, B. & DeLeon, E. (2014). The effect of government contracting on nonprofit human service organizations: Impacts of an evolving relationship. *Human service organizations: Management, leadership & governance, 38,* 258–270.

Office of Federal Procurement Policy (OFPP). *Memorandum for chief acquisition officers senior procurement executives (May, 2007). Using performance based acquisition to meet program needs—Performance goals, guidance, and training.* Retrieved from http://www.whitehouse.gov/sites/default/files/omb/assets/procurement/pba_revised_052207.pdf.

Rossi, P., Lipsey, M. & Freeman, H. (2004) *Evaluation: A systematic approach.* 7th Edition, Thousand Oaks, TA: Sage Publications.

Savas, E. S. (2001). *Privatization & public private partnerships.* New York, NY: Chatham House.

Standards Board (GASB) (1994). *Concepts statement No 2 of the Governmental Accounting Standards Board on Concepts Related to Service Efforts and Accomplishment Reporting.* Norwalk, CT: Governmental Accounting Standards Board. Retrieved from http://www.gasb.org/cs/BlobServer?blobkey=id&blobnocache=true&blobwhere=1175824063642&blobheader=application/pdf&blobcol=urldata&blobtable=MungoBlobs.

5

Contracting with Nonprofit Organizations

Christopher R. Prentice and Jeffrey L. Brudney

INTRODUCTION

From a traditional perspective, government production and delivery of goods and services is straightforward. Where economic or private markets fail to provide needed goods, government usually emerges to produce them. Guided by principles such as equity, transparency, and representativeness, government ensures that taxpayer-funded public goods and services, such as education, national defense, interstate highways, and municipal fire protection, are broadly available and generally inexhaustible. Unconcerned with profit and accountable to the citizenry whose taxes fund public purposes, government endeavors to provide services in an effective and efficient manner. In this process, government often relies on other organizations as partners to help deliver services. Although contracting for service delivery predates the founding of the United States, over the past half-century or so this practice has accelerated with growing amounts of services, governments, organizations, and funding involved. This chapter examines one primary facet of this growth: government contracting with nonprofit organizations for the delivery of publicly financed goods and services.

CHARACTERISTICS OF NONPROFIT ORGANIZATIONS

Nonprofit organizations in the United States number 2.3 million, 1.6 million of which are registered with the Internal Revenue Service (Roeger et al., 2012). Nonprofits are a major force in the U.S. economy, contributing 5.4 percent of GDP (McKeever & Pettijohn, 2014) and accounting for 10.5 percent of employment (Roeger et al., 2012). In 2013 private giving to nonprofits totaled over $335 billion, and volunteer labor added an estimated value of $163 billion as more than one-quarter of Americans reported volunteering in that year (McKeever & Pettijohn, 2014). Nonprofits operate in various mission areas, such as education, health, environment, religion, human services, recreation and sports, public safety, housing, and culture and arts among others. The nonprofit landscape of today is as representative as Alexis de Tocqueville described it in the 1830s:

Americans of all ages, all conditions, and all dispositions constantly form associations. They have ... associations of a thousand ... kinds, religious, moral, serious, futile, general or restricted, enormous or diminutive. The Americans make associations to give entertainments, to found seminaries, to build inns, to construct churches, to diffuse books, to send missionaries to antipodes; in this manner they found hospitals, prisons, and schools. If it is proposed to inculcate some truth or foster some feeling by the encouragement of a great example, they form a society. Wherever at the head of some new undertaking you see the government in France, or a man of rank in England, in the United States you will be sure to find an association. (1945, II, p. 106)

Although it is difficult to summarize the characteristics of an entire sector of economic activity, several theorists, including Salamon and Anheier (1992a), provide a cogent description of the nonprofit sector. Their description helps us to understand not only the distinctive characteristics of nonprofit organizations but also why government chooses to engage with them in the delivery of public services. Salamon and Anheier (1992a) identify five characteristics of nonprofits. These organizations are formally constituted, non-governmental in basic structure, self-governing, non-profit distributing, and voluntary to some meaningful extent.

- *Formally constituted*: Although nonprofit activity often begins and arises to address a communal issue, nonprofit organizations are formalized entities dedicated to particular purposes. Formalization includes obtaining a state charter of incorporation and/or attaining IRS recognition of tax-exempt status, naming a board of directors, meeting regularly, and setting procedures.
- *Non-governmental*: Nonprofits are not instruments of government; they are private organizations that provide a public benefit. Though nonprofits receive a substantial portion of their revenue from government directly in the form of grants and contracts, and indirectly through tax-exemptions, they are not government-run.
- *Self-governing*: Nonprofits have bylaws, boards of directors, and additional internal procedures to ensure the independent governance of the organization. These elements create legal and ethical boundaries that prevent control by outside entities.
- *Non-profit distributing*: Nonprofits are mission-oriented organizations. Although nonprofits are legally allowed, even normatively encouraged to make a profit (that is, bring in revenues in excess of expenses) to maintain fiscal health and organizational stability, profits are cycled back into the organization's programs. Nonprofits do not have shareholders (stockholders) like for-profit organizations, and are thus legally prohibited from distributing dividends (a concept known as the non-distribution constraint).
- *Voluntary*: Nonprofit organizations are voluntary for two reasons: first, nonprofits typically receive at least some of their revenue from contributions, and second,

nonprofits operate with and/or are governed by volunteers. "The presence of some voluntary input, even if only a voluntary board of directors, suffices to qualify an organization as in some sense 'voluntary'" (Salamon & Anheier 1992a, p 136).

According to Salamon and Anheier (1992b, p. 268), these "five core structural or operational features . . . distinguish the organizations that comprise the nonprofit sector from other types of social institutions." Given these characteristics, we begin to understand why government might view nonprofit organizations as desirable partners in the delivery of services. First, and perhaps most obviously, the public (government) and nonprofit sectors are grounded on a philosophy of not seeking or realizing a profit from their activity. Second and related, by contrast to the for-profit or business sector, government and nonprofit organizations tend to operate in public policy domains where it can be difficult to earn a profit even if this motivation were salient. Third, both the public and the nonprofit sectors attempt to meet the human and social needs of the populace, usually without regard for citizens' ability to pay for the requisite services, for example, job training, literacy, counseling, food, etc. Fourth, both sectors are accustomed to working under the confines of tight budgetary restrictions. Based on these similarities, governments might well seek to contract with like-minded and -motivated nonprofit organizations for the delivery of services.

GOVERNMENT CONTRACTING WITH THE NONPROFIT SECTOR: THEORETICAL BACKGROUND

"Three-failures theory" (Steinberg, 2006) offers more specific answers regarding why government chooses to contract with nonprofit organizations for the delivery of certain types of services. According to this theory, government contracts with nonprofit organizations to overcome a market failure or inefficiency that would otherwise result from relying on for-profit business firms to provide goods and services when the motives of these potential partners, as well as citizens' ability to evaluate the services, are in doubt. The theory proposes that government will prefer nonprofit organizations as contracting partners over for-profit firms when it is difficult for the consuming public to judge service quality or results. As economist Henry Hansmann (1987, p. 29) argued, when "owing either to the circumstances under which a service is purchased or consumed or to the nature of the service itself, consumers feel unable to evaluate accurately the quantity or quality of the service a firm produces," they will ultimately prefer that a nonprofit organization provide the service rather than a business firm. In such circumstances, a for-profit firm has both the incentive and the opportunity to take advantage of customers by providing less service than was promised and paid for (Hansmann, 1987).

By contrast, consumers are likely to perceive and appreciate nonprofit organizations as more trustworthy for two reasons: the "halo effect" and the non-distribution constraint. The "halo effect" refers to the popular perception of nonprofit organizations as altruistic, likely owing to nonprofits' historical roots in providing alms to the poor. As we discussed above, the non-distribution constraint refers to the restrictions on private benefit and private inurement in nonprofit organizations. Nonprofits are required by law to cycle profits back into mission-related activities and are not allowed to pay dividends to the "owners" or "shareholders." Indeed, the concept of ownership is more nebulous in the nonprofit sector and is often grounded in the belief that because nonprofits receive favorable tax treatment, they have a responsibility to operate on behalf of the public. Without shareholder profit as a motivating factor as in for-profit firms, nonprofits are constrained in their ability "to benefit personally from providing low-quality services and thus have less incentive to take advantage of their customers" (Hansmann, 1987, p.29).

Burton Weisbrod (1977) presents an additional rationale for government contracting with nonprofit organizations for the delivery of goods and services: because government tends to provide public goods and services only to the level that satisfies the typical or "median" voter, residual demand by those individuals who want more public goods or services goes unsatisfied. In this view, nonprofit organizations arise to meet this demand. Thus, "Many nonprofit firms provide services that have the character of public goods" (Hansmann, 1987), which not only supports the potential for goal congruence between government and nonprofits that we described earlier but also offers an explanation for why governments choose to support nonprofit enterprise in policy areas that have the character of public goods and where government is unable or unwilling to provide services.

Three-failures theory proposes that governments contract with nonprofit organizations to deliver goods and services for which it is difficult to evaluate service quality or amount, or to fill the gap left by the public and market sectors. Nonprofits provide goods and services in excess of the wants of the typical median voter and in areas that do not yield profits. Yet, due to several voluntary sector failures (Salamon, 1987), such as lack of funding, resource insufficiencies, and disorganized and inefficient practices, the nonprofit sector itself fails to meet the goals that government has for it in their entirety.

Three-failures theory begins to provide the theoretical background for government contracting, but it cannot offer a complete explanation. To understand this changing dynamic we turn to the rise in "Third-Party Government."

THIRD-PARTY GOVERNMENT

Third-party government refers to the shift in the delivery of public goods and services from direct government provision to indirect means through the use of private actors often through contracting relationships. In this model, government and nonprofits emerge as complementary rather than alternative actors (Salamon, 2002), providing a range of services through a mix of delivery systems. As Smith and Gronbjerg (2006, p. 221) explain, "The extent and nature of government-nonprofit relations are perhaps most evident and concrete in the mix of auspices under which a wide range of common goods and services are delivered. Where government services are privatized so that private entities deliver services financed by government through line-item subsidies, grants, contracts, or fee-for-service arrangements, and where the bulk of service providers are nonprofits (e.g., human services in the United States), government-nonprofit relations involve complex interdependencies and substantial transaction benefits—and costs—to both parties."

The rise of third-party government is usually attributed to the growth of the "Welfare State," where government took on greater responsibility for public problems (Agranoff, 2003). This substantial expansion has resulted in significant increases in government social welfare spending and assistance in the fields of health, social services, housing, education, and employment training (Salamon, 1993). Although government assumed greater responsibility, political, organizational, and economic forces have led governments to avoid direct service provision in favor of contracting with nonprofit organizations to provide human and social services. "Philosophically, policy makers are enacting decisions that not only restrict but in many cases remove government from providing services directly to citizens. In part, this is being driven by market and political ideologies that have their roots in perceptions about greater efficiencies and innovations arising from the private sector and broad support for smaller government" (Van Slyke, 2007).

From 1990 to 2001 federal-level contracting increased by 24 percent in real terms, which is astonishing given the significant defense cutbacks resulting from the end of the Cold War (Goldsmith & Eggers, 2004). So significant was the increase in contracting as a means of service delivery that "federal contractors outnumbered federal employees by more than two to one and contract-generated federal jobs soared by more than 700,000 between 1999 and 2002. During the same period, the number of civil service employees actually fell by 50,000" (Goldsmith & Eggers, 2004, p. 11). According to the Office of Management and Budget (OMB) in a fiscal year 2005 report, the federal government spends about $100 billion more annually for contractors than it does for employee salaries. OMB's fiscal year 2015 report emphasizes that the historical trend toward an increased reliance on contractors has continued unabated over the past decade. Salamon (2002) documented a "massive proliferation . . . in the instruments or means used to address public problems. Whereas earlier government activity was largely restricted to the direct delivery of goods or services by government bureaucrats, it now embraces a dizzying array of alternative arrangements."

The devolution of service delivery to third parties goes beyond the delegation of clearly defined ministerial duties and exhibits a sharing of governmental functions with third-party actors, including nonprofit organizations. In fact, "the major share of the discretion over the operation of public programs routinely comes to rest not with the responsible governmental agencies, but with the third-party actors that actually carry the programs out" (Salamon, 2002, p. 2). Van Slyke (2007, p. 158) refers to this trend as "a transformation from governance by authority to governance by contract." Milward and Provan (2000) illustrate this point further by differentiating "government" from "governance":

> The essence of governance is its focus on governing mechanisms (grants, contracts, and agreements) that do not rest solely on the authority and sanctions of government. These mechanisms or tools are used to connect networks of actors, who operate in various domains of public policy such as child welfare, health, or economic development. (Milward & Provan, 2000, p. 360)

Government's choices of third-party partners and mechanisms for managing this partnership are crucial. Government contracting with nonprofit organizations for the delivery of publicly-financed services reveals these challenges.

NONPROFIT ORGANIZATIONS AS GOVERNMENT CONTRACTING PARTNERS

When government contracts with other organizations for the delivery of services, it faces the possibility of opportunistic behavior on the part of its partners: as self-interested economic actors, vendors or contracting partners have a rational incentive to exploit contracts to their own advantage, sometimes at the expense of the contracting government's goals (Brown et al., 2006). An important strategy to combat such opportunism is to secure goal congruence between the contracting government—the "principal" and its "agent"—the organization with which it contracts to deliver the service. In a contracting relationship, principals (government) enjoy only indirect and fragmented authority over agents (vendors) where goal alignment is weak, and strong mechanisms for monitoring performance are absent. These "indirect, arm's length relationships between principal and agent allow for behaviors by the agent that the principal may find difficult to control," which results in ineffective contract performance (Provan & Milward, 1995).

To combat these problems, the literature advises that the principal should structure the control mechanism, i.e., the contract, to incentivize agents (vendors) to fulfill their responsibilities under the contract and monitor their performance to ensure compliance. Government (as the principal) should create contracts that encourage vendors to produce the desired outcomes through a mix of incentives and authority, and monitor the agent's activities and measure outcomes to ensure quality standards. Several issues complicate implementation of these best practices, though: in complex service areas information asymmetries are prevalent in which the agent has more or better information than the principal, for example, in service domains where outcomes are difficult to measure or in highly technical arenas where principals lack expertise.

With this background, we can understand why government would turn to nonprofit organizations as contracting partners. Nonprofits are not as prone to "moral hazard"— situations in which an agent takes advantage of information asymmetries to act inappropriately for private gain (for example, provide a good or service at a lower quality to derive greater profits)—as for-profit businesses. In so doing, the agent takes advantage of the principal, who is unable to monitor the agent's work and bears a greater risk. Nonprofits have less incentive to behave opportunistically, i.e., act in a self-interested manner at the expense of the principal (government), because they benefit from the popular perception that they are trustworthy, mission-oriented organizations that do not distribute proceeds to shareholders. Nonprofits, especially charities, seek value creation and problem amelioration over gross profit. Furthermore, as discussed earlier, nonprofits provide public-like goods and services and are, therefore, more likely to share goal congruence with contracting governments.

We can summarize the implications for government selection of nonprofit organizations as contracting partners. In policy areas with sharp information asymmetries, i.e., where the organization providing the service has much more knowledge of the costs and quality of the service than the contracting government, or when the outcomes of service delivery are difficult to measure, such as in mental health services, government contracting with nonprofit organizations is often the preferred choice. For example, human and social services typically do not yield large profits and often require personnel with highly technical knowledge (for example, graduate degrees) and certifications (for example, social work) to evaluate the outcomes. Moreover, unlike for-profit organizations that have a relentless focus on efficiency and profits, nonprofits share government's mission orientation and are less inclined to act opportunistically at the expense of the contracting government.

Traditionally, contracting for mental health and other social services is conducted via fee-for-service arrangements where inputs and processes are the focus of the contract. Because outcomes are difficult to capture and indicators are few, these fee-for-service arrangements are structured based on service delivery procedures, including defined time and labor allocations, and are assessed based on the number of units of service delivered by the vendor: the means of service delivery as specified in the contract, as opposed to the outcome of the service, becomes the focus of the contract. Although effective in monitoring the activities of the agent, such process-oriented contracts may stifle innovation and shift attention from problem amelioration and results to "inputs," i.e., cases processed, costs per case, number of hours per case, etc.

Perhaps as a result, another view of contracting has emerged in government-nonprofit partnerships, especially in human and social service delivery marked by unfavorable market conditions, complexity, and information asymmetry: "relational contracting" (Brown et al., 2006). Relational contracting goes beyond the transactional and structural components of traditional contracts to emphasize the social aspects emerging from government-nonprofit partnerships, such as the frequency and depth of communication, the existence and cultivation of trust, and the building of a relationship between principal and agent. In relational contracting the formal mechanism of control (i.e., the contract) is complemented by the informal mechanisms of shared values and norms to align principal and agent interests and control agent behavior. We now turn to the issue of how these various tendencies of government to contract with nonprofit organizations for the delivery of services are borne out in practice in the United States.

NONPROFIT REVENUES AND THE SCOPE OF GOVERNMENT CONTRACTING WITH NONPROFIT ORGANIZATIONS

Nonprofit revenues are heavily dependent on government grants and fee-for-service arrangements. As shown in Table 5.1, figures from the National Center for Charitable Statistics at the Urban Institute show that government support for nonprofits in the form of contracts and awards accounts for approximately one-third of total nonprofit revenues. Reliance on government funding varies by policy subsector, with health and human services nonprofits being most reliant on government funds and arts organizations the least. Government funding, primarily grants, accounts for 13 percent to 21 percent of nonprofit revenues other than for nonprofits in the health and human services field. Arts organizations, international and public affairs organizations, and animal welfare organizations generate only about 1 percent of their revenue from government fee-for-service arrangements. This variation notwithstanding, the gross nonprofit financial picture is driven largely by health and human services nonprofits, which generate 72.9 percent of all nonprofit revenues and account for 72.8 percent of all nonprofit expenses. Human services nonprofits generate 48 percent of their revenues from government sources with a relatively equal split coming from fee-for-service arrangements (25 percent) and from

Table 5.1
Revenue Sources for Reporting Public Charities, 2010

	All subsectors	Arts, culture, & humanities	Education	Animals	Health	Human Services	Int'l & Public Affairs	Other
Fees for services & goods from private	50	34	61	29	56	28	8	27
Fees for services & goods from government	24	1	3	1	33	25	1	5
Private contributions	13	45	17	49	4	20	69	44
Government grants	8	12	12	14	3	23	19	16
Investment income	3	5	6	3	2	2	2	5
Other income	2	3	2	5	1	2	2	3
Total government support	32	13	15	15	36	48	20	21

Source: The Nonprofit Almanac 2012 (Roeger et al., 2012). Numbers are expressed as percentages and may not sum to 100 due to rounding.

grants (23 percent). Government support accounts for 36 percent of total revenue for health-related nonprofits, with over 90 percent of these funds coming in the form of fee-for-service arrangements.

Between 1965 and 1970 federal expenditures for social services soared, almost tripling, from $812 million to $2.2 billion primarily through contracting with nonprofit human service agencies (Smith, 2010). Federal funding as a percentage of total government funding for social services accounted for 38 percent in 1965 and rose to 65 percent by 1980. "A large percentage of the increase in public funding of social services was channeled through nonprofit agencies in the form of government contracts" (Smith, 2010, p. 555). After a temporary dip during the Reagan administration, federal spending on social services rebounded and contracting with nonprofit organizations grew, especially with the expansion of Medicaid in the 1980s and welfare reform legislation (Temporary Assistance to Needy Families) in 1996. "Overall, a large percentage of this additional service funding was spent in support of services provided by nonprofit organizations, including day care, welfare to work, job training, and counseling" (Smith, 2010, p. 557). In the 1990s and early 2000s government contracting with nonprofits also grew in social service program areas such as at-risk youth, community service, drug and alcohol treatment, prisoner reentry, and community care (Smith, 2010).

The substantial increase in public spending between 1960 and 1995 was matched by an increased use of nonprofit organizations to provide the desired services (Gronbjerg, 2001; Boris et al., 2010). Although data collected by the International City/County Management Association tends to show rather stable use of nonprofit providers from 1992 through 2007 (Warner & Hefetz, 2009), most research documents an increased reliance on nonprofit service-providers in state and local governments over time. So integral are nonprofits to the delivery of social services that some government administrators observed:

> that if nonprofits were no longer willing or able to contract with governments to provide services, those services would stop or be severely disrupted. In particular, 45% of Delaware state government managers said they would not be able to provide services if their current nonprofit providers stopped contracting with the state. (Boris et al., 2010)

By 1997 approximately 52 percent of federal, state, and local government funds for social services went to nonprofits (Boris et al., 2010; Salamon, 2002). "In June 2009, New York State had nearly 31,000 active contracts, worth $14.6 billion, with nonprofit organizations" (Boris et al., 2010, p. 3). In New York City alone, for the year 2011 government facilitated nearly 55,000 contracts worth close to $15 billion, 2,200 of which were contracts with nonprofit agencies representing roughly $4 billion (Miltenberger, 2013).

According to findings from the Urban Institute's 2013 National Survey of Nonprofit-Government Contracts and Grants shown in Table 5.2, government reliance on nonprofits has continued (Pettijohn & Boris, 2013). Estimates from 2012 hold that local, state, and federal governments worked with nearly 56,000 nonprofit organizations to deliver services through two primary funding mechanisms, contracts, and grants, which totaled over $137 billion. Human service contracts and grants with nonprofit organizations accounted for nearly 30,000 contracts and $80.5 billion (Pettijohn & Boris, 2014). These estimates are down from 2009 numbers, which showed roughly 33,000 contracts worth approximately $100 billion in the area of human services (Boris et al., 2010), a result of the recent 2008 recession and constrained budgets at all levels of government.

Table 5.3 displays government funding of nonprofit activities in greater detail through the number and dollar amount of grants awarded to nonprofits by federal government agencies. The Federal Award Assistance Data System contains data on grants, loans, insurance, and direct payment transactions made by federal government departments to for-profit organizations, nonprofit organizations, and state and local government agencies. With respect to federal government awards to nonprofit organizations, the Department of Health and Human Services (DHHS) awarded by far the greatest number of grants in 2012, accounting for roughly half of the number of awards. Of the more than $29 billion in federal grants awarded to nonprofit organizations in 2012, DHHS accounted for $16.7 billion. Second on the list is the Agency for International Development (USAID), which awarded almost $5.3 billion in 2012 to nonprofits; the Department of State is third on the list with over $1 billion awarded. While the Department of Agriculture and the Department of Veterans Affairs awarded hundreds more grants than USAID, the average value of each award was significantly lower: The average award given by USAID was roughly 18 times the size of the average awards given by the Departments of Agriculture and Veterans Affairs.

Table 5.2
Dollar Amount of Contracts and Grants

Type of Organization	Number	Percent	Mean ($)	Median ($)	Total ($ millions)	Percent
Arts, culture, & humanities	7,189	12.9	152,074	33,600	1,081	0.8
Education	3,828	6.9	1,392,814	157,034	5,223	3.8
Environment & animals	2,359	4.2	560,871	101,800	1,306	1.0
Health	6,729	12.1	5,586,483	545,082	36,448	26.5
Human services	29,483	52.9	2,826,338	387,732	80,565	58.6
Other	6,114	11.0	2,203,786	274,688	12,769	9.3
Overall	55,702	100.0	2,543,870	250,000	137,392	100.0

Source: Urban Institute, National Survey of Nonprofit-Government Contracts and Grants (2013). Reproduced from Pettijohn & Boris (2013).

Table 5.3
2012 Federal Awards to Nonprofit Organizations

Agency	Number of Awards	Sum of Awards($)	Average Award ($)
Department of Health & Human Services	29,585	16,708,720,652	564,770
Agency for International Development	3,095	5,298,653,183	1,712,004
Department of State	840	1,059,699,657	1,261,547
Department of Labor	1,046	791,877,603	757,053
Department of Education	1,664	537,761,725	323,174
Department of Defense	1,140	506,739,354	444,508
National Science Foundation	1,141	484,036,654	424,221
Department of Housing & Urban Development	960	453,993,799	472,910
Department of Justice	933	433,711,677	464,857
Department of Agriculture	3,966	426,312,993	107,491
Environmental Protection Agency	2,480	313,089,550	126,245
Department of Veterans Affairs	3,699	299,889,551	81,073
Department of Commerce	1,035	278,577,405	269,157
National Aeronautics & Space Administration	2,132	273,369,719	128,222
Corporation for National & Community Service	1,113	221,701,601	199,192
Department of Interior	2,102	210,354,233	100,073
Department of Energy	469	190,996,551	407,242
Department of Treasury	794	187,357,480	235,967
Department of Transportation	166	168,036,622	1,012,269
National Endowment for the Humanities	1,930	68,957,987	35,729
Small Business Administration	354	52,494,276	148,289
Department of Homeland Security	85	35,005,954	411,835
Appalachian Regional Commission	161	19,852,371	123,307
National Endowment for the Humanities	63	9,952,663	157,979
National Foundation on the Arts & the Humanities	425	5,107,268	12,017
Nuclear Regulatory Commission	6	1,120,661	186,777
Total	61,384	29,037,371,189	473,044

Source: Table created by the authors with data from the Federal Assistance Award Data System. Only those agencies with grants totaling $1 million or more are shown

Grants constitute only one source of government funding for nonprofit organizations. As illustrated above, government contracts are also a major source of nonprofit revenue. Data from the Federal Procurement Data System (FPDS) shown in Table 5.4 provide a snapshot of how the federal government spends these contract dollars as well as some insight into how federal contract dollars are subcontracted to other levels of government. Analysis of these data shows that in 2012 nonprofit organizations were awarded 175,610 federal contracts amounting to almost $19 billion. The Department of Defense awarded the most contracts (55,687) and accounted for almost half of the total dollars contracted to nonprofits in 2012 ($9.1 billion). The Departments of Energy and Veterans Affairs awarded contracts to nonprofits totaling roughly $1.4 billion each, good enough for the second and third most amounts contracted to nonprofit organizations, respectively. As with the grant data (Table 5.3), the average contract amount varied greatly. The General Services Administration awarded the second most contracts (51,851) totaling $468 million, but with an average contract value of just $9,036. This contract amount is especially low compared to the average contract levels for the Departments of Energy ($643,954) and Defense ($164,209).

Table 5.4
2012 Federal Contracts to Nonprofit Organizations

Agency	Number of Contracts	Sum of Contracts ($)	Average Contract ($)
Department of Defense	55,687	9,144,309,744	164,209
Department of Energy	2,272	1,463,064,217	643,954
Department of Veterans Affairs	17,323	1,348,099,887	77,821
Department of State	7,031	966,091,727	137,405
Department of Health & Human Services	7,957	956,747,143	120,240
Department of Homeland Security	5,284	828,519,008	156,798
National Aeronautics & Space Administration	2,463	559,272,032	227,069
General Services Administration	51,851	468,545,915	9,036
Department of Interior	5,368	462,262,265	86,114
Department of Transportation	1,871	378,359,364	202,223
Department of Justice	4,858	339,406,214	69,865
Department of Commerce	1,436	334,014,730	232,601
Department of Housing & Urban Development	968	279,050,608	288,275
Department of Agriculture	3,646	271,502,981	74,466
Department of Treasury	1,805	204,294,893	113,183

Department of Education	513	188,479,299	367,406
Department of Labor	722	183,298,809	253,876
Agency for International Development	388	174,959,257	450,926
Environmental Protection Agency	1,591	144,350,327	90,729
Social Security Administration	367	108,226,615	294,895
Small Business Administration	102	35,266,034	345,745
Office of Personnel Management	283	32,332,215	114,248
National Science Foundation	116	14,270,993	123,026
Nuclear Regulatory Commission	205	12,524,694	61,096
Smithsonian Institution	148	12,273,818	82,931
Overseas Private Investment Corporation	10	11,154,779	1,115,478
Court Services & Offender Supervision	93	10,149,490	109,134
Broadcasting Board of Governors	425	10,060,315	23,671
National Archives & Records Administration	87	8,909,952	102,413
Federal Communications Commission	24	8,279,821	344,993
Securities & Exchange Commission	129	6,176,325	47,878
National Transportation Safety Board	13	2,732,827	210,217
Pension Benefit Guaranty Corporation	26	2,635,920	101,382
Peace Corps	33	2,434,312	73,767
Federal Energy Regulatory Commission	28	2,371,457	84,695
Commodity Futures Trading Commission	18	1,923,478	106,860
Federal Trade Commission	37	1,464,145	39,571
Federal Election Commission	3	1,286,142	428,714
Consumer Product Safety Commission	41	1,204,697	29,383
Selective Service System	8	1,173,865	146,733
National Labor Relations Board	31	1,010,051	32,582
Total	175,610	18,986,801,896	108,119

Source: Table created by the authors with data from the Federal Procurement Data System. Only those agencies with contracts totaling $1 million or more are shown.

Signed into law in 2006, the Federal Funding Accountability and Transparency Act (FFATA) was intended to increase government accountability to citizens and to reduce wasteful spending. This Act led to the creation of another federal data collection effort to track information on sub-awards given by prime award recipients to subcontractors, such as nonprofit organizations. The FFATA Sub-award Reporting System (FSRS) requires federal prime grant contractors to report sub-award data for any subcontract greater than $25,000. As shown in Table 5.5, the FSRS data indicate that over $780 million in subcontracts was awarded to nonprofit organizations in 2012. Originally awarded through federal contracts to for-profit organizations, nonprofit organizations, and state and local governments, these funds were subcontracted to nonprofit organizations. The bulk of these subcontracted dollars originated with the Department of Health and Human Services ($428 million), followed by the Agency for International Development ($189 million) and the Department of Defense ($128 million). Although these data are preliminary and likely underestimate the volume of subcontracts to nonprofit organizations, they nonetheless illustrate the importance of nonprofit organizations in government contracting for the delivery of goods and services.

BENEFITS OF GOVERNMENT CONTRACTING WITH NONPROFIT ORGANIZATIONS

Given the characteristic shortcomings of contracts for regulating behavior, governments often prefer to enlist nonprofit organizations rather than business firms as contracting partners for several reasons. First, like government, nonprofits are not created to maximize shareholder wealth. Although nonprofits must generate excess revenues to survive and thrive, they are not legally allowed to distribute those "profits" to investors (non-distribution constraint), but are required to reinvest excess financial returns into current or future organizational operations. For-profit business firms must be concerned with shifting residual value (i.e., profit) to shareholders. When contracting with government, for-profits "will treat performance standards set by government as a constraint and will use any discretionary room that is left to them in the contractual arrangements to maximize financial returns" (Moore, 2002, p. 318), or as Witesman and Fernandez (2013, p. 692) put it, they "are more likely to opt for reducing costs at the expense of the government's interests."

Second, nonprofits generally share government's commitment to promoting the public interest (Hansmann, 1987; Salamon, 1995; Witesman & Fernandez, 2013). Unlike for-profit organizations that understandably pursue their own economic interests, nonprofits are legally, socially, and historically bound to pursue communal interests (Witesman & Fernandez, 2013). When US nonprofits incorporate in their state or apply for federal recognition under section 501(c)(3) of the Internal Revenue Code, public charities in particular are legally required to forego private benefit and operate in the public interest. To obtain tax-exempt status before the IRS, nonprofits must demonstrate that their mission, programs, and revenue generation serve communal interests.

Table 5.5
2012 Federal Subcontracts to Nonprofit Organizations

Agency	Number of Subcontracts	Sum of Subcontracts ($)	Average Subcontract ($)
Department of Health & Human Services	715	427,972,716	598,563
Department of Defense	73	189,038,515	2,589,569
Agency for International Development	390	127,980,867	328,156
National Aeronautics & Space Administration	32	7,995,847	249,870
Department of Education	20	7,844,839	392,242
Department of Agriculture	19	6,073,724	319,670
Department of Transportation	15	5,010,285	334,019
Social Security Administration	7	3,528,957	504,137
Department of Homeland Security	19	2,602,355	136,966
Department of Energy	9	968,025	107,558
Environmental Protection Agency	16	872,942	54,559
Department of Labor	6	565,673	94,279
Department of Veterans Affairs	4	439,897	109,974
Department of Interior	7	362,537	51,791
Department of Justice	1	94,801	94,801
General Services Administration	4	88,850	22,213
Department of Housing & Urban Development	1	36,338	36,338
Total	1,338	781,477,169	584,064

Source: Table created by the authors with data from the Federal Procurement Data System.

Third, nonprofit organizations are embedded in local communities, with several related benefits (Witesman & Fernandez, 2013). Nonprofits with significant social capital networks offer government actors the opportunity to achieve "short-term political gains and longer term reductions in transaction costs" (Witesman & Fernandez, 2013; Bryce, 2006). With most nonprofits being locally based, board and staff members may have established relationships with government officials and community leaders not shared by for-profit contractors (Witesman & Fernandez, 2013). Furthermore, social capital networks offer the "opportunity for a bottom-up approach to dealing with regional issues rather than a top-down approach" (Benton 2013, p. 221).

Fourth, nonprofit organizations leverage volunteer labor to lower production costs and increase public involvement (Gazley & Brudney, 2007). Volunteers are vital to the nonprofit labor force and contribute significantly to nonprofit productivity. According to surveys conducted by the Bureau of Labor Statistics (2013), about 62.6 million

Americans volunteered through or for an organization at least once in the year ending in September 2013, more than one-quarter of the US adult population (25.4 percent). In 2012 Americans volunteered 7.9 billion hours, worth an estimated $175 billion according to the Independent Sector's (2014) estimated value of an average volunteer hour ($22.55). Volunteers provide benefits that go beyond the economic, including commitment, outreach, and fundraising capability. Although volunteer programs are not "free" but require nonprofit time and resources, research consistently finds that this investment is well worth the support costs: "With a relatively small investment of resources, volunteers have the potential to increase the level and quality of services that an agency can deliver to the public" (Brudney, 2010, p. 756). Successful volunteer programs give nonprofit organizations a distinct advantage over for-profit organizations in the delivery of contracted services.

Fifth, nonprofits offer specialized expertise in certain service domains required by government (Gazley & Brudney, 2007), particularly human and social services (Brown & Potoski, 2005). In these subsectors, where service outputs are difficult to monitor and measure, nonprofits are seen as cheaper alternatives to for-profits (Witesman & Fernandez, 2013). Nonprofits have the potential to leverage diverse talents and community resources and are perceived to have less red tape, which ideally should allow for greater experimentation and innovation in service delivery (Salamon, 2002).

DRAWBACKS TO GOVERNMENT CONTRACTING WITH NONPROFIT ORGANIZATIONS

These advantages notwithstanding, several potential drawbacks jeopardize the success of government contracting with nonprofit organizations to deliver publicly funded goods and services. First, although goal alignment between public organizations and nonprofit contractors is touted as an advantage, perfect alignment should not be assumed. Whereas governments are accountable to multiple stakeholders, nonprofits are oftentimes single-interest advocates (Cooper, 2003). The nonprofit sector collectively serves a very broad array of particular interests that yield substantial benefit to communities, but, individually, nonprofit organizations typically produce specific goods that serve narrow interests. In contrast to government, no single nonprofit provides for all charitable causes in a jurisdiction. Although, as a sector, nonprofit organizations provide public-like goods that serve communal interests, individually their missions and programs may not perfectly align with government responsibility to multiple, diverse constituencies.

Second, "many nonprofits have multiple programs and contracts, creating opportunities for them to shirk on a particular contract by diverting funding and resources toward other priorities" (Witesman & Fernandez, 2013, p. 692). Nonprofits funded through multiple grants or contracts are obligated to these respective commitments. For the nonprofit organization, bearing accountability to multiple stakeholders while still pursuing its own unique mission presents a difficult management task, and tempts nonprofit managers to prioritize one funder, one program, or one contract over another. The management challenges associated with responding to the various stakeholders have led some scholars to label this condition "multiple accountabilities disorder" (Koppell, 2005; Ebrahim, 2010), with uncertain consequences for the governments that let contracts to them.

Third, though opportunistic behaviors are oftentimes associated with for-profit organizations seeking to maximize shareholder wealth, nonprofits are also resource-seeking organizations intent on preserving organizational capacity and growing future financial sustainability. Because nonprofits can reinvest profits in the organization, the incentives to grow revenues and cut costs remain (Steinberg, 1986). Based on a desire to maximize budgets, nonprofit organizations may "behave opportunistically in a manner similar to their profit-seeking counterparts" (Witesman & Fernandez, 2013, p. 692). Scholars recognize that nonprofit organizations may drift significantly from their focus on their original mission in favor of revenue from government contracts (Witesman & Fernandez, 2013; Brown & Potoski, 2005). Such "mission drift" can deflect nonprofits away form the core competencies that led government to contract with them in the first place. We should also be aware that goal achievement rather than efficiency is the foremost objective of the nonprofit, and that employee compensation may lag behind the other sectors of the economy. As a result, the ability to attract and retain top quality management and to achieve cost-savings may suffer.

GOVERNMENT CONTRACTING WITH NONPROFIT ORGANIZATIONS: RESULTS FROM THE FIELD

Findings from an empirical study by Witesman and Fernandez (2013) comparing the advantages of nonprofit organizations versus for-profit businesses in contractual relationships with government provide insight into this practice at ground level. Based on analysis of contractual relationships between local governments and nonprofit and for-profit service providers, Witesman and Fernandez (2013) test hypotheses that nonprofit organizations are more trustworthy than for-profit firms, and that they have a specialization advantage in providing public-like goods.

Witesman and Fernandez (2013) use survey data collected on dyadic contractual relationships between local governments in the United States and private service providers (for-profit and nonprofit) for a range of services. Their 439 respondents (48 percent response rate) were chief executives or professional managers of local governments engaged in these contractual arrangements. Study findings reveal mixed support for the hypothesis that governments trust nonprofit contractors more than for-profit firms. For example, local governments award nonprofit organizations contracts for services with higher levels of task uncertainty, which suggests an implicit level of trust that nonprofits will not behave opportunistically. In addition, the average duration of government contracts is nearly double for nonprofits than for-profits: about six years compared to about three and a half years. Local governments monitor nonprofit contractors less frequently than their for-profit counterparts, again an indication of greater trust. Yet, nonprofit organizations are not subjected to less rigorous screening in the contracting process than for-profit firms, and they are not granted greater discretion in decision-making.

Witesman and Fernandez (2013) also examined local government officials' views regarding differences in contract performance between nonprofit and for-profit contractors. They hypothesized that the nonprofit contractors would have a comparative advantage with respect to five key indicators of contract performance: cost, quality of service, responsiveness to government requirements, compliance with the law, and customer satisfaction. The results demonstrated that the nonprofit organizations held a significant performance advantage only in perceived customer satisfaction. According to Witesman and Fernandez (2013, p. 705), "these results are in line with previous findings indicating no relationship between organizational form and performance."

CONCLUSION

This chapter has explained how private actors such as nonprofit organizations are integral to providing public goods and services through contracting and other relationships with government. This new governance model is changing the way governments operate. As Donahue and Zeckhauser (2011, p. 25) write, "At one time good government may have merely entailed running bureaucracies efficiently and accountably. Now, to a large and growing extent, it depends on knowing how to capitalize on private capacity." Based on both theory and data, we have shown in this chapter that effective contracting by governments with nonprofit organizations means more than simply transferring funds for service delivery to another entity and waiting for reports of desirable results. Despite the virtues of nonprofit organizations that we have described in this chapter, nonprofits, like all organized enterprise, have their problems as well.

To guide government practitioners as they explore and implement contractual relationships with nonprofit agencies, we close with five key points:

- Government contracting with nonprofit organizations is not an abdication of government authority. Instead, it is using that authority creatively, for example, through strategic contract design, monitoring, and evaluation, to achieve shared results.
- Government contracting with nonprofit organizations does not mean that every good or service can or should be contracted to private actors, whether for-profit, nonprofit, or government. The characteristics of the good or service to be provided are crucial to the make-or-buy decision.

- Government contracting with nonprofit organizations should not be concerned exclusively with sparing public budgets. Rather, contracting is about working together to achieve effective, efficient, and accountable services with committed partners.
- Government contracting with nonprofit organizations should be undertaken with partners aligned with government missions and goals. Evaluating and checking the meaning and priority accorded to public purposes by nonprofit contractors constitute essential government tasks.
- Government contracting with nonprofit organizations need not, and should not, be entered in a vacuum. Voluminous evidence is available. This chapter offers a place to start.

REFERENCES

Agranoff, R. (2003). *Leveraging networks: A guide for public managers working across organizations.* Arlington, VA: IBM Endowment for the Business of Government.

Benton, J. E. (2013). Local government collaboration: Considerations, issues, and prospects. *State and Local Government Review*, I(4), 220–223.

Boris, E., de Leon, E., Roeger, K., & Nikolova, M. (2010). *Human service nonprofits and government collaboration: Findings from the 2010 national survey of nonprofit government contracting and grants.* Washington, DC: Urban Institute.

Brown, T., & Potoski, M. (2005). Transaction costs and contracting: The practitioner perspective. *Public Performance & Management Review*, 28(3), 326–351.

Brown, T., Potoski, M., & Van Slyke, D., (2006). Managing public service contracts: Aligning values, institutions, and markets. *Public Administration Review*, 66(3), 323–331.

Brudney, J. (2010). Designing and managing volunteer programs. In D. Renz & Associates (Ed.), *The Jossey-Bass handbook of nonprofit leadership and management* (pp. 753–793). San Francisco, CA: Jossey-Bass.

Bryce, H. (2006). Nonprofits as social capital and agents in the public policy process: Toward a new paradigm. *Nonprofit and Voluntary Sector Quarterly*, 35(2), 311–318.

Bureau of Labor Statistics. (2013). In *Volunteering in the United States, 2013*. Washington, DC: author. Retrieved from www.bls.gov/news.release/volun.nr0.htm.

Cooper, P. (2003). *Governing by contract: Challenges and opportunities for public managers.* Washington, DC: CQ Press.

Donahue, J. & Zeckhauser, R. (2011). *Collaborative governance: Private roles for public goals in turbulent times.* Princeton, NJ: Princeton University Press.

Ebrahim, A. (2010). The many faces of nonprofit accountability. In D. Renz & Associates (eds.) in *The Jossey-Bass handbook of nonprofit leadership and management* (pp. 101–121). San Francisco, CA: Jossey-Bass.

Federal Assistance Award Data System (July 2014). Retrieved from www.usaspending.gov/data.

Federal Procurement Database System (July 2014). Retrieved from www.usaspending.gov/data.

Gazley, B. & Brudney, J. (2007). The purpose (and perils) of government-nonprofit partnership. *Nonprofit and Voluntary Sector Quarterly*, 36(3), 389–415.

General Services Administration (July 2014). Retrieved from http://www.gsa.gov/portal/content/157105.

Goldsmith, S. & W. Eggers. 2004. *Governing by network: The new shape of the public sector.* Washington, DC: Brookings Institution Press.

Gronbjerg, K. (2001). The U.S. nonprofit human service sector: A creeping revolution. *Nonprofit and Voluntary Sector Quarterly*, 30(2), 276–297.

Hansmann, H. (1987). Economic theories of nonprofit organization. In W. Powell (Ed.), *The nonprofit sector: A research handbook* (pp. 27–42). New Haven, CT: Yale University Press.

Independent Sector. (2014). *Independent sector's value of volunteer time*. Washington, DC: Author. Retrieved from www.independentsector.org/volunteer_time.

Koppell, J. (2005). Pathologies of accountability: ICANN and the challenge of multiple accountabilities disorder. *Public Administration Review*, 65(1), 94–108.

McKeever, B., & Pettijohn, S. (2014). *The nonprofit sector in brief 2014: Public Charities, Giving, and Volunteering*. Washington, DC: Urban Institute.

Miltenberger, L. (2013). Collaboration, contracting, and contradictions: How nonprofit leaders can begin to think about collaborating with the government. *Journal of Leadership Studies*, 7(1), 54–60.

Milward, H.B. & Provan, K. (2000). Governing the hollow state. *Journal of Public Administration Research and Theory*, 10(2), 359–380.

Moore, M. (2002). Privatizing public management. In J. Donahue & J. Nye (Eds.), *Market-Based governance: Supply-side, demand-side, upside, downside* (pp. 296–322). Washington, DC: Brookings Institution Press.

Office of Management and Budget. (2004). Fiscal Year 2005 Analytical Perspectives. *Budget of the United States Government*. Washington, DC: U.S. Government Printing Office.

Office of Management and Budget. (2014). Fiscal Year 2015 Analytical Perspectives. *Budget of the United States Government*. Washington, DC: U.S. Government Printing Office.

Pettijohn, S. & Boris, E. (2013). *Contracts and grants between nonprofits and government*. Washington, DC: Urban Institute.

Pettijohn, S. & Boris, E. (2014). *Contracts and grants between human service nonprofits and government: Comparative analysis*. Urban Institute.

Provan, K. & Milward, H.B. (1995). A preliminary theory of interorganizational network effectiveness: A comparative study of four community mental health systems. *Administrative Science Quarterly*, 40(1), 1–33.

Roeger, K., Blackwood, A. & Pettijohn, S. (2012). *The nonprofit almanac 2012*. Washington, DC: Urban Institute Press.

Salamon, L. (1987). Of market failure, voluntary failure, and third-party government: Toward a theory of government-nonprofit relations in the modern welfare state. *Nonprofit and Voluntary Sector Quarterly*, 16(2), 29–49.

Salamon, L. (1993). The marketization of welfare: Changing nonprofit and for-profit roles in the American welfare state. *Social Service Review*, 67(1), 16–39.

Salamon, L. (1995). *Partners in public service: Government-nonprofit relations in the modern welfare state*. Baltimore, MD: Johns Hopkins University Press.

Salamon, L. (2002). The resilient sector: The state of nonprofit America. In L. Salamon (Ed.), *The State of Nonprofit America* (pp. 1–64). Washington, DC: Urban Institute Press.

Salamon, Lester L. & Helmut Anheier, H. (1992a). In search of the non-profit sector I: The question of definitions. *Voluntas: International Journal of Voluntary and Nonprofit Organizations*, 3(2), 125–151.

Salamon, Lester L. & Helmut Anheier, H. (1992b). In search of the non-profit sector II: The problem of classification. *Voluntas: International Journal of Voluntary and Nonprofit Organizations*, 3(2), 267–309.

Smith, S. (2010). Managing the challenges of government contracts. In D. Renz & Associates (Eds.), *The Jossey-Bass handbook of nonprofit leadership and management* (pp. 553–579). San Francisco, CA: Jossey-Bass.

Smith, Steven S. & Kristen Gronbjerg, K. (2006). Scope and theory of government-nonprofit relations. Pages 221–242. In W. Powell & R. Steinberg (Eds.), *The nonprofit sector: A research handbook* (2nd Edition), (pp. 221–242). New Haven, CT: Yale University Press.

Steinberg, R. (1986). The revealed objective functions of nonprofit firms. *The RAND Journal of Economics*, *17*(4), 508–526.

Steinberg, R. (2006). Economic theories of nonprofit organizations. In W. Powell & R. Steinberg (Eds.), *The nonprofit sector: A research handbook* (2nd Edition), (pp. 117–139). New Haven, CT: Yale University Press.

Tocqueville, A. de. (1945). *Democracy in America*, Volume II. (H. Reeve Trans.). New York, NY: Random House. (Original work published 1835.)

Van Slyke, D. (2007). Agents or stewards: Using theory to understand the government-nonprofit social service contracting relationship. *Journal of Public Administration Research and Theory*, *17*(2), 157–187.

Warner, M.E. & Hefetz, A. (2009). Cooperative competition: Alternative service delivery 2002–2007. *The Municipal Year Book 2009*. Washington, DC: International City/County Management Association.

Weisbrod, B. 1977. *The Voluntary Nonprofit Sector: An Economic Analysis*. Lexington, MA: Lexington Books.

Witesman, E. & Fernandez, S. (2013). Government contracts with private organizations: Are there differences between nonprofits and for-profits? *Nonprofit and Voluntary Sector Quarterly*, *42*(4), 689–715.

6

Public Private Partnerships

Implications for Public Procurement

Wendell C. Lawther

INTRODUCTION

Many have noted the declining state of a wide range of infrastructure in the United States (e.g. Puentes, 2008), including roads, bridges, wastewater treatment plants and courthouses. Identifying the source of funds to repair or build new infrastructure has led many state and local governments to consider adopting a Public Private Partnership (P3) approach.

P3s may take a variety of forms or approaches, including the Design-Build-Finance-Operate-Maintain type, also known as the Concessionaire form (Martin & Saviak, 2014). This is the most complex form, in which the role of the private partner has the most impact, as almost all of the efforts needed to build or repair infrastructure are performed by the private partners. Many of these efforts, especially those associated with financing a project and performing operations such as collecting tolls in the case of a transportation P3, are unfamiliar to public procurement officials. The complexity of P3s, the lack of familiarity with appropriate processes, analyses, and procurement approaches, and the greater risk of inadequate expertise should lead public procurement officials to consider adopting optimal processes for P3s prior to initiating a P3 approach.

Given the lack of familiarity of many state and local officials with P3s, it is assumed that the role of the public procurement official is also not well defined in many cases. There is the opportunity, then, for the procurement official to work closely with project managers as well as hired consultants in delivering a final project. This role may evolve and be different depending on each specific P3. Overall, however, the following analysis assumes the procurement official should be recognized as a member of the public team, acting to protect the public interest as much as possible.[1]

DEFINITIONS: P3S VERSUS CONTRACTING

P3s can be defined as (NCCP, 2014):

> A contractual arrangement between a public agency (federal, state or local) and a private sector entity. Through this agreement, the skills and assets of each sector (public and private) are shared in delivering a service or facility for the use of the general public. In addition to the sharing of resources, each party shares in the risks and rewards potential in the delivery of the service and/or facility.

P3s are more complex than traditional contracting arrangements. First, agreements are ongoing and skills are shared in that expectations, tasks and efforts are expected to evolve and change throughout the contractual relationship. In contrast, governments specify goods purchased using an Invitation for Bid, and will have much more control over identifying goods/services purchased using the Request for Proposal approach. Second, private partners will more actively participate in all decisions leading to the completion of the P3 project, especially if they are expected to provide initial financing. Also, as long as specified performance standards and goals are met, private partners have more control over how to create the product or deliver the service. Third, the nature of the risk and the extent to which it is shared among all partners can be much more complex with P3s. With typical governmental services such as garbage collection, if the service is not delivered as specified, the private contractor solves the problem. The risk or probability that something may go wrong is completed assumed by the private contractor. In contrast, with P3s, the risks, as well as rewards, are often shared by the public and private partners. Calculating the amount of risk and understanding the extent to which it is shared are efforts that the public procurement official can undertake, or at least review the efforts consultants and others make.

TYPES OF P3S

As indicated in Table 6.1, P3s can take a variety of forms. Moving from the top of the table to the bottom, from O&M to DBFOM types, the degree of participation in decision-making by the private partners becomes much greater. The use of outside consultants and expertise by public partners in the creation or procurement of the P3 is likely to increase as well.

The following discusses the optimal P3 creation process, one in which public procurement officials can participate throughout. The intent is to provide an introduction or overview to what are considered best practices or the optimal processes. To the extent

Table 6.1
Major Types of P3s
(Adopted from Martin & Saviak, 2014)

- Operate & Maintain (OM)

    The private sector partner operates and maintains a transportation or other facility under a contract with a government. The government provides the financing and compensates the private sector when the facility is open and available for use.

- Design-Build (DB)

    The private partner both designs and builds (or rehabilitates) a transportation or other facility. The government provides the financing and compensates the private sector partner when the facility is delivered or completed.

- Design-Build-Finance (DBF)

    The private sector partner both designs and builds (or rehabilitates) a transportation or other facility and also arranges for short term construction financing. The government compensates the private sector partner when the transportation or other facility is delivered or completed.

- Design-Build-Finance-Maintain (DBFM)

    The private sector partner designs, constructs (or rehabilitates) and maintains a transportation or other facility and also arranges for long term financing. A long-term contract is created. The government compensates the private sector partner when the transportation or other facility is open and available for use, as long as agreed upon performance standards are met.

- Design-Build-Finance-Operate-Maintain (DBFOM)

    The private sector partner designs, builds, operates and maintains a transportation or other facility, and also arranges for long term financing. The private sector partner is compensated by revenue often in the form of user charges generated by the transportation or other facility or through payments made by the government, as long as the facility is open and available for use. This type of P3 is also referred to as a "concession."

that a specific jurisdiction is not adopting one or more of the practices below, for example benefit cost analysis, the public procurement official can suggest that such analysis occur. For those practices more relevant to procurement, such as using Request for Qualifications and/or some form of competitive dialogue, procurement officials can act to acquire needed expertise.

THE P3 CREATION PROCESS

Generally, the P3 creation process can be divided into four phases:

1. Planning efforts, in which decisions are made to support a given project;
2. A P3 is chosen as the preferred approach to complete the project;

3. Pre-contract award steps, in which the private partner is awarded the contract;
4. Post contract award relationships, including those relevant to construction and operations and maintenance (if applicable).

Decisions made in one phase affect decisions made in subsequent phases. Ideally, a well-conceived business case completed during the planning phase, for example, will result in a stronger P3 agreement: one less prone to errors, and result in better performance during the operations and maintenance phases.

Phase One and Two: The Planning Phase and Choice of P3 Approach

The start of the P3 process is a planning phase that includes reaching a decision that the roadway or other infrastructure is needed. The second phase encompasses steps and actions that result in a decision to choose a P3 as a means of building a roadway or other infrastructure as preferable compared to traditional or alternative means of doing so. These two phases combined consist of all efforts and decisions made prior to the procurement phase, the start of which is marked by the issuance of a Request for Qualifications or Request for Information.

There are at least four processes or analyses that should occur during these two initial phases: A) Determination of the need for given infrastructure; B) Benefit/cost analysis; C) Value for money analysis; and D) Business case development. To maximize accountability and transparency, all research performed during this phase should be released to relevant stakeholders including the general public.

A. Need for the Infrastructure

A variety of sources support the need for agencies and relevant stakeholders to determine the need for the infrastructure.[2] The Australian National Guidelines, for example, state that the choice of proceeding with a specific capital project should result from a determination that existing infrastructure is insufficient to achieve government or agency goals (Infrastructure Australia, 2008).

The decision to build a new roadway or expand/repair an existing roadway, for example, should result from an analysis made as part of the review process associated with Metropolitan Planning Organizations (MPOs). State Departments of Transportation should contribute to this review as part of the planning relevant to their future work plans. For other types of infrastructure, sufficient planning efforts should be undertaken.

B. Benefit/Cost Analysis

Benefit/Cost (B/C) Analysis (Sallman et. al., 2012) is defined as "a systematic process for calculating and comparing benefits and costs of a project for two purposes:

- To determine if it is a sound investment (justification/feasibility); and
- To see how it compares with alternate projects (ranking/priority assignment)."

Various commissions and authors have called for greater use of benefit/cost analysis (for example, ENO P3 Working Group, 2014). The Productivity Commission (Australia) (2014: 39), as part of a discussion of good governance practices, recommends:

> instituting effective processes, procedures and policy guidelines for planning and selecting public infrastructure projects, including rigorous and transparent use of cost–benefit analysis and evaluations, public consultation, and public reporting of the decision.

To validly assess the value of a P3 contract, benefits and costs in addition to those identified by a value for money (VfM) analysis should be performed. This more encompassing B/C analysis identifies benefits that are termed non-financial because they are separate from revenue collection or the financial aspects of VfM, and because they can add to the value of a P3 project (European PPP Expertise Center, 2011a). A rebuilt roadway can relieve congestion, lessening the commute time of travelers on a daily basis. If the roadway can be built sooner by using a P3 approach instead of alternatives, then these non-financial benefits (NFBs) should be recognized, even if the VfM analysis does not conclude that a P3 project will produce a net financial benefit.

To the extent possible, these NFBs should be quantified. For example, the Sea to Sky Highway P3 project (British Columbia) identified specific user benefits resulting from upgrades to the existing 81.5-mile highway. These upgrades have led to two types of benefits: increased safety and reduced travel times, resulting in travel time savings. Over the life of the P3 contract, from 2009 to 2030, savings from fewer accidents were estimated at $222M, while travel time savings were estimated at $327M (Partnerships British Columbia, 2005).

B/C analysis has limitations and should not be the only source of analysis that leads to the choice of a P3 or the traditional approach. It does not sufficiently assess, for example, difficult to measure or non-quantifiable benefits and costs. It may be biased in favor of recurring behavior or events, e.g., average travel time, and not give sufficient weight to non-recurring events such as traffic crashes or inclement weather (Sallman, 2012). Given these challenges, B/C analysis should only be one part of an overall business case analysis, as discussed below.

C. Value for Money Analysis

Value for Money (VfM) analysis can be defined as:

> The optimum combination of life-cycle costs and quality (or fitness of purpose) of a good or service to meet the user's requirement (US DOT, 2012).

Its purpose is to enable policy planners to determine if a P3 approach to building a roadway, for example, will result in a cost-saving compared to the traditional design-bid build traditional approach. If the VfM is not performed correctly, especially containing poorly devised risk assessment (Ontario Auditor General, 2014) based on assumptions that bias the result in favor of a P3 contract, a higher than anticipated cost for the project is likely. Furthermore, accountability of public officials who have approved the project suffers. In general, VfM is "not universally required by enabling legislation, nor are standard methods consistently applied" (ENO, 2014).

Several aspects of VfM can contribute to faulty analysis if not performed accurately. Three of the most prominent are: Life-Cycle Cost Analysis; Risk determination; and Choice of Discount Rate.

D. Life-Cycle Cost Analysis

Life-cycle cost analysis (LCCA) must be part of the calculations that compare the P3 approach to alternatives; as with a DBFO P3 approach, capital costs are combined with operational costs throughout the life of the partnership. In many cases, higher capital costs, due to the higher cost of private sector financing, are offset by lower operating costs. Without the use of LCCA, VfM cannot be determined if the P3 approach choice includes partnering with the private sector for operations and maintenance responsibilities.

E. Risk Analysis

As cited by many sources, including Infrastructure Australia (2008), optimal risk analysis

> seeks to assign project risks to the party in the best position to control them and therefore minimize both project costs and risks. The party with greatest control of a particular risk has the best opportunity to reduce the likelihood of the risk eventuating and to control the consequences if it does.

Risk analysis can be considered less than optimal if 1) risks are assessed incorrectly; 2) risks are not assigned to the partner best able to control them; and/or 3) risk transfer from the public to the private partner does not occur as originally anticipated. All three of these factors or aspects are interrelated.

A discussion of risk categories and the process of assessing risks in each of these categories can be found elsewhere.[3] Similarly, there are many descriptions of risk typically assigned to private and public partners, including those that may be shared. Conceptually, optimal risk occurs when there is a balance between risk and reward. To the extent that risks are over estimated, the resulting analysis biases a specific project in favor of using the P3 approach (Ontario AG, 2014). To the extent that risks are seriously underestimated, as has been the case with overly optimistic forecasts of travel on a new roadway, for example, higher than anticipated public costs are likely.

If all of the risk has been assigned to one partner, and evidence suggests that sharing should have occurred because the partner is not able to effectively manage the risk[4], then optimal risk is less likely to occur. To the extent that risks cannot be correctly assigned because there is too much uncertainty to assess them correctly, public and private partners should agree to share the risk (Bensaid & Marty, 2014).

F. Discount Rate Choice

The choice of the discount rate (DR) chosen as part of the VfM is a crucial determinant of the final analysis. The higher the discount rate chosen, the greater the risk that concluding analysis will bias a P3 option compared to alternative means of building a roadway. To the extent that there is no one accepted or "correct" discount rate,[5] there is a greater need to apply sensitivity analysis to the VfM calculations, applying a range of discount rates to identify a range of VfM based conclusions.

Moreover, the more the DR is above the current inflation rate, or the current cost of borrowing money, the greater the likelihood that the public will perceive that the VfM analysis is invalid, and that any decision to proceed with a P3 approach may reflect a lack of accountability to the public interest. As discussed by the California legislative analysis of the Presidio Parkway Business Case that included applying a discount rate of 8.5 percent, accepting the legislature's recommendation of a 5 percent DR would have resulted in the choice of a DBB or DB option over the DBFOM option that was chosen (Taylor, 2012).

> Discount rate can be defined as:
>
> a percentage by which a cash flow element in the future is reduced per year, applied exponentially. It is used to estimate how much money would have to be invested currently, as a rate of return equal to the discount rate, to yield the cash flow in the future. (DeCorla-Souza, 2013)

Analyzing various factors should contribute to the choice of a discount rate. A riskier project requires a higher internal rate of return (IRR) than a lower risk project, as the interest paid to obtain funding from equity investors and banks would be higher than if the project were less risky.

Choosing a discount rate that only reflects the cost of borrowing capital, and not reflecting the use of that capital for construction or operations costs, is preferred. Estimations of the risk premium added by bidders for construction overruns, for example, can be made separately from the choice of a discount rate. Overall, given the complexity of risk assessment, the best approach is to run a sensitivity analysis using a variety of risk assumptions and discount rates, and report the results in the overall business case analysis.

G. Business Case Analysis

The analyses discussed above all have limitations. A commitment to an overall business case analysis incorporates B/C analysis and VfM analysis with a goal of overcoming these limitations and more fully supporting the P3 approach choice (World Bank Institute, 2013).

There are a variety of names that are given to business case analysis, including scoping study and feasibility analysis. The business case can also contain a variety of analyses, including different combinations of benefit/cost assessment and VfM (Canada). The benefit of requiring a business case to be crafted includes making sure that the public partners have performed sufficient "due diligence," resulting in furthering public support, increasing accountability, and avoiding perceptions of making decisions that are not in the public interest (Edwards et al., 2004). To the extent that the above-mentioned aspects of the planning phase have already occurred, the business case analysis may largely consist of a summary of these efforts. To the extent that previous steps have omitted key information or data, these can be captured in the business case analysis (Partnerships British Columbia, 2012).

Phase Three: The Procurement Process—Pre Award

After the project has completed the planning phase and the P3 approach is deemed to be preferable, then the pre award procurement process begins. Goals of this process include:

1. Choosing the private partners who will provide the most benefits compared with costs and the best value for money.
2. Maximizing the flexibility necessary to arrive at the most optimal means to build the infrastructure, allowing for suggestions of innovation and creativity by bidders.
3. Lowering the time and cost needed to complete the procurement process, i.e., lowering transaction costs.
4. Avoiding power in balances among public and potential private partners while negotiating, known as "Deal Drift."
5. Maximizing adherence to the public interest over the 30–50 year life of the contract or partnership.

To some extent efforts to achieve these goals will conflict, as for example lowering transaction costs may lead to choosing less than optimal private partners. Choosing the most flexible procurement process, involving negotiation among more than one bidder teams, could result in less amount of time spent during pre-award as well as better VfM. The optional procurement process must result from achieving as much as possible a balance among competing goal achievement efforts.

Negotiation among top rated bidders, in essence inviting bidders to help solve the problem or meet the need, should be maximized. Such negotiation is likely to be more extensive than that found when using a Request for Proposal approach. Competitive Dialogue, used in Europe, is an example of recommended processes. Other examples include Invitation to Negotiate—used in Florida (Lawther, 2007; Rothman, 2004) and Alternative Technical Concepts (http://www.fhwa.dot.gov/construction/cqit/atc.cfm).

A. Competitive Dialogue

Competitive Dialogue, created in 2004 by the European Union, is designed specifically to address "particularly complex contracts," and is explicitly linked to the creation of infrastructure P3s (Burnett, 2009). Complexity is defined as relevant to one or both of two instances when contracting authorities:

- are not objectively able to define the technical means ... capable of satisfying their needs or objectives; and/or
- are not objectively able to specify the legal and/or financial make up of a project. (European Commission, n.d.)

Technical complexity includes the lack of ability to determine which of several possible solutions may be best. The financial complexity of a project includes the willingness of a contracting authority, e.g., a transportation agency, to build a roadway at the least cost possible by allowing the bidders to suggest the means of doing so. Competitive Dialogue provides the flexibility to negotiate the lowest cost approach as supported by financial markets, including changing the contract from a DBFOM to an alternative approach if appropriate (European Commission, n.d.). Competitive Dialogue allows public officials to remain open to innovative/creative ideas coming from the proposer; alternative procurement means do not (Burnett, 2009).

Other relevant aspects of Competitive Dialogue include:

- Contracting authorities can discuss all aspects of the contract with bidders (minimum of three).
- Discussions or negotiations can occur in stages.
- It ends when the contracting agency determines its needs have been met; each bidder issues a last and best final offer.
- After the final offer, the evaluation of all bidders' proposals occurs; there is no additional negotiation allowed with the preferred bidder.

A common procurement alternative, often present in a Request for Proposal process, results in a scaled listing of bidder proposals, with one achieving the highest evaluation score and others ranked below it. Typically negotiation occurs with the preferred bidder, with the potential for negotiations to occur with the second ranked bidder if those with the highest ranked are deemed unsuccessful. This process can lead to protracted negotiations with the preferred bidder, as no real competition exists: the likelihood of negotiating with the second preferred bidder is slight (Office of Governmental Commerce, 2006).

Phase Three: Key Contract Issues

The elements of an optimal P3 contract should build upon the analysis made in the planning stage and should contain those aspects that provide a framework for the relationships among all partners during the post contract award period. As such, these elements should be as clear and as certain as possible, outlining the roles and responsibilities of the public and private partners as much as possible.

The most significant elements relevant to the design of a P3 contract are those relevant to performance requirements and payment mechanisms (World Bank Institute, 2012). The choices of payment mechanisms associated include:

- User fees payment mechanism
- Availability payment mechanism with performance measures and standards. (Farquharson, Torres de Mastle, & Yescombe, 2011; Bensaid & Marty, 2014)

With the user fee payment type of P3, the private partner or concessionaire performs design, build finance, operate and maintain functions (DBFOM) over a long-term contract, and collects all fees or tolls to pay for incurred costs, including financing and profit. In doing so, all demand risk is assumed, along with the technical and construction risks. It is assumed that the acquisition of this risk is a sufficient incentive to maximize efficiencies during operations and maintenance periods, as well as throughout construction.

In contrast, the public partners assume all demand risk using the availability payment (AP) approach. All infrastructures for which no user fees are charged to patrons entering the facility, such as courthouses, schools, and hospitals, employ the AP approach. Given that there is no link between usage and payment, without the implementation of a much more formal performance measurement system there is a lack of incentives for the private partners to operate as efficiently and effectively as possible.

An alternative to these two approaches involves the sharing of risk between public and private partners, as well as employing performance measures to ensure maximum efficiency. Demand risk and relevant revenue sharing is discussed in the following section, followed by a more in-depth analysis of availability payments and performance management system characteristic and issues.

A. User Fee Issues and Contract Alternatives

SHARING DEMAND RISK

Sharing demand risk alternatives, if the P3 project collects user fees such as tolls, can take many forms. Public partners can subsidize part of construction costs, providing payments to meet construction milestones. In order to reduce tolls to more publically acceptable levels, a subsidy for operating costs could be provided in lieu of the projected toll shortfall. Similarly, grants or subsidies can occur, identifying either a fixed or variable amount to support operating costs.

Revenue guarantees, which may occur to lessen the potential for private partner bankruptcy or the need for renegotiation, must be chosen carefully. If the public sector were willing to guarantee 100 percent of what is needed to cover operating costs and pay debt and equity investors, the availability payment approach may be preferable. The guarantee, then, should be less than 100 percent of what is needed to cover all expenses and profit. Guarantees can take the form of a fixed amount, a percentage of expected revenues, or a sliding scale, with a higher percentage during the ramp up period than in later years of operations (Yescombe, 2007).

USER CHARGE RATES AND CHANGES

Key contract issues include rate setting and adjustment of user fees. Options range from the private partners having full control over rate setting to full government regulation, with rates dictated by the public partners (Eno, 2014). The key issue is identifying under what circumstances the user fees will be allowed to change, either at the rate of inflation, for example, or due to increase in costs or other reasons (World Bank Institute, 2012).

Optimal user fees and change rates are difficult to determine as the unknown factor is the traveling public's "willingness to pay." If rates are too high, then ridership is likely to fall; if rates are too low, then insufficient revenue results. The history of the Dulles Greenway P3 reflects a series of changes in fees over time as the private partners attempted to identify rates that maximized usage (Boardman & Vining, 2010).

If public partners share demand risk, then allowing private partners maximum control over rate setting would risk rates that diminish ridership, requiring higher revenues to be paid by public partners. In contrast, allowing public partners complete control over rate setting may result in no rate increases, as illustrated by the situation faced by the Indiana Turnpike prior to leasing the roadway to the Indiana Toll Road Concession Company (Gilroy & Aloyts, 2013).

Removing some control over rate setting from any partners in a P3 project lessens the risk of decisions made that do not result in optimal revenue collection. State statutes that support and require rates to rise at least by the rate of inflation provide some public interest protection.[6] The more demand risk is shared, that is, retained by the public partners, the greater the emphasis on and importance is placed on the performance measures and standards, as discussed in the next section. The challenge is to provide sufficient incentives to maintain optimal operational performance.

B. Availability Payments and Performance Measurement Issues

Availability payments (APs) are periodic payments, made over the life of a P3 contract, that respond to specific efforts made by the private partner. These efforts can occur during the time periods devoted to operations or maintenance. In its simplest form, during the operations period, if a roadway remains open for a specified time period, or a courthouse or school is open for service delivery, then a corresponding AP will be made. If lanes on a roadway are closed for any reason, or the school is closed because the heating system is not functioning, then the AP will be reduced according to a specified formula. This situation may reflect conditions of "pure availability": unobstructed travel by motorists or use of the infrastructure (Dochia & Parker, 2009).

Another category of APs refers to "constructive availability": the use of

> Performance, safety and quality criteria—specified in the contract, often providing the public owner with stronger metrics and management tools to assure a high quality service than it may be able to apply to services it self-performs. (Dochia & Parker, 2009)

During the operations and maintenance periods, APs are tied to performance measures or Key Performance Indicators (KPIs) (Garvin et al., 2011). Data must be collected and monitored relevant to the KPIs, with corresponding levels of APs related to the KPIs achieved. If the data is not collected, or if monitoring of KPIs does not occur, then the use of APs are simply another way of the public sector borrowing funds (Farquharson, Torres de Mastle, & Yescombe, 2011).

C. Benefits of Availability Payments

Using an AP approach can include the following potential benefits:

- The use of Key Performance Indicators (KPIs) ensures that private partner performance will remain at high, specified levels.
- The potential for private partner bankruptcy is likely reduced.
- Public contributions to the overall cost of the P3 are capped.
- Private profit is also capped, eliminating the likelihood of "windfall" profits.

- Financing costs are less, since public bonds and other debt mechanisms can be accessed at a lower cost.
- The cost of debt is lower, as debt service coverage ratios are lower.
- Greater transparency and public support for the P3 project can be more easily achieved because payment amounts are known.
- Maintenance and future capital renewal costs are fully funded.

D. Challenges/Potential Problems with Availability Payments

Availability risk may increase. Availability risk can be defined as:

> an underperformance linked to the state of the PPP assets [that] results in services being partially or wholly unavailable, or where these services fail to meet the quality standards specified in the PPP contract. (European PPP Expertise Centre, 2011b)

During operations, the private partner may meet minimum performance standards to limit availability risk, but will have no incentive to go beyond these standards as the payment received remains constant. Furthermore, if more travelers are using the road—or more patrons enter a courthouse—operations and maintenance costs may increase, further reducing profit (Ugarte, Guiterrez, & Phillips, 2012).

Additional related challenges refer to the KPIs chosen and the resulting enforcement or contract management system created. Optimal KPI choice results in measures that reflect achievement of project and societal goals. The choice of penalties and enforcement of them by public partners must be an ongoing, accepted part of the relationship among partners after contract award. The risk is that, with an AP P3 approach, a true partnership will not occur, and the relationship among the public agencies and private contractors reflect more than found in privatization contracts and not P3s.[7]

E. Availability Payments and Key Performance Indicator Choices and Issues

Garvin et al. (2010:5) offer useful definitions of performance measures and key performance indicators.

Performance measures are derived from the programmatic levels of service sought by the transport agency and imposed contractually as broad classifications of desired outcomes required of the contractor.

Key performance indicators are more specific milestones in or components of performance measures that serve as precursors to indicate progress toward the eventual achievement of the desired performance measures.

KPIs can be further categorized by:

- Project Faults: roadway may be judged constructively unavailable even if travel on the roadway still occurs, e.g., failure to meet pavement smoothness standards; reduction in payments as a result can be adjusted by segment and time of day.
- Non Compliance Points: failure to meet minimum performance requirements; failure to meet maintenance requirements. (Harder, 2009)

To further assess relevant issues, it is useful to identify different categories or types of KPIs or performance measures.[8] Each category can be distinguished by the degree of control that the P3 project has over the potential outcomes or outputs. At the broadest or highest level, societal goals such as safety or congestion mitigation may be likely. More relevant to a P3 contractual arrangement are agency goals and P3 project goals. To the extent that KPIs or performance measures designed to achieve all three goals are the same or can be aligned, the P3 has greater potential for being judged effective or successful.

An optimal Performance or Operations Management System must contain the following components: 1) performance measures; 2) performance standards; 3) data collection and reporting policies and procedures, and penalties and/or incentives. Optimally, performance measures should be identified in the RFP or ITN document. Standards can be identified as the result of negotiation among partners prior to contract award. Data collection and reporting policies should be identified, but the private partner could propose the precise procedures after contract award, with approval by the public partners.

Phase Four: Post Contract Award

The optimal relationships and actions during the post contract award time period should be characterized by all partners effectively working toward the P3 project and relevant societal goals while maintaining high levels of transparency and accountability. To the extent that these are governed by efforts made during the previous phases, the greater the likelihood of success in implementing the remaining years of the P3 agreement.

The post contract award process can be divided into two periods: Construction (years 1–5); and Operations and Maintenance (years 6–30). A more detailed discussion of the construction time period can be found elsewhere (for example, Lawther & Alford, 2008). The relationships that are created during construction can be carried over into the O&M period.

A. Operations and Maintenance

The O&M period should be characterized by:

- A specified governance structure and process, reflecting an ongoing positive relationship among all partners

- Implementation of the Performance or Operating Management System established during the pre-award period
- Continued, periodic interaction with stakeholders.

B. Governance Issues: Structure and Process

Characteristics of an optimal O&M governance structure and process include:

- Identification of appropriate roles and role expectations of all partners
- Formal, periodic meeting times of P3 Team
- Consistent agenda and review processes
- Standardized decision-making processes
- Creation of an organizational culture that is flexible, innovative, and evolutionary.

Role expectations for public partners include those aspects traditionally identified as contract monitoring, management, or administration (Davison & Wright, 2007). Public partner representatives must review private partner efforts, assess them according to performance specifications, and issue incentives or penalties. The creation of the team that represents the public partners, ideally created before the contract is awarded, must be properly resourced and adequately trained. If it is not, the review of private partner performance, for example, may not be as sufficient as needed (Farquharson et al., 2011; US GAO, 2002). The availability payment approach involves greater involvement of the government partner management team than if demand risk is transferred totally to the private partners.

Private partners will be required to provide performance reports as specified by the performance management system identified in the P3 Contract. A process must be established to link performance reviews with payments. This process should be formalized and documented to enable appropriate audit findings, with a specific review of each performance report by the designated contract management team member and a subsequent interaction with the team member in charge of approving payments. If this process does not exist, the risk is that payments will be issued without collection of performance data and/or formal review and assessment of what data is provided (Office of the Auditor General, British Columbia, 2012).

Overall, the optimal partnership creates a culture that allows for some flexibility to enable sensible approaches to be taken to problems and unforeseen issues (Farquharson et al. 2011). The very best partnerships are based on a positive, deliberate, and structured approach to establishing and maintaining the partnership. The approach should be based on a simple philosophy—magnets work better than handcuffs. The establishment of an effective partnership requires a detailed understanding of the common and the uncommon ground between both partners. It is also required to both partners understand each other in some detail with respect to motivation and preferences. The whole objective here is to avoid an "us and them" situation and instead develop a situation of mutual respect and cooperative actions towards success on both sides (McQueen, 2013).

C. Stakeholder Involvement

Traditional public involvement in infrastructure development has occurred during the planning stages of projects. What has been missing, however, is public involvement in the post contract award or O&M time period. During the O&M phase, efforts change to include a greater focus on uses of the roadway or infrastructure, as well as on interacting with key stakeholders. These efforts should build upon public education and outreach efforts that had previously occurred, allowing all partners to manage expectations about the outcome of the project (National Audit Office, 2006).

The framework proposed by the National Audit Office, United Kingdom, recommends that user satisfaction surveys be implemented periodically, obtaining views on the performance of the private partners. Past and present concerns or complaints should be elicited, along with views on how well past concerns have been resolved. Overall, some measure of on-going satisfaction with the private partners should be identified (National Audit Office, 2006).

CONCLUSION

For the public procurement official who wishes to take an active role in P3 creation and procurement, two approaches seem appropriate—both aimed at filling gaps in the knowledge held by other state and local officials that implement P3s. First, he/she can acquire additional knowledge not presently held and perform the needed analysis. Among the topics addressed in this chapter, knowledge about Competitive Dialogue or a version of this procurement approach would seem invaluable. Learning how to perform benefit/cost analysis, VfM, and/or risk analysis would also assist policy makers in making decisions that are in the best interest of their state or local communities. Adding to current knowledge about performance measurement, creating performance management systems, and carrying out tasks similar to standard contract management practices could be added to this list.

A second approach involves a watchdog role, acquiring enough knowledge about the topics addressed to review and question the analyses performed by consultants hired to advise local officials, as well as to potentially assist their analysis. For example, the lifecycle cost data on which VfM and risk assessment is based could be reviewed for validity and accuracy. If analyses or studies such as a business case are not performed and there is a strong political push to adopt a P3 approach, these omissions can be noted and conveyed to public policy makers. Overall, the public procurement official can act in the traditional role of protecting the public interest, even suggesting that a P3 approach may not be the best to adopt for a given project.

KEY POINTS

- Identifying the source of funds to repair or build new infrastructure has led many state and local governments to consider adopting a Public Private Partnership (P3) approach. The complexity of P3s, the lack of familiarity with appropriate processes, analyses, and procurement approaches, and the greater risk of inadequate expertise, should lead public procurement officials to consider adopting optimal processes for P3s prior to initiating a P3 approach.
- The P3 creation or procurement process should begin with identifying the need for the infrastructure or facility project, followed by analyses such as benefit/cost analysis and value for money (VfM), all contributing to a business case development. Appropriate or valid VfM must include life-cycle cost analysis, optimal risk analysis, and the choice of a discount rate that does not unduly bias the choice of a P3 approach.
- Once a P3 approach has been chosen, the pre award process must include competitive dialog or a similar flexible approach that maximizes negotiation among three or more offerors prior to the bid award decision. Relying on traditional negotiation approaches that include negotiation only with the highest bidder is likely to encounter power imbalances such as "deal drift," as well as not maximizing the flexibility necessary to arrive at the most optimal means to build the infrastructure.
- Key contract issues include the choice of payment mechanisms and performance management systems. If user fees or tolls are used to provide payment to the private partners, then they assume all demand risk. In contrast, the use of availability payments, in which the public partners assume all risk, or alternatively demand risk is shared among public and private partners, requires identification of performance measures and a management system to ensure project success.
- In the post award P3 time period, an optimal governance structure creates a culture that allows for some flexibility to enable sensible approaches to be taken to solve problems and tackle unforeseen issues. An often-overlooked aspect of what may be a 30-year relationship is the establishment of ongoing viable interaction with clients or customers and key stakeholders. Periodic satisfaction surveys, plus a formal citizen advisory committee, should be established.
- Given the lack of expertise found among state and local officials concerning P3s, the role of the public procurement official can be twofold. He/she can acquire knowledge to perform the needed analysis. Alternatively, a "watchdog" role, one that reviews all materials created by consultants and ensures that the optimal processes are followed can be assumed to ensure maximum adherence to the public interest.

NOTES

1. See, for example, the discussion found in Thai, 2004.
2. Even if the P3 type considered is for Operations and Maintenance, in many cases rehabilitating existing structures and/or building new facilities is part of the P3 agreement.
3. See, for example, Akintoye, Beck and Hardcastle, 2003.
4. More discussion of risk sharing is found later in the chapter.
5. See the review of various approaches to determine an acceptable discount rate, including those by Australia and Partnerships British Columbia, in Federal Highway Administration (2013).
6. See, for example Florida Statute [338.165 (3)].
7. For a discussion of the difference in relationships between privatization contracts and P3s, see Forrer, Kee, Newcomer, and Boyer, 2010).
8. For more detailed discussion see Lawther and Martin, 2014.

REFERENCES

Akintoye, A., Beck, M. & Hardcastle, C. (2003). *Public private public partnerships: Managing risks and opportunities.* London: Blackwell Science.

Bensaid, J & Marty, F. (2014). What makes public private partnerships work? An economic analysis. *Prisme* No 27, June. Retrieved from http://www.centre-cournot.org/what-makes-public-private-partnerships-work-an-economic-analysis.

Boardman, A. & Vining, A. (2010). P3s in North America: Renting money (in Canada), selling roads (in the USA). In G. Hodge, C. Greve, & A. Boardman, (Eds.), *International handbook on public-private partnerships* (pp. 354–398). Cheltenham, UK: Edward Elgar.

Burnett, M. (2009). Using competitive dialogue in EU public procurement: Early trends and future developments. European Institute of Public Administration, *SCOPE* (2), 17–23. Retrieved from http://www.eipa.eu/files/repository/eipascope/20100114121857_Eipascope_2009_2_Article2.pdf.

Davison, W. D. & Wright, E. (2007). *Contract administration* (2nd ed.). Herndon, VA: National Institute for Governmental Purchasing.

DeCorla-Souza, P. (2013). *Value for money analysis: Constructing the public sector comparator and the shadow bid.* P3-Value Webinar, July 12. Slide 21. Retrieved from http://www.fhwa.dot.gov/ipd/pdfs/p3/p3_vfm_analysis_webinar_071113.pdf.

Desscan, P. and McCann, S. (2012). *Competitive dialogue: A critical monologue.* Retrieved from: www.morgan-cole.com.

Dochia, S. & Parker, M. (2009). *Introduction to private public partnerships with availability payments.* Philadelphia, PA: Jeffrey A. Parker and Associates. Retrieved from http://www.pwfinance.net/document/research_reports/9%20intro%20availability.pdf.

Edwards, P., Shaoul, J., Stafford A. & Arblaster, L. (2004). *Evaluating the operation of PFI in roads and hospitals.* London: Certified Accountants Educational Trust. Retrieved from http://image.guardian.co.uk/sys-files/Society/documents/2004/11/24/PFI.pdf.

Eno Center for Transportation. (2014). *Partnership financing: Improving transportation infrastructure through public private partnerships.* Retrieved from https://www.enotrans.org/publications.

European Commission. (n.d.) *Explanatory note—competitive dialogue classic directive.* Directorate General Internal Market and Services. Retrieved from http://www.europadecentraal.nl/wp-content/uploads/2013/01/explanatory-note-competitive-dialogue.pdf.

European PPP Expertise Centre. (2011a). *The Non financial benefits of PPPs: A review of concepts and methodology.* Luxembourg. June. Retrieved from http://www.eib.org/epec/resources/epec-non-financial-benefits-of-ppps-public.pdf.

European PPP Expertise Centre. (2011b). *The guide to guidance: How to prepare, procure and deliver PPP projects.* Luxembourg: European PPP Expertise Centre. Retrieved from: http://www.eib.org/epec/resources/guide-to-guidance-en.pdf.

Farquharson, E., Torres de Mastle, C. and Yescombe, E. (2011*). How to engage with the private sector in public private partnerships in emerging markets.* Washington, DC: The International Bank for Reconstruction and Development/The World Bank. Retrieved from http://www-wds.worldbank.org.

Forrer, J., Kee J., Newcomer, K. & Boyer, E. (2010). Private-public partnerships and the public accountability question. *Public Administration Review, 70*(3), 475–484.

Garvin, M., Molenaar, K., Navarro, D. & Proctor, G. (2011). *Key performance indicators in private public partnerships.* Washington DC: Federal Highway Administration. Retrieved from http://international.fhwa.dot.gov/scan/index.cfm /.

Gilroy, L. & Aloyts, D. (2013). *Leasing the Indiana toll road: Reviewing the first six years under private operation.* Reason Foundation, Policy Brief 108. Retrieved from http://reason.org/files/indiana_toll_road_lease.pdf.

Harder, P. (2009, December) *Availability payments: An alternative PPP payment mechanism.* Presentation made at the IBTTA 2009 Transportation Finance Summit. Retrieved from http://ibtta.cms-plus.com/files/PDFs/Harder_Patrick.pdf.

Infrastructure Australia. (2008). *National public private partnership guidelines: Overview.* Commonwealth of Australia. Retrieved from http://www.infrastructureaustralia.gov.au/public_private/files/National_PPP_Guidelines_Overview_Dec_08.pdf.

Lawther. W. (2007). Flexible procurement approaches that facilitate relationship change and negotiation: The use of the invitation to negotiate. *Journal of Public Procurement, 7*(2), 173–193.

Lawther, W. & Adler, J. (2008). *Contracting for construction services: Understanding capital improvement contract management.* Herndon, VA: NIGP.

Lawther, W. & Martin, L. (2014) Availability payments and key performance indicators: Challenges for effective implementation of performance measurement systems in transportation public private partnerships. *Public Works Management and Policy, 19*(3), 219–234.

Martin L. & Saviak J. (2014). *Contracting & public-private partnerships (P3s): A guide for state & local government officials and administrators.* Jacksonville, FL: Government Services Partnership Institute.

McQueen, B. (2013). *Public private partnerships for the provision of new highways: Some thoughts for Florida.* Unpublished manuscript.

National Audit Office (2006). *A framework for evaluating the implementation of private finance initiative projects: Volume 1.* London: National Audit Office. Retrieved from http://www.nao.org.uk/wp-content/uploads/2006/05/Framework_PFI_Projects_i.pdf.

Office of the Auditor General, British Columbia. (2012). *Audits of two p3 projects in the sea to sky corridor.* Vancouver, British Columbia. Retrieved from http://www.bcauditor.com/pubs/2012/report4/audits-two-p3-projects-sea-sky-corridor.

Office of the Auditor General, Ontario. (2014) *Infrastructure Ontario—alternative financing and procurement.* Annual Report 2014, 3.05. Retrieved from http://www.auditor.on.ca/en/reports_en/en14/2014AR_en_web.pdf.

Office of Governmental Commerce. (2006). *Olympic delivery authority: Delivery partner procurement using competitive dialogue: A lessons learned study.* United Kingdom. Retrieved from http://webarchive.nationalarchives.gov.uk/20110601212617/http:/www.ogc.gov.uk/documents/CompetitiveDialogueProcedureODALessonsLearned.pdf.

Partnerships British Columbia. (2005). *Achieving value for money: The Sea to Sky highway improvement project.* Retrieved from http://www.partnershipsbc.ca/pdf/SeatoSkyFinal.pdf.

Partnerships British Columbia. (2012). *Methodology for quantitative procurement options analysis discussion paper.* Vancouver, BC. Retrieved from http://www.partnershipsbc.ca/files-4/documents/ProcurementOptionsAnalysisDiscussionPaperOctober142011.pdf.

Productivity Commission (2014). *Public infrastructure*. Commonwealth of Australia, Inquiry Report No. 71. Retrieved from www.pc.gov.au.

Puentes, R. (2008) *A bridge to somewhere: Rethinking American transportation for the 21st century*. Washington, DC: The Brookings Institution, Metropolitan Policy Program. Retrieved from http://www.brookings.edu/research/reports/2008/06/transportation-puentes.

Rothman, R. (2004, November 5). *Negotiations in Florida*. Presentation made at the Florida Association of Public Procurement Officials. Jacksonville, FL. Retrieved from https://www.fappo.org/.

Sallman, R., Flanagan, E., Jeannotte, K., Headen, C. & Morales, D. (2012). *Operations benefit/cost analysis desk reference*. Cambridge Systematics, Oakland, CA. Retrieved from http://www.ops.fhwa.dot.gov/publications/fhwahop12028/index.htm.

Taylor, M. (2012). *Maximizing state benefits from public private partnerships*. Legislative Analyst's Office, State of California. Retrieved from http://www.lao.ca.gov/reports/2012/trns/partnerships/P3_110712.pdf.

Thai, K. (2004). *Introduction to public procurement*. Herndon, VA: NIGP

Ugarte, C., Guiterrez, G. & Phillips, M. (2012). *A roadmap to funding infrastructure development*. International Transport Forum, Discussion Paper 2012–9, Prepared for the Roundtable on: Public Private Partnerships for Funding Transport Infrastructure, Sources of Funding, Managing Risk and Optimism Bias. Retrieved from http://www.internationaltransportforum.org/jtrc/DiscussionPapers/DP201209.pdf.

U.S. Department of Transportation (2012). *Value for money: Assessment for private public partnerships: a primer*. Federal Highway Administration, Office of Innovative Program Delivery. Retrieved from http://www.fhwa.dot.gov/ipd/pdfs/p3/p3_value_for_money_primer_122612.pdf.

U.S. General Accountability Office. (2002). *Transportation infrastructure: Cost and oversight issues on major highway and bridge projects*. Washington, DC: Author, GAO-02-702T. Retrieved from http://gao.gov/products/GAO-02-702T.

World Bank Institute. (2012). *Public private partnerships reference guide version 1.0*. Washington, DC: Author. Retrieved from http://www-wds.worldbank.org/.

World Bank Institute (2013). *Value-for-money analysis—practices and challenges: How governments choose when to use ppp to deliver public infrastructure and services*. Retrieved from http://wbi.worldbank.org/wbi/Data/wbi/wbicms/files/drupal-acquia/wbi/VFM_0.pdf.

Yescombe, E.R. (2007) *Public private partnerships: principles of policy and finance*. Burlington, MA: Elsevier.

7

Monitoring and Evaluating Contracts

Clifford McCue and Bill Davison

The goal of any contract is to ensure that the agency receives the right quantity of the right material or service of the right quality in the right time at the right place, and to do this within the identified budget and without claim. A government's ability to provide the goods and services demanded by its citizens requires not only good contract planning and formalization, but also good contract monitoring and evaluation to insure that the contractor is performing to the standards identified in the contract. Unfortunately, governments have not always done a good job of establishing effective contract monitoring and evaluation plans to insure that they receive exactly what they ordered.

According to the Governmental Accountability Office (2009), a number of federal agencies have done a poor job monitoring contract compliance and evaluating contractor performance. The GAO audited various civilian agencies (Departments of Education, Energy, Health and Human Services, and Housing and Urban Development) and found that 68 percent of the contracts reviewed (87 contracts worth $1.4 billion) failed to properly monitor and/or evaluate contractor performance. The GAO noted that the results of poor contract monitoring and evaluation included (1) increases in contract costs ranging from several hundred dollars to over $1 million; (2) increases in the time necessary to complete the contract from several days to 2 years; and (3) failure to complete a contract task or the entire contract. The study noted that there were a number of critical issues that resulted in the failure to comply with contract requirements, and the GAO recommended that agencies establish better contract monitoring processes and develop strategies to evaluate contract compliance to avoid problems with contract quality, time, and costs.

In 2011, the GAO conducted another study of federal agencies and found that agencies had not made much progress with the recommendations of the 2009 study. In fact, the 2011 study found that poorly designed contract monitoring and evaluations processes were still affecting contractor performance. Some of the more interesting findings were:

- Contractors were not performing to standards expressed in the contract;
- Poor enforcement of rules, regulations, and/or contract provisions because agency personnel were not properly trained in contract evaluation;
- Over reliance on rules and regulations rather than contract outputs/outcomes;

- Failure to ensure that corrective action was taken in cases of contract noncompliance; and,
- Failure to identify the risk and level of review necessary for each phase of the contract monitoring and evaluation process.

The study concluded that good contract management and evaluation requires consistent follow-up, including performance review and feedback, and keeping track of contract deliverables to insure that any potential or real problems in contract performance can be quickly identified and any deficiencies addressed to avoid contract surprises. The GAO recommended that all federal agencies develop a contract monitoring and evaluation plan.

CONTRACT MONITORING AND EVALUATION PLAN

It is important to note at this point that contract monitoring and contract evaluation are two distinct aspects of insuring that the contractor complies and/or has complied (evaluation) with all the terms and conditions of the contract. In other words, contract monitoring and evaluation requires an established process, whether periodic or continuous, that measures and confirms contractor compliance with the terms, conditions, and requirements of a contract. Contract monitoring and evaluation plans are an essential component in contract administration because it provides a systematic way for ensuring that all elements of the contract are delivered satisfactorily. According to the State of Georgia (2003), the contract monitoring plan has several elements.

There are several types of monitoring and evaluation methods to choose from, and selecting the correct method is just as important as developing a good monitoring plan. By understanding the procedural and legal aspects of each method, the appropriate method can be selected that would mitigate risks and identify performance issues. In some states, development of a contract monitoring plan is required as part of a contract. For example, the State of Iowa requires that all contracts have contract monitoring language included the standard terms and conditions, as discussed below (State of Iowa Uniform Terms and Conditions for Service Contracts, Chapters 117 and 119):

> Monitoring clause. The contract shall include a clause or clauses describing the methods to effectively oversee the party's compliance with the service contract by the department or establishment receiving the services during performance, including the delivery of invoices itemizing work performed under the service contract prior to payment. Monitoring should be appropriate to the nature of the contract as determined by the department or establishment. Acceptable methods of monitoring may include the following:

Table 7.1

Elements of a Contract Monitoring Plan

1. Identify and document each contract deliverable for:
   a. delivery time,
   b. quantity,
   c. quality,
   d. cost, and
   e. place of delivery.
2. Identify potential problems, i.e. late delivery, insufficient quality, cost overruns, change orders.
3. Identify the method of evaluation on how acceptance will be determined for each deliverable (i.e. report, test, survey).
4. Develop a contract monitoring plan that identifies the type and level of monitoring necessary to monitor contract progress:

   A. Incorporate the likely problems and develop a monitoring strategy that minimizes the occurrence of the potential problems.
   B. Tracks the progress of contract deliverables and contract issues (typically through a contract management system, spreadsheet, or other electronic tracking applications).
   C. Maintain information in a manner that is accessible to all members of the project team.
5. Identify the method and level of surveillance necessary to minimize problems:

   A. Conduct careful monitoring of contractor performance and maintain written records.
   B. Require and utilize progress reports, including contractor-reporting requirements.
6. Conduct a "kick-off" or post award meeting with the contractor and review the contract-monitoring plan and establish an appropriate meeting schedule.
7. Have an internal plan to resolve any performance issues (Corrective Action Plan, Performance Fees).

Source: State of Georgia (2003), Components of an Effective Contract Monitoring System

> Random sampling
> Periodic inspection
> Customer input

Review clause: The contract shall include a clause or clauses describing the methods to effectively review performance of a service contract, performance measurement should be appropriate to the nature of the contract as determined by the department or establishment. The measures below are not intended as an exhaustive or prescriptive list; they are provided as examples. The review clause for performance may include:

> Outcome measures
> Output measures
> Quality measures

A review plan determined by the department or establishment to be appropriate for the purposes of the service contract and that includes methods to effectively review the performance of a service contract.

ELEMENTS OF A CONTRACT MONITORING PLAN

1. Identify and document each contract deliverable, specification, method of evaluation (i.e. report, delivery, and expected results), timeframe, budget, and performance criteria

The first step in the contract monitoring and evaluation process is to identify the type of contract deliverables. Governments purchase everything from routine, low value items to highly risky and complex projects. Clearly, contract monitoring and evaluation requirements differ greatly across this spectrum. A number of factors drive the monitoring and evaluation approach utilized, and it is important to consider the nature of each contract requirement and then decide on the appropriate approach. There are a number of key criteria that can affect the decision on the monitoring and evaluation approach utilized, but generally most approaches include the following:

- Complexity: How complex is the contract, typically in terms of a technical specification (building construction) or the range of services required (a training program for a welfare-to-work program at a local government training center)?
- Repeatability: Is the contract going to be repeated each year or is it a one-time purchase? That is, is there going to be an ongoing concern (laptop computers) or is it a one-time purchase, such as an ERP software bridge?
- Risk and Contract Value: The value of the contract or the risk of contract failure must be weighed against the costs of contract non-compliance. Remember, a contract may be low in value but may still carry significant risk, such as failure of the local agency training program.
- Commonality: The commonality of what is being contracted; is the government the only one that requires the item (e.g. fighter planes) or is it something many governments require, such as temporary labor or furniture.

One way to look at contract deliverables and to identify the appropriate monitoring and evaluation approach is to use a logic model. The logic model provides a simple way to categorize the various potential deliverables in any contract.

According to the W.K. Kellogg Foundation (2004):

> the program logic model is defined as a picture of how your organization does its work—the theory and assumptions underlying the program. A program logic model links outcomes (both short- and long-term) with program activities/processes and the theoretical assumptions/principles of the program.

Table 7.2
Contract Types

Contract Type	Examples
Commodities, Small Purchases	MRO (maintenance, repair and operating supplies) Term contracts, i.e. office supplies, one-time orders for durable goods under $5000
Capital Outlay	Durable goods over $5000
Professional Services	Architects, consultants
Contracted Services	Custodial services, food service
Software	Custom developed and shrink-wrap
Construction	Any type and any dollar amount—New construction or remodeling
Leases	Leased space or equipment—lease without intent to own

Source: Davison-Sebastian 2009

The logic model deliverables can be viewed as inputs, activities, outputs, and outcomes:

1. Inputs (resources) typically include the financial, organizational, and human resources that are used in the delivery of a contract deliverable.
2. Activities are the resources consumed by the contractor and the agency in completing the contract specifications, including the administrative resources used during the contract process. Activities can be classified as the methods, tools, technology, and action steps that are necessary to complete the contract. These activities must directly bring about the identified changes or results identified on the contract.
3. Outputs are the direct products or services delivered by the contractor and may include types, levels and targets to be delivered. Outputs measure the volume produced (quantitative data) that you can count, test, or otherwise measure.
4. Outcomes are the specific consequences or results anticipated in the contract. Outcomes measure the quality or effectiveness of the services delivered (qualitative data). It can be challenging to create meaningful deliverables for services. The service may have a short-term and long-term outcome. Those outcomes that are attainable within 0 to 1 years are termed short-term outcomes, where intermediate outcomes are typically achievable within 1 to 3 years, and those that take longer then 3 years. Outcomes are called long-term outcomes. Long-term outcomes normally involve an ongoing relationship between the contractor and the agency.

One way to help operationalize the inputs and activities used in logic model is to develop a work breakdown structure (WBS). The WBS allows you to identify:

A. What is needed?
B. When is it needed?

C. Where is it needed?
D. Who needs the outcome?
E. Why is the outcome needed?
F. What will be done with the outcome?
G. What will occur as a result of the outcome?
H. How will you determine if the outcome has been achieved?

Then once the inputs and activities are identified the next step is to identify the outputs/outcomes of the model. These outputs/outcomes should comply with the SMART principles when identifying desired results for each step of the WBS:

A. Specific
B. Measurable
C. Attainable
D. Relevant
E. Timely.

For example, if you awarded a contract for the Social Services department for job counseling, an *output* may be the number of persons who receive counseling and the percentage of the last quarter's caseload with jobs. A short-term *outcome* might involve determining how successful the training program for the unemployed was compared to no training in getting the client a job. A long-term outcome might involve how long the client was employed, what types of jobs they acquired, and what follow-up training they needed to perform successfully. Identifying the output and outcomes are critical to successful contractor performance measurement, and the plan should account for both the qualitative and quantitative aspects of each when identifying contract deliverables.

Acceptance Considerations

Once the type of deliverable has been determined, the monitoring plan must identify an accurate method to determine acceptance. The output or outcome must be evaluated to determine if it meets the contract specifications. Acceptance is the formal acknowledgment that the goods or supplies/services conform to the requirements specified in the contract. Ultimately, acceptance of a good or service has legal consequences for both parties. Once a product or service is accepted, the contractor is entitled to payment and the agency has limited options for rejection after acceptance. It is critically important that the contract specify what exactly is to be delivered and the quality of that deliverable. Remember, use may result in implied acceptance. To avoid potential problems, a contract-monitoring plan should be developed to determine if the contractor is making progress toward final acceptance. Acceptance should only occur after the completion of contractually specified tests or evaluations. Once the contractor's work has been accepted, the contractor is entitled to be paid and transfers the title of any good or service being purchased to the agency; the agency's right to recover for patent defects is also severely constrained. It is critical that the process for determining acceptance is in the contract documents to avoid any disputes. A monitoring plan should specify:

- How acceptance will be determined.
- The time of acceptance, whether before delivery, at the time of delivery, or after delivery.
- The place of acceptance, for example, "at the source," which means the point where the actual work is being performed; "at destination," which means at the point where items are being delivered; or some other location.
- Responsibility for acceptance should be specified in the contract. It may rest with the contracting officer, receiving personnel, or other designees who should issue a receiving report, "Certification of Acceptance," or "Inspection Report."

Identification of Potential Problems

The goal of contract management for any good or service is successful contract completion. Successful contract completion is defined by the National Institute of Government Purchasing (NIGP) as successful procurement of the right item, in the right quantity, for the right price, at the right time, with the right quality, from the right source (Thai, 2007). Davison and Sebastian proposed, "advance knowledge of the likelihood of occurrence and the severity of consequences of contract problems will allow procurement professionals to identify the likely contract administration problems for a specific contract type" (Davison-Sebastian, 2009). From this, procurement professionals could proactively identify and prepare for known contract risks, work with suppliers throughout the contract to mitigate problems, and ultimately avoid the waste of valuable resources normally spent reacting to problems.

Davison and Sebastian (2009) surveyed members of the National Institute of Government Purchasing to assess which types of contract administration problems (Table 7.3) were perceived as most likely for seven types of contracts (Table 7.2).

Knowledge of potential contract problems can provide contract managers with information about which contract administration problems are perceived as most likely to occur for a given type of purchase, and which type of purchase is likely to encounter the most contract administration problems. Armed with this information, public purchasing personnel can prepare specifications, contracts, and contract monitoring plans to avoid or minimize the adverse impact of contract administration problems. For example, the research showed that construction contracts encountered the highest number of problems, and delays and change orders were the most frequently encountered problem (Davison & Sebastian, 2009).

Table 7.3
Typical Contract Administration Problems

Contract Problem	Examples
Wrong product	Purchase order or contract clearly identifies correct product, but vendor ships incorrect. No dispute involved.
Delay	Purchase order has clearly stated completion date. Completion date delayed (any length of time) due to agency or vendor (with or without cause).
Change order	Change in the scope of work (additional work, money, time), after contract award. Can be requested by either party for any reason.
Personality conflict	Personality conflicts between agency project manager or staff and vendor project manager or employees. Disagreement between the parties that cannot be easily resolved. May involve scope of work, materials supplied, payment schedules, or any other aspect of the contract.
Definition of acceptance	Completion of project is delayed due to non-acceptance of final product. Example: difference in either party's definition of what was supposed to be delivered or provided.
Poor performance	Contract clearly states a level of expected performance (this is not in dispute) and quality problems with vendor's performance of work occur.
Sub-Contractors	The vendor uses subcontractors not on his payroll to perform any or all of the work. Prior approval, for use of subcontractors, was received
Other sources	There are very few vendors that can perform the work.
Risk of failure	The project has a high risk of failure. i.e. new technology, new equipment, new vendor. Project never been done before. Tight timeline or budget
Cost	Project has a high cost.

Source: Davison-Sebastian 2009

Evaluation Methods and Testing Considerations

Inspection and testing may be necessary to determine if the agency has received the correct quantity and quality of the good or service identified on the contract. The risk of receiving the wrong product or quality of a service must be balanced against the cost for conducting a test when recommending a testing approach. Contracts for the acceptance of outputs may be inspected and monitored differently than those covering the delivery of outcomes because of associated contract risks and costs to perform. There are three important facts about testing:

- All requirements for testing must be clearly stated in the specifications or the statement of work (SOW) in the bid or RFP or contract documents and identified on the monitoring plan.
- Both monitoring and testing are costly, but the benefits far outweigh the expense when defects can be detected before equipment failure or personal injury.
- Inspection, testing, and acceptance are conclusive except for latent defects or fraud.

Description of Testing Methods

The monitoring plan must include the contract specifications and how acceptance will be evaluated. Specifications provide details on the right quantity of the right material, of the right quality in the right time needed, and acceptance clauses in the contract are used to determine how and when acceptance will occur. The following issues should be addressed in a part of the monitoring plan:

- Inspection obligation of both parties
- Inspection and testing methods
- Rejection process
- Acceptance process.

Inspection Obligations of Both Parties

Right to Inspect: The agency has the right to inspect and test all products and services listed in the contract in a reasonable manner, at any time, including during manufacture, and at any place during the timeframe of the contract. However, inspections and tests cannot cause an unreasonable delay in the work. If the time and place are specified in the contract and changes made by the agency cause an increase in the supplier's costs, the agency is responsible for the increased costs. The agency is not required to inspect or test.

Inspection Costs: Each party is responsible for any costs incurred. If a product fails an inspection due to contractor fault, the contractor is liable for re-inspection costs.

Inspection Type: There are basically two types of tests that can be conducted,—the contractually specified test and the unspecified test. For the Contractually Specified Testing, the contract will contain a testing specification establishing a level of performance, the agency cannot use a different test that would require the supplier to perform at a higher level that the original test specification. The contract-monitoring plan will specify the type of testing. For the Unspecified Testing, the agency does not have to specify the testing method in the contract. The test must be reasonable and have the ability to determine if the specifications have been met.

Inspection Testing Methods

After evaluating the risk of receiving the wrong product, an inadequate level of effort in producing the product, and the cost of contract compliance has been determined, then the contract compliance method can be decided. The method may differ depending on the type of deliverable (output or outcome) purchased and its importance. For example, the method for most outputs is to visually inspect for shipping damage, verification of receipt of the correct product and the correct quantity. Additional methods such as sampling and in process may be used for determining acceptance for outcomes, such as contracted and professional services or construction and software.

Measuring an outcome may involve the analysis of the user-provided data on the service quality. This type of measurement requires a higher level of effort to perform. In a street maintenance contract, for example, the number of potholes repaired is a measure of output, whereas an outcome analysis might focus on the smoothness of the repair or on the reduction of hazards to pedestrians. The specifications of the criteria on how the outcomes will be measured should be included in the monitoring plan. The monitoring plan will also specify the type of testing method and the consequences of failing a test.

EXCEPTION

In this inspection method, compliance is assumed and is performed only if there is a complaint from the end user. This method is cost effective when the risk of receiving a wrong product is low, and there are numerous suppliers; an example would be purchases that measure outputs, such as commodities, large quantities, low value, and purchases from reliable contractors. There is little risk or consequence of accepting products that do not conform to specifications.

AFTER DELIVERY AND FINAL

Inspection occurs at the delivery location and prior to use. This method is cost effective when the risk of receiving a wrong product is low, and there are numerous suppliers; an example would be for the purchases that measure outputs that require testing or more detailed visual such as; commercial goods. The level of inspection is usually dependent on the product complexity or how important the product is. This is usually limited to visually inspecting for shipping damage, verification of product description with packing list, and verification of quantity.

IN PROCESS

In process occurs at the supplier's location or at the delivery location, while the work is in process. The purpose is to verify the product is on schedule. This method is effective for products with long build times, unique products (no other sources), such as construction, or outcomes such as software or training.

IN USE

In use occurs at the delivery location after delivery. The method used to determine compliance is use of the product for a specified time. This method is effective for purchases that measure outcomes, such as contracted and professional services.

SAMPLING

A sample of an entire shipment is tested in accordance with contractually specified tests. If the test sample fails, the entire shipment may be rejected. The contract will specify the testing methods, the quality tolerances, and the acceptable number of defects. This type of inspection is useful for contracts that measure outputs.

SURVEYS

Surveys are a good tool for determining acceptance for outcome-based projects. Polling of end-users to determine if contract progress or goals are being met is useful for professional services such as a training consultant. The attendees fill out a survey to help determine if the training goals were met. For contracted services, such as custodial services, the end user will complete a form to determine if the area is clean.

Determining the Type and Level of Monitoring

The contracting officer needs to determine the appropriate level of monitoring based on the likelihood of occurrence of problems and the severity of the problem if it does occur. Each method requires a different level of effort by the agency.

The contracting officer has the following monitoring methods available:

- Monitoring by exception
- Follow-up monitoring
- Random monitoring
- Scheduled monitoring
- Direct monitoring.

MONITORING BY EXCEPTION OR RELIANCE ON CONTRACTOR SYSTEM (NO NEWS IS GOOD NEWS)

No monitoring is done except in the case the end-user complaint. The product or service is assumed to be satisfactory. While essential services should be directly monitored, monitoring by exception is appropriate for services that users evaluate continuously as a matter of course. Generally, very large service contracts, both in terms of scope and dollars, would not be suitable for monitoring by exception. Contracts for commodities or low value lend themselves to monitoring by exception. Contractors that are ISO 9000 certified would also be candidates.

FOLLOW-UP MONITORING

Follow-up monitoring is the method most often used and its purpose is to answer general and specific questions such as:

- Does the work being performed meet contract requirements?
- Is the contractor or delivery of product on schedule?
- Are the agency agencies satisfied with the service, product, or contractor?

In contracts that measure outputs such as commodities, capital outlay purchases would benefit from this approach.

RANDOM MONITORING

Random monitoring is direct from or a follow-up of the contractor's performance undertaken without the contractor's advanced knowledge over the course of the contract. Good candidates for this type of monitoring are contracts that are long term, have outcome measurements, no history of performance problems, and multiple contractors, such as contracted service contracts (food service, custodial).

SCHEDULED MONITORING

Regularly scheduled reviews of contracts can help identify and correct service problems. The agency usually collects data on service levels from the end users and then meets with the contractor to discuss the results. Good candidates for this type of monitoring are contracts that are; long term, have outcome measurements, have a history of performance problems, mission critical, such as contracted service contracts (food service, custodial).

DIRECT MONITORING

Direct monitoring is intended to ensure that the work is being performed according to established procedures or standards. Direct monitoring requires daily observation and interaction between the agency contract field manager and the contractor. Good candidates for this type of monitoring are contracts that are long term, have output or outcome measurements, have a high likelihood of performance problems, and high severity if the problem occurs, are mission critical, such as construction and software contracts often utilize this method.

2. Maintain information that is accessible and tracks deliverables (typically through a contract management system, spreadsheet, or other electronic tracking applications)

Once a contract is awarded, a contract track monitoring system should be established that insures the contractor is providing the goods or services in accordance with the terms and conditions of the contract. A Deliverables Tracking System, whether electronic or paper-form, is used to monitor contractual activities, including deliverables tracking, subcontracting, purchasing, receiving, shipping, and billing. Examples of deliverables include conveyance of goods by a certain date, engineering designs by a particular date, purchase of goods from a third party, subcontracted goods or services, and shipment of goods. In addition to tracking shipping and delivery statuses, the tracking system should be integrated with all other monitoring systems for contract management purposes.

By establishing a monitoring system that is integrated with the agencies' financial system, including purchasing, you will be able to:

- Link costs to specific projects and deliverables;
- Identify payment requirements and payment cycles for financial management purposes;
- Transfer demand into the planning and execution system;
- View accounts payable information, including invoice and payment details for a purchase order created from the tracking system;
- View accounts receivable in formation, including invoice and payment receipt details for a billing event initiated from the tracking system;
- Create procurement documents and shipment requests directly in the tracking system.

3. Require on-going progress reports, both from the contractor and contract administrator

Project monitoring and evaluation should be the main purpose of progress reporting. A good project report should provide a summary of the project goals, identify progress made toward achieving a specific goal during the reporting period, highlight significant costs and scheduling issues, and list future objectives to be carried out. Generally, progress reports are prepared at intervals, most frequently at quarterly intervals of the fiscal year. The intervals are often specified in the initial project proposal.

Agencies use progress reports to maintain contact with contractors to inform the agency about the progress of the contract. The agency then uses these reports to report on their work to managers and others within their own agency. Progress reports are useful tools for management in keeping track of work progress on contracts, and they also provide a structure for monitoring their own commitments and levels of support.

4. Identify the level of surveillance needed to minimize problems

Documenting Performance

A major part of contract monitoring and evaluation is keeping and maintaining accurate records of contractor performance. There should be filing systems, located in a centrally located and convenient location, that contain information which allows all concerned parties, including the contractor, to determine what was expected and received under the contract, especially when disputes arise with the contractor. The following are samples of reports that document performance:

- Observation Record
- Complaint Record
- Discrepancy Record
- Unsatisfactory Performance Report
- Summary Evaluation Report
- Contractor Status Report
- Surveys.

Observation Record—The monitor records what is observed. For a construction example, it was a clear day, temps in the 70s, no workers on sight. This method is useful for long-term service contracts and construction. Progress or lack of can be recorded over a period of time.

Complaint Record—When previous history indicates that the risk of poor performance is low (good contractor, ISO 9000 certified or low value contract. "No news is good news").

Discrepancy Record—Useful for product with detailed specifications, when it is important to identify discrepancies early before use or expiration of warranty (capital outlay, construction or software).

Unsatisfactory Performance Report—Useful for long-term contracts or professional services. Surveys indicate ongoing poor performance. Also linked to previous reporting. If identified problems are not corrected. This is often a precursor to termination notice.

Contractor Status Report—Update on status of performance (meeting schedule) circulated to team for approval or for a chance to dispute progress.

Sampling—Written procedures detailed what will be sampled, the acceptable quality level, lot size, level of surveillance, sample sizes, sample selection procedures, performance criteria, evaluations procedure, and consequences of failure.

Surveys—A good tool for determining acceptance for outcome-based projects is to poll end-users to determine if contract progress or goals are being met. Professional services consultant 9 meeting attendees fill out). Contracted services (end-users fill out) is the area clean?

5. Conduct a "kick-off" or post award meeting with the contractor and establish a regular meeting schedule or follow the schedule specified in the contract

According to the Treasury of the Republic of Cyprus's *Public Procurement Best Practice Guide,* after an award is offered to the contractor, and before the contractor begins the contract, a meeting between the two parties (and in many cases all relevant stakeholders) should be held to make sure that all of the concerned parties have a complete understanding of the specific goals and the expected outcomes of the contract. In addition, all parties must agree on the intended outcomes, contract performance reporting requirements, and all appropriate administrative procedures that must be used to insure contract compliance. Depending on the nature and complexity of the specific contract (such as relevant risks, contract value, duration, special requirements, and previous experience from the management of similar contracts), there needs to be an official meeting, which is known as the "kick-off meeting." This meeting is conducted between the key stakeholders of the agency (i.e., Project Manager, members of the Procurement staff, and/or the team that worked on the original solicitation) and the contractor's counterparts. The time period between the signature of the contract and the kick-off meeting is usually set forth in the terms of the contract and, ordinarily, does not exceed 45 days.

The Republic of Cyprus further suggests that the main purpose of the kick-off meeting is to clarify all the relevant terms and conditions identified in the contract (or discussed on the solicitation documents) to avoid any potential interpretation issues during contract implementation. By clarifying all the critical issues upfront, all parties have a clear picture of the terms and requirements of the contract, as well as with regard to the roles and responsibilities of the parties. Often, it is assumed that both the contractor and agency have a full and clear understanding of the expected outcomes identified in the contract. However, the kick-off meeting that follows the signature of the contract ensures that all those involved or those who will be involved directly in the procedures of contract monitoring and evaluation have a common understanding of all its requirements. The table below provides a list of the most common contents included in such a meeting. Please note that the items discussed on Table 7.4 are not exhaustive and topics can be added or removed in order to cover all the necessary components of the specific contract.

Table 7.4

Typical Agenda for a Contract Kick-off Meeting

Introduction: All of the key stakeholders should introduce themselves by describing their current job and responsibilities and their role in relation with the execution of the contract.

Contract Scope: Discussion on the contract scope in order to clarify exactly what the agency expects to achieve from the execution of the specific contract. Despite the fact that the contract scope has already been defined in the solicitation documents and the contractor has detailed in their method of delivery/implementation of the contract scope, at this moment in time it is good and useful that both sides provide the necessary clarifications to avoid the appearance of any problems during the implementation of the contract.

Terms of Contract: A summary reference to the terms and conditions of the contract with emphasis on special conditions. This reference helps to avoid any misunderstanding in the later stages of implementation, allowing the contractor to better understand the terms of the contract before they commences work on the contract.

Requirements: A discussion about the technical requirements and the reporting requirements in the framework of the contract. The technical requirements may also be covered during the discussion on the contract scope. However, proper explanations must be given to the contractor regarding the specifications that the deliverables must satisfy in order to be accepted by the agency. Also, the contractor must realize the importance of the reports that they are required to provide and how important it is that these reports respond to the contract requirements.

Contract Administration: Discussion on the contract administration procedures with emphasis on the monitoring of the contractor and the progress of the work, as well as the management of claims for variations or amendments to the contract.

Determine who will conduct monitoring

Self-reporting or direct monitoring by agency.

Self-reporting is the quickest, easiest and least expensive type of monitoring to implement. Clear and auditable performance standards are necessary. The contractor must describe the methodology used for each type of self-reporting. Some types of self-reporting monitoring are: adherence to required government laws, testing results, sample testing. A disadvantage is that the contractor may not report negative results, and auditing results may be complex, time consuming, or costly.

Direct Monitoring is more costly and requires that the contract management staff or agency have a level of experience necessary to conduct and interpret any outcomes or test results.

Rights and Obligations: A brief reference to the rights and obligations of both parties with the emphasis on the procedures of the contractor performance evaluation. The contractor must be given clear explanations regarding the way in which monitoring and evaluation of contract performance will be made during the implementation of the contract as well as during its closure. The contractor must also be informed that any failure in the performance of their duties based on the contract or non-satisfactory performance during the execution of the contract may lead to his exclusion from any future undertaking of any public contract for a specific period.

Potential Problems: The agency should raise issues that may generate future problems, and solutions must be proposed jointly on how to handle them.

Payments: Clarification to the contractor about the invoicing and the payment procedure requirements of the agency. The matter of payments becomes especially serious in a case where payments are associated with the achievement of specific goals on the part of the contractor or with specific milestones. Also, in a case where the payments are associated with the charging of hourly rates, a discussion must take place regarding the respective procedure based on which the hourly rates shall be certified (e.g., submission of Timesheets). In a case where the contract includes provision for the indemnification of the contractor for certain expenses that they incur in the context of contract implementation, there should be a discussion of the respective procedure on the basis of which the certification of expenses and the indemnification will be made.

Acceptance of Deliverables: Discussion with the contractor regarding the procedures to be applied for the acceptance and approval of contract deliverables.

Competencies/Powers: The agency representatives must explain the limits of their competencies and power in the framework of the contract management and administration and obtain the same information from the representatives of the contractor.

Source: Treasury of the Republic of Cyprus's *Public Procurement Best Practice Guide*

As noted in the table above, this kick-off meeting is critical to the ultimate success of any contract, and it establishes the performance criteria that are used to judge the success of the contractor in delivering what was identified on the contract. Therefore, official minutes of the meeting must be drafted by the meeting secretary and sent to all individuals attending the meeting. Minutes serve to ensure that critical decisions and subsequent actions resulting from a meeting are not lost or forgotten. Once all parties at the meeting have approved the minutes, they become an official part of the contract file. Like any good set of minutes, the following information should be included: date, time and place of the meeting, participant names and titles, contract issues identified, decisions made about the issues and how they were resolved, responsibilities and deadlines to take further actions.

This meeting is the first official communication between agency and contractor following the signature of the contract, and essentially signals the commencement of the Contract Monitoring and Evaluation process on the part of the agency and the commencement of the project implementation on the part of the contractor.

Have an internal plan to resolve any performance issues and a conflict resolution and corrective action plan

How conflict and contract problems are going to be resolved must be addressed in the contract-monitoring plan. When resolving conflicts, follow these steps:

- Think before reacting
- Listen actively
- Assure a fair process
- Attack the problem
- Accept responsibility
- Use direct communication
- Look for interests
- Focus on the future
- Options for mutual gain.

In order to effectively resolve problems, it is important to have a corrective action plan. The corrective action plan should include the following steps.

1. State the problem or weakness succinctly, including the root cause. Determine what should be happening by asking what is actually happening. Why is the problem occurring, what is the root cause? What is the effect of this problem?
2. How can this be fixed?
3. Have "owners" who are accountable for results.

4. Break the solution into discrete, measurable actions that address the root cause.
5. Identify accountable person for each action.
6. Set achievable deadlines.
7. Monitor progress.

CONCLUSION

A successful contract does not happen by accident. A successful contract requires teamwork and close communication by the end user and the contracting office. The end user must identify the project goals: the right product, the right quality, the right quantity, the right price and the right time (5 Rs). Together, they identify the potential problems based on the project goals that may threaten the success of the project. The contracting office has many tools at its disposal to aid in successful project completion. Together, they select the appropriate monitoring tools for each step of the process and develop a monitoring plan that identifies strategies to achieve each of the project goals and avoid or minimize potential problems.

KEY POINTS

- Contract administration should ensure that the agency receives the right quantity of the right material, or service of the right quality in the right time, at the right place, and do so within the identified budget and without claim.
- Develop a contract-monitoring plan for the purpose of establishing a process, whether periodic or continuous, to measures and confirm contractor compliance with the terms, conditions, and requirements of a contract.
- Define, identify and document each contract deliverable.
- The contract-monitoring plan must identify an accurate method to determine acceptance. The output or outcome must be evaluated to determine if it meets the contract specifications.
- Develop a list of potential contract problems, which provides contract managers with information about which contract administration problems are perceived as most likely to occur for a given type of purchase, and which type of purchase is likely to encounter the most contract administration problems.
- The contract monitoring plan must include the contract specifications and how acceptance will be evaluated, and identify the type of testing method and the consequences of failing a test.
- The contract officer needs to determine the appropriate type and level of monitoring based on the likelihood of occurrence of problems and the severity of the problem if it does occur.
- A major part of contract monitoring and evaluation is keeping and maintaining accurate records of contractor performance.

- At the contractor kick-off meeting, the role of the government agency and the contractor needs to be specified.
- The contract-monitoring plan needs to contain a conflict resolution and corrective action process addressing how conflict and contract problems are to be resolved.

REFERENCES

Cyprus, Treasury of the Republic (2014). *Public procurement best practice guide.* Retrieved from http://www.publicprocurementguides.treasury.gov.cy/OHS-EN/HTML/index.html?6_2_from_assign_to_implementation_.htm.

Davison, B., & Sebastian, R. J. (2009). The relationship between contract administration problems and contract type. *Journal of Public Procurement,* 9(2), 261–285.

Davison, B., & Wright, E. (2004). *Contract administration.* Herndon, VA: National Institute of Government Purchasing.

Department of Administrative Services [Iowa] (September 2013) *Administrative Rules, Chapter 117 Procurement of Goods and Services General Use.* Retrieved from https://das.iowa.gov/procurement/agencies/administrative-rules.

Government Accountability Office (2009). *Contract management: Extent of federal spending under cost-reimbursement contracts unclear and key controls not always used.* GAO-09-921: Published: Sep 30, 2009. Washington, DC: Author.

Government Accountability Office (2011). *Contract audits: Role in helping ensure effective oversight and reducing improper payments.* GAO-11-331T, Published November, 9, 2011. Washington, DC: Author.

McNamara, Carter (2008). *Basic guide to outcomes-based evaluation for nonprofit organizations with very limited resources.* Washington, D.C.: United Way of America.

National Institute of Government Purchasing (2000). *Contract management* (1st ed.). Herndon, VA: Author.

State of Georgia, Department of Audits and Accounts, Performance Audits Operations Division (July 2003), *Components of an effective contract monitoring system.* Retrieved from http://www.dca.ga.gov/housing/housingdevelopment/BestPractices_ContractMonitoring.pdf.

Thai, K.V. (2007). *Introduction to public procurement* (2nd ed.). Herndon, VA: National Institute of Government Purchasing.

W.K. Kellogg Foundation (2004), Using logic models to bring together planning, evaluation, and action: Logic model development guide. Battle Creek, Michigan. Retrieved from http://www.smartgivers.org/uploads/logicmodelguidepdf.pdf.

Part III

Government Contracting

Ethics, Management, and Governance

8

Governance and Contracting

Julia L. Carboni

INTRODUCTION

Contracting is an increasingly important aspect of governance in the United States. Broadly conceptualized, governance encompasses laws, rules and administrative structures related to the provision of publicly supported goods and services (Lynn, Heinrich & Hill, 2000). Over the last 30 years, government has shifted production of many public services to private parties, often through contracts. Public managers at all levels of government must grapple with how to manage contracted goods and services to ensure contractors are held accountable to public goals. However, contract management functions are often poorly specified and underfunded, especially for complex services. The purpose of this chapter is to untangle some complexity associated with managing contracts for complex services.

Formal contracts are not a proxy for management, but rather are a tool in the public manager's toolkit that provides formal structures for interaction for a government funder and a contractor. The importance and purpose of formal contracts varies depending on the nature of the contracted service, contractor characteristics and *ex post* (post award) market characteristics. Contracts should be designed and managed with an eye for ways in which these characteristics might offer incentives that facilitate or hinder contractor performance. Ineffective contract management undermines the ability of the state to ensure publicly demanded outcomes. This chapter will outline key contract management considerations for public managers who administer contracts.

CONTRACT MANAGEMENT LITERATURE

Contract management is an evolving concept in the realm of governance studies. Early work emphasized production costs. The prevailing assumption of early contract scholarship was that contracting itself would produce desired performance by ensuring transparency and efficiency, particularly where contracts are highly specified and enforceable and alternative options for providers exist (Donahue, 1989; Savas, 1987, 2000; Sclar, 2000). Empirical results on contracting efficiency are mixed (Boyne, 1998; Hirsch,

1995; Hodge, 1998). Mixed results suggest that government contracting may not meet economic assumptions of competitive markets or clearly specified contracts. Additionally, governments contract out services for political or ideological reasons rather than, or in addition to, efficiency reasons. This means that public managers must consider additional factors to ensure contractors are held accountable to public demand. Markets alone will not ensure service production efficiency or effectiveness. Public managers must also develop management strategies that account for suboptimal conditions.

Managing contracts in suboptimal conditions requires investment in contract management capacity of government because suboptimal conditions increase risks for non-compliance of contractors. Contract design and appropriate management strategies are crucial to produce desired performance in suboptimal conditions (see Brown & Potoski, 2003; Brudney et al., 2005; Cooper, 2003; Hefetz & Warner, 2004; Hodge, 1998; Romzek & Johnson, 2002, 2005). Prior to contract award, management strategies emphasize contract design to eliminate as many contingencies as possible, and selection of contractors that could properly implement public services in an efficient and effective manner rather than simply choosing the lowest cost bidder. In post-award contract management, emphasis shifts to developing management structures to minimize costs associated with market transactions and ensure desired performance either through conventional monitoring or relational approaches (see Brown & Potoski, 2003; Van Slyke, 2003, 2007). In both monitoring and relational contract management approaches, the aim of government is to reduce the likelihood contractors will not perform, and emphasis is placed on the relationship between government funder and contractor.

More recent work also considers characteristics of the *ex post* markets that contract relationships are embedded in (Bertelli & Smith, 2010; Carboni, 2015a, 2015b). Rather than focusing only on dyadic relationships between government funders and contractors, this work considers how position in the overall system influences contract performance and, subsequently, management considerations. For example, the number of substitutable alternatives in *ex post* markets may influence contractor incentives for performance. Where government has many alternatives, it reduces its dependence on any single contractor providing more incentive for contractors to underperform because government alternatives are limited. Available alternatives may also influence whether government threats to terminate contracts are credible. Where many alternatives exist, threats become more credible. Other work examines how the structural arrangement of providers influences systemic risk (Carboni, 2015a; Carboni & Milward, 2012). Where risk is high, shocks can impair system functioning, potentially leaving clients without services if the system is disrupted. From a governance perspective, system failures can have disastrous consequences, as clients would be left without legally mandated services.

So how should public managers manage contracts? Public managers should understand service characteristics, exchange characteristics, contractor characteristics and market conditions for contracted services and match governance structures accordingly to minimize the risk that contractors will underperform or that systems will be disrupted. Public managers should also consider the management capacity of their government. The following sections explore these issues.

SERVICE CHARACTERISTICS

Contracting out is rooted in the idea that the private sector can produce services more efficiently than government. Early work on contracting out emphasized production efficiency gains through use of competitive markets and emphasized simple services with tangible, measurable outcomes such as trash collection (Boyne, 1998; Savas, 1987). This work assumed that government funding of services would equate with control over how services are delivered and does not account for transaction costs associated with administering and managing contracts. Production and transaction costs are tied to the nature of the service—whether it is simple or complex.

The first question a contract manager should examine is whether the contracted service is simple or complex. Simple services are characterized by certainty about process or outcomes. These services align with the idea that government can maintain control through a formal contract because certainty allows government to fully specify and enforce contracts. Certainty reduces risk for government that a contractor might shirk, or not fulfill responsibilities for which it is paid by government. Contracts for simple services should be managed by monitoring contractor behavior. For example, with garbage collection services, we can easily estimate costs and know whether a service is effective by observing that trash was collected. However, pure simple services are rare. Most contracts involve complex services characterized by some degree of uncertainty about the service that creates risk for nonperformance of contractors. Costs, process and/or outcomes may be difficult to identify *ex ante* (prior to award). For example, how do we assess whether a contractor has provided acceptable foster care administration? Is the absence of tragedy a reliable signal? The remainder of the chapter will address managing contracts for complex services.

Uncertainty inherent in contracts for complex services raises questions about government's ability to maintain control over contractors. This has implications for governance. Contracts for complex services require more careful attention than simple services. Ideally, government should work on shifting risk to contractors by emphasizing what government has most certainty about process or outcome. This incentivizes contractors to behave according to government desires because they bear risk if things go wrong. In other words, shirking hurts them. When this is not possible, government should develop relational contracts with contractors to increase trust among parties and reduce the risk of malfeasance.

According to theory, where behavior and/or outcomes are easy to identify and measure, conventional strategies such as monitoring are likely to be effective because performance management is based on the notion that contracts can be specified and performance can be observed. As contracts become more incomplete and contractor behavior more difficult to observe and measure, transaction costs associated with contract management increase (Brown & Potoski, 2003; Miller, 1992, 2004; Sclar, 2000). In those situations, relational contract management strategies may be more appropriate to fill in "gaps" of formal contracts.

As services become more complex, government's role as contract manager becomes to create cooperative exchanges rather than to monitor and control contractors (Kettl, 1993; Sclar, 2000). Building a good relationship with a contractor is a tool public managers can employ to increase coordination with contractors and reduce uncertainty about contractor performance. Relational contract theory emphasizes collaborative processes, trust, and shared norms that facilitate mutual adaptation to changing conditions and alternative means for dispute resolution where trust may substitute for monitoring (DeHoog, 1990; Sclar, 2000; Smith, 1996; Van Slyke, 2007). Theoretically, relational contracts reduce the risk of opportunistic behavior and may be an effective substitute for command and control strategies, particularly in long-term relationships characterized by repeated interactions (Fernandez, 2007; Hill, 1990; Mayer et al., 1997; Uzzi, 1996). In practice, contract managers may employ both monitoring and relational contract management strategies rather than selecting a single approach.

CONTRACTOR CHARACTERISTICS

Contractor characteristics may also influence contract behavior and appropriate management strategies. Specifically, contractor motivations and dependence on government funder may shape behavior and influence the way public managers should approach contract management. Where contractor's organizational mission is not aligned and contractors are not dependent on government, public managers may assume that contractors will be more likely to maximize their own utility, perhaps at the expense of a government principal. This idea is rooted in principal agent theory (Jensen & Meckling, 1976). Agents (contractors) enter contracts in order to gain some utility from principals (government funders). If the wishes of principals and agents are aligned, no principal-agent problem exists. However, where principal and agent wishes differ, principal agent problems arise, typically in the form of adverse selection or moral hazard. This is especially true for complex services characterized by uncertainty in production and/or outcomes. Adverse selection occurs when a principal contract with an agent to produce a good or service without knowing the full set of risks involved. The principal may be unaware of risk because the agent withheld or misrepresented information prior to the contract award. Moral hazard arises when agents act opportunistically to maximize self-interest at the expense of principals. Unequal risk sharing and information asymmetry may lead to moral hazards in contracts for complex services.

From a principal-agent perspective, contract design and management strategies should emphasize avoiding and/or overcoming problems of adverse selection and moral hazard. Principals can overcome problems of adverse selection by ensuring *ex ante* competition for contracts and by requiring detailed contract proposals and plans for implementing the contract (Brown & Potoski, 2003; Romzek & Johnson, 2002, 2005). During the contract design phase, principals should focus on developing contracts with high specificity so that the contract is precise and comprehensive (Hart & Moore, 1990, 2007; Sclar, 2000; Savas, 2000). Once the contract has been awarded, agents should be rigorously monitored for contract compliance (Brown & Potoski, 2003; Brown, Potoski & Van Slyke, 2007, 2010; Hefetz & Warner, 2004; Savas, 2000). Monitoring may also help principals overcome problems of moral hazard. Theoretically, if principals rigorously monitor agents, they will be more likely to identify instances of opportunistic behavior and pursue legal sanctions outlined in the contract. Other prescriptions to limit or avoid moral hazard involve development of incentives that align principal and agent interests (Heinrich, 2000) and investing in contract management capacity by having dedicated contract monitoring staff who are experts on contract administration and the good/service to be contracted out (Brown & Potoski, 2003; Kettl, 1993; Romzek & Johnson, 2002, 2005).

Where contractor mission is aligned with government expectations or contractor interests are encapsulated in government interests, public managers may assume that contractors will be more likely to perform according to government demand. In the case of goal alignment, contractors may be trusted to perform because it is in their interest to do so. Performance is based on factors intrinsic to contractors. This idea is rooted in stewardship theory, which suggests organizations may behave according to principal wishes even if it may not be in their rational interest to do so. This theory is based on sociological and psychological approaches to governance rather than the economic approaches that dominate agency theory (Davis et al., 1997). When stewards are identified, management strategies should focus on cultivating relationships and giving stewards autonomy rather than emphasizing control (Donaldson & Davis, 1991; Davis et al., 1997).

In the case of encapsulated interests, contractors can be trusted to perform according to government expectations because it is in their interest to do so. For instance, a contractor may be dependent on government for funds to continue operations. In this case, contractors may have an agent orientation rather than a steward orientation, but will perform according to government demand to continue the flow of resources. Here, performance is externally motivated. In other words, contractors do not perform in accordance with principal demands because they find it rewarding. Rather, they perform because they are dependent on government and wish to maintain the contracting relationship into the future.

However, it is unclear how stewards (vs. agents) might be identified *ex ante* on a large scale. Recent empirical work has attempted to address this issue (see Van Slyke, 2007), but much work remains to be done to systematically predict which contractors will behave as responsible stewards and which contractors will behave as opportunistic agents. For individual public managers, understanding the motivations and values of their contractors will go a long way toward predicting behavior and selecting appropriate management strategies. This is another example of why investment in contract management capacity is wise. For public managers to understand contractor motivations, they must spend time and resources to understand contractor motivations.

MARKET CHARACTERISTICS

Often, government employs multiple contractors to deliver the same or similar services, effectively creating a networked structure of interdependent exchanges (Carboni, 2015a). Where multiple contract relationships exist, they are embedded within a larger structure of interaction—the *ex post* market. From a governance standpoint, considering characteristics of *ex post* markets is important because market structure may influence contractor response to government demands. Additionally, systemic risk in the structure may put service production in jeopardy if the system experiences shocks, even if individual contractors are providing acceptable services (Carboni & Milward, 2012).

There are several important characteristics of *ex post* markets that might affect contractor performance. First, government may be the sole buyer of services (monopsony) or it may face competition with other buyers for services. An example of the former is a single payer healthcare system where government buys all healthcare services and is theoretically able to regulate price and competition among sellers. An example of the latter is a system where government competes with private buyers. In the government funded Medicaid and Medicare health plans, government competes in a market with private insurance programs, reducing its ability to regulate price and competition among sellers. Competition with other buyers may reduce the dependence of a contractor on the government funder. Alternatives for the contractor may provide less incentive to perform.

Second, the number of contractors may vary. As the number of substitutable contractors increases, government decreases its dependence on a single exchange partner (Thibaut & Kelley, 1959). The presence of alternative exchange partners for government reduces dependence of government on a single actor similar to the way alternatives for contractors reduce contractor dependence on government. For example, if government relies on two actors rather than one actor to administer foster care programs, it creates substitutable alternatives for itself. The structure of exchange may lead to better performance among foster care administrators because they want to maintain the flow of resources (i.e. clients) to their program. When contractors are replaceable, they may be more likely to perform according to the terms of the contract. They are also more likely to take seriously government threats to sanction or terminate contracts (Bertelli & Smith, 2010).

Third, *ex post* markets may or may not have joint service production. In joint production arrangements, contractors collaborate to serve clients. This type of arrangement is an important service delivery model when one organization is unable to meet the full spectrum of client needs (Milward & Provan, 2000, 2006). A prominent example in the public management literature is government-funded services for mentally ill persons. In joint service production arrangements, accountability may be unclear because it is difficult to identify specific outcomes for which each contracted party is responsible (Milward & Provan, 2000), providing incentives for contractors to shirk. In *ex post* markets without joint production, government relies on multiple contractors working independently to produce services. In these systems, contractors are able to provide a full spectrum of services independently. For example, a state government may contract with multiple private prison companies that each provide a full spectrum of services and do not interact with each other. In settings without joint service production, the lines of accountability are clearer and it is less difficult for government to assess whether a contractor is performing because a contractor is responsible for the full spectrum of services instead of just a component.

Joint production is also important to consider at the system level. As joint production increases, contractors become more dependent on each other to produce services. In turn, government reliance on complex networks to deliver services increases the risk for systemic failure. Where organizations are heavily intertwined, the failure of a single organization may cause the system to collapse, particularly if that organization is central to the network (Carboni & Milward, 2012). Systemic risk also exists in systems without joint production. External shocks such as the Great Recession could cause groups of organizations to fail even if they did not have high individual risk to fail prior to the shock. Systemic contractor failure could leave clients without mandated services if government does not have the capacity to immediately reabsorb clients. This situation could be dire in some settings like juvenile justice where contractors are responsible for juvenile justice.

Fourth, the "hollowness," or degree of separation between government funders and contractors, may vary (Milward & Provan, 2000). In some instances, government contracts out management functions to a third party (i.e. network administrative organization) and has no contact with contractors, while in others government directly manages contractors. Direct management of contractors increases a government funder's access to information about contractor performance. Provan and Milward (1995) found that centralized networks of providers where external control is direct and not fragmented are most effective for delivering services. Theoretically, additional layers of accountability may increase potential for opportunistic behavior, particularly if contractors can credibly blame performance problems on another level of the hierarchy. When public managers interact with contract managers rather than service providers, they need to think about how to ensure performance at the contract manager level and the service production level.

A fifth characteristic that may influence contractor incentive to perform in service delivery networks is whether government funders or clients select service contractors. When clients select service contractors, they may choose based on a number of factors including proximity, access, or something else unrelated to contract performance. Ostensibly, when government chooses contractors for clients, it has more information about contract performance and can choose the highest performing contractors, particularly where there is some slack in the system, thus incentivizing contractor performance.

Ex post market characteristics such as availability of buyers and sellers, joint production, whether there are direct links between funders and contractors and contractor selection are likely to influence contractor incentives to perform. These characteristics should be considered jointly with characteristics about individual contractors outlined in the previous section. For example, availability of substitutable alternatives for government may reduce the risk of nonperformance where contractors' motivations do not align with government demands. In this case, maintaining substitutable alternatives may serve a similar function as developing resource intensive relational contracts. There is some empirical evidence that while both relational and structural strategies are effective governance tools, they may be redundant; combining them has little additional benefit for improved performance (Rowley et al., 2000).

CONCLUSION

Contracting is increasingly used as a governance tool to implement public policy, particularly for complex service delivery. For public managers, this means they must shift from managing service production to managing relationships with contractors. How these relationships should be managed is contingent on a number of factors including service characteristics, contractor characteristics and *ex post* market conditions. Simple services should be governed using simple structures with clearly specified and enforceable contracts. Complex services should be governed using more complex structures that account for variance in contractor characteristics and market conditions.

In terms of contractor characteristics, contractor motivations are particularly important. If contractor motivations are aligned with government, contractors may behave as stewards, faithfully upholding public values and responding to public demands even if it is not in their best interests to do so. These relationships should be managed with an eye toward building trust and relationships. Where contractor motivations are not aligned with government, public managers should focus on providing contractors with incentives to perform such as shifting risk to contractors or making sure contractor interests are encapsulated in the interests of government. Public managers might also develop relationships where the costs of monitoring are high with the acknowledgment that organizational motivations vary and the potential for nonperformance is higher than with contractors who share public values and motivations.

Multiple market characteristics may influence incentives for contractor performances including availability of buyers and sellers, joint production, whether there are direct links between funders and contractors and contractor selection. Public managers should understand how each of these factors might influence contractor behavior and develop management strategies accordingly. Understanding how *ex post* market characteristics shape contractor incentives is perhaps the greatest weakness in scholarly and practitioner literature. Until very recently, these factors have not been considered in scholarly or practitioner literature.

In conclusion, public managers are still accountable for ensuring implementation of public policy, but their role has gradually shifted from rowing to steering over the last three decades. This shift comes with a new set of challenges on how to manage public services. Effective management necessitates consideration of service characteristics, contractor characteristics and market characteristics. These characteristics should be considered jointly when developing contract management capacity and strategies to manage contracts. This chapter sheds light on specific issues to consider when managing contracts for complex services.

KEY POINTS

- Contracts are an increasingly important part of governance, particularly in policy implementation.
- Public managers are still responsible for ensuring policy implementation, but their role has shifted from managing service production to managing contract relationships.
- Contracts are a tool of governance that structures formal interactions between government funders and contractors.
- Contracts are not a proxy for management. Public managers should develop contract management strategies that are specific to service characteristics, contractor characteristics, and market conditions.

REFERENCES

Bertelli, A. M. & Smith, C. R. (2010). Relational contracting and network management. *Journal of Public Administration Research and Theory, 20*, i21–i40.

Boyne, G.A. (1998). Bureaucratic theory meets reality: Public choice and service contracting In U.S. local government. *Public Administration Review, 58*, 474–484.

Brown, T. & Potoski, M. (2003). Managing contract performance: A transaction costs approach. *Journal of Policy Analysis and Management. 22*(2): 275–297.

Brown, T., Potoski, M. & Van Slyke, D. (2007). Trust and contract completeness in the public sector. *Local Government Studies, 33*(4), 607–623.

Brown, T., Potoski, M. & Van Slyke, D. (2010). Contracting for complex products. *Journal of Public Administration Research and Theory, 20*, i41–i58.

Brudney, J., Fernandez, S., Ryu, J., & Wright, D. (2005). Exploring and explaining contracting out: Patterns among the states. *Journal of Public Administration Research and Theory 15*(3), 393–419.

Carboni, J. L. (2015a). Contract exchange structures: Measures for multi-mode affiliation networks. *Complexity, Governance and Networks. 2*(1), 45–46.

Carboni, J. L. (2015b). Ex post contract market structure: Implications for performance over time. *American Review of Public Administration.* DOI: 10.1177/0275074015608753.

Carboni, J. L. & Milward, H. B. (2012). Governance, privatization and systemic risk in a disarticulated state. *Public Administration Review, 72*, s36–s44.

Cooper, P. J. (2003). *Governing by contract: Challenges and opportunities for public managers.* Washington, DC: CQ Press.

Davis, J. Schoorman, F. & Donaldson, L. (1997). Toward a stewardship theory of management. *Academy of Management Review, 22*(1), 20–47.

DeHoog, R. (1990). Competition, negotiation or cooperation: Three models for service contracting. *Administration and Society, 22*(3), 317–40.

Donahue, J. (1989). *The privatization decision: Public ends, private means.* New York, NY: Basic Books.

Donaldson, L., & Davis, J. H. (1991). Stewardship theory or agency theory: CEO governance and shareholder returns. *Australian Journal of Management, 16*, 49–64.

Fernandez, S. (2007). What works best when contracting for services? An analysis of contracting performance at the local level. *Public Administration, 85*, 1119–1140.

Hart, O., & Moore, J. (1990). Property rights and the nature of the firm. *Journal of Political Economy, 98*(6), 1119–1158.

Hart, O., & Moore, J. (2007). Incomplete contracts and ownership: Some new thoughts. *The American Economic Review 97*(2),182–186.

Hefetz, A., & Warner, M. (2004). Privatization and its reverse: Explaining the dynamics of the government contracting process. *Journal of Public Administration Research and Theory, 14*(2), 171–90.

Heinrich, C.L. (2000). Organizational form and performance: An empirical investigation of nonprofit and for-profit job-training service providers. *Journal of Policy Analysis and Management, 19*(2), 233–261.

Hill, C. W. (1990). Cooperation, opportunism, and the invisible hand: Implications for transaction cost theory. *Academy of Management Review, 15*, 500–513.

Hirsch, W. Z. (1995). Contracting out by urban governments: A review. *Urban Affairs Review, 30*(3), 458–472.

Hodge, G. (1998). Contracting public sector services: A meta-analytic perspective of the international evidence. *Australian Journal of Public Administration, 57*, 98–111.

Kettl, D. (1993). *Sharing power: Public governance and private markets.* Washington, DC: The Brookings Institution.

Jensen, M., & Meckling, W. (1976). Theory of the firm: Managerial behavior, agency costs and ownership structure. *Journal of Financial Economics, 3*, 305–360.

Lynn, L. E., Heinrich, C.J. & Hill, C. (2000). Studying governance and public management: Challenges and prospects. *Journal of Public Administration Research and Theory, 10*(2), 233–261.

Mayer, R. C., Davis, J. H., & Schoorman, F. D. (1995). An Integrative Model of Organizational Trust. *The Academy of Management Review, 20*(3), 709–734.

Miller, G. (1992). *Managerial dilemmas.* Cambridge, UK: Cambridge University Press.

Miller, G. (2004). Monitoring, rules, and the control paradox: Can the good soldier sveijk be trusted? In R. Kramer & K. Cook (Eds.), *Trust in organizations: Dilemmas and approaches* (pp. 99–126). New York, NY: Russell Sage Foundation.

Milward H.B. & Provan K. (2000). Governing the hollow state. *Journal of Public Administration Research and Theory, 10*, 359–79.

Milward, H.B. & Provan, K.G. (2006). *A manager's guide to choosing and using collaborative networks*. Washington, DC: IBM Center for the Business of Government.

Provan, K. G., & Milward, H. B. (1995). A preliminary theory of interorganizational network effectiveness: A comparative study of four community mental health systems. *Administrative Science Quarterly*, 40(1), 1–33.

Romzek, B. & Johnson, J. (2002). Effective contract implementation and management: A preliminary model. *Journal of Public Administration Research and Theory, 12*,(3), 423–453.

Romzek, B. & Johnson, J. (2005). State social services contracting: Exploring the determinants of effective contract accountability. *Public Administration and Review, 65*(4), 436–449.

Rowley, T., Behrens, D., & Krackhardt, D. (2000). Redundant governance structures: An analysis of structural and relational embeddedness in the steel and semiconductor industries. *Strategic Management Journal, 21*(3), 369–386.

Savas, E. (1987). *Privatization: The keys to better government*. Chatham, NJ: Chatham House Publishers.

Savas, E. (2000). *Privatization and private-public partnerships*. Chatham, NJ: Chatham House Publishers.

Sclar, E. (2000). *You don't always get what you pay for: The economics of privatization*. Ithaca, NY: Cornell University Press.

Smith, S. R. (1996). Transforming public services: contracting for social and health services in the US. *Public Administration*, 74(1), 113–127.

Thibaut, J.W., & Kelley, H.H. (1959). *Social psychology of groups*. New York, NY: John Wiley & Sons.

Uzzi, B. (1996). The sources and consequences of embeddedness for the economic performance of organizations: The network effect. *American Sociological Review, 61*(4), 674–698.

Van Slyke, D. M. (2003). The mythology of privatization in contracting for social services. *Journal of Public Administration Research and Theory, 63*(3), 296–315.

Van Slyke, D. M. (2007). Agents or stewards: Using theory to understand the government-nonprofit social service contracting relationship. *Journal of Public Administration Research and Theory, 17*, 157–87.

9

Ethics in Contracting

William Sims Curry

The awarding of illicit government contracts is the preeminent mechanism for compensating corrupt corporate representatives who provide money, vehicles, event tickets, sexual favors, vacations, or other gratuities to unethical public servants. The Federal Bureau of Investigations (FBI) has authority to investigate such corruption within the legislative, executive, and judicial branches of the federal government as well as within state and local governments. An excerpt representative of the FBI's activities with respect to public corruption at the federal, state, and local level is provided below (U.S. Federal Bureau of Investigation, 2014):

> The vast majority of public servants who work at the local, state, and federal levels of government are honest and dedicated folks who strive every day to do the right thing for their constituents, their communities, and their country.
>
> Unfortunately, there is a small subgroup of public servants who, whether elected, appointed, or contracted, are only concerned about a very specific constituency—themselves. And because this type of corruption strikes at the heart of government, eroding public confidence and undermining the strength of our democracy, the investigation of public corruption is the FBI's top criminal priority.

Contract corruption has been an affliction on government agencies since the earliest history of the United States. Prior to the civil war, government procurement was largely conducted at the state and local level. Federal contracting practices largely began evolving during the civil war. As the war proceeded, contracting for war materials began to shift from states to the federal government and established the beginning of the present behemoth federal contracting system. Contract corruption was prevalent at this early stage in American history. Civil war corruption was well documented by the Select Committee (also known as the "Van Wyck Committee" and the "Committee on Government Contracts"), as reported in the *The New York Times*. While historical, yet considerably more recent than the corrupt practices during the civil war, the Teapot Dome Scandal is also worthy of mention from a historical perspective in any discussion of ethics in government contracting (Diner, 1975).

Despite the history of ruined careers, disastrous impacts on families, fines, imprisonment, and suicides, government representatives and company officials continue to conspire by trading contracts for favors. A case originating in 2006 has been referred to as the "largest domestic bribery and bid-rigging scheme in the history of federal contracting cases." This recent enmeshment involves corrupt federal government officials and corporate representatives illegally plundering taxpayer money through bribes and kickbacks in return for the award of government contracts (U.S. Federal Bureau of Investigation, 2013, July). A more disturbing case, the facts of which are still being revealed, involves numerous naval personnel, including two Navy admirals who were being investigated, placed on leave, and had their access to classified information suspended. These actions represent the initial results from an entanglement involving the exchange of both classified and unclassified information being provided to a government contractor in exchange for prostitutes and cash. While this environment of corruption and debauchery might dissuade students considering careers in contract management, or for recent entrants from continuing a career in this field, it is apropos to cite the fact that the monumental majority of government and private sector contracting professionals are in pursuit of a legitimate profession in an honest and trustworthy manner.

CONTRACT CORRUPTION DURING THE CIVIL WAR

To illustrate the occurrence of contract corruption during the earliest times in the United States, several cases investigated by the Select Committee on Government Contracts of the US House of Representatives (Select Committee) are summarized here The New York Times, 1862). The House of Representatives appointed the Select Committee in the spring of 1861 to investigate contractor fraud during the civil war. Representative Charles Van Wyck of New York chaired the committee. One of the more notorious cases investigated by the Select Committee involved the Secretary of the Navy's employment of Mr. George D. Morgan, the Secretary's brother-in-law, to buy or charter ships required by the Union during the war effort. The arrangement between the Secretary and his brother-in-law involved no fixed salary, but Mr. Morgan was to receive two and one-half percent of the purchase price for each vessel. It is curious that the Select Committee recognized the folly of paying a percentage on the price, as noted in the following excerpt from the report:

> Besides, if the method of payment by commissions had any effect upon the agent, it is apparent that the higher the price paid for ships the greater the compensation.

This commission compensation arrangement is virtually identical to the cost-plus-a-percentage-of-cost (CPPC) type of contract that was commonly used throughout World War I. Although the perils of CPPC contracting were recognized early in the Civil War, this contract type was not prohibited until after World War I and remains prohibited to the present day (Federal Acquisition Regulation, 2015). The outrage caused by the selection of Mr. Morgan to purchase vessels for the Navy is precisely expressed in the passages quoted from the Select Committee report:

> On the 8th of May last [1861] the purchasing of vessels for the Navy Department at the Port of New York was taken from Commodore BRESSE, the Commandant of the Brooklyn Navy-yard, and shortly after transferred to Mr. GEORGE D. MORGAN, of New York, under an arrangement between him and the Secretary of the Navy of a most singular and extraordinary character, and one the Committee feel called upon to pronounce most reprehensible in its nature and demoralizing to the public service.
>
> Mr. MORGAN had never had the slightest experience in the new and responsible duties which he was called upon to discharge, either in the naval service, the building or buying and selling of ships, or in any pursuit calling for knowledge of their construction, capacity, or value, never having spent an hour in either. The Department itself seemed to have so little confidence in the ability of Mr. MORGAN to judge of the quality and fitness of the articles he was constituted sole agent to buy, that it expressly enjoined upon him to rely in these particulars upon the judgment of three gentlemen of position in the navy, who were detailed for the special service of protecting the Government from mistakes in this regard by the new agent thus constituted. For everything which entered into the fitness or propriety of the purchase, the Department fell back upon itself.
>
> The evidence was abundant before the Committee that if it had been necessary to obtain the services of any gentleman outside of the Navy itself, those gentlemen, combining from experience and education the knowledge most calculated to fit them for this duty, independent of outside aid, could have been secured without the slightest difficulty, for a salary not exceeding $5,000 for the year.

The alleged ignorance of Mr. Morgan, whose experience was gained in the wholesale grocery business, regarding expertise in purchasing vessels was evidenced by the findings of the Select Committee of his being deceived by ship's owners. An example of his ignorance was his being deceived regarding the cost to the owners of building a particular ship. The ship had been afloat for merely two months and the cost to build it was $35,600. By taking advantage of Mr. Morgan's lack of experience and ignorance about shipbuilding, the owners convinced him that the cost to build the ship was $60,000. Mr. Morgan chartered the ship for two months at a net price of $15,000 and then purchased it for $55,000. The clear profit to the owners was $34,400: an amount nearly equal to the build cost. It might be argued, however, that Mr. Morgan may not have been as ignorant as alleged since the more he paid for vessels the greater his commission. The evidence appears unambiguous that Mr. Morgan was selected to replace the Commandant of the Brooklyn Navy Yard, Commodore Bresse, based on his connection to the then

Secretary of the Navy rather than his expertise in purchasing naval vessels. Although it was reported that a full-time, fully qualified buyer of naval vessels could have been hired for $5,000 per year, Mr. Morgan kept $8,000 of the sale price of this one vessel for him, and the ship's owners received $47,000. Through his arrangement for purchasing and chartering vessels for the Navy, Mr. Morgan received compensation of $95,000 which was equivalent to a rate of about $300,000 per year. Readers are reminded that the moneys referred to here are in 1861 dollars.

One other example of the employment of mandatory "middlemen" or "go-betweens," as they were referred to, in purchases made to support the war effort was for the procurement of horses and mules. The Select Commission concluded "that the Quartermaster himself was in collusion with corrupt and unprincipled men, who combined together to swindle the Government." The price that the Quartermaster's Department would pay for horses and mules was $119 each and $150 each for artillery horses. The original owners or legitimate dealers for the horses and mules, who were not permitted to sell directly to the government, received from $85 to $105 for cavalry horses, $108 and $110 for mules, and $125 for artillery horses. In addition to pocketing the difference between the price the middlemen paid and the price the government paid, these favored individuals oftentimes had either the authority to inspect the horses themselves or select their own inspectors. There were also reports of direct bribery and fraudulent branding. An inspector named James Neil was found to rebrand the $119 cavalry horses and resell them as artillery horses for $150. A Select Committee observation regarding the quality of some of the purchased horses is provided below:

> Of course, when horses were purchased through such agencies the Government was certain to be defrauded, not only in the payment of the large sums going to the middle men, but in the quality of the stock purchased. Large numbers of utterly worthless horses were imposed on the Government, all at the maximum price. Old, broken-down omnibus, wagon and dray horses, and mules, were picked up with avidity by contractors.

Fraudulent procurement practices during the civil war were not limited to vessels, horses, and mules purchased in New York. The Select Committee also looked into corrupt procurement practices regarding army supplies, guns, and other materials needed to support the war effort.

OTHER HISTORICAL PROCUREMENT FRAUDS

One might believe that government officials would have learned valuable lessons from the nefarious contracting practices discovered during the civil war. The government readily perceived the folly of paying the cost of purchasing vessels plus a percentage of that cost during the civil war. The more the government paid for vessels, the greater the commission received by the middlemen. Yet, during World War I, a popular contract type was the previously mentioned CPPC contract that was selected to induce contractors to produce new products for which they were not familiar (Musicus, 1994). Certain government contractors soon learned that the more they spent to produce products, the higher the profit they earned. If the contractor incurred costs of $100,000 to manufacture tanks under a CPPC contract with a 10 percent fee, it would earn $10,000. If the contractor incurred costs of $200,000, however, it would earn $20,000. Whether government officials historically awarded CPPC contracts through incompetency or in collusion with contractors is not fully understood. The government's prohibition against CPPC contracts has been almost entirely successful. Collusion through other means, however, continues to the present.

TEAPOT DOME SCANDAL

Teapot Dome, the name which was once considered as synonymous with the sordid side of American politics, deserves a space in the infamous history of government contract corruption. Teapot Dome, in Wyoming, and Elk Hills, in California, were similar oil rich tracks of government owned land earmarked for use exclusively by the Navy. Although control of these naval oil reserves was transferred to the Navy from the Interior Department during President Wilson's administration, control was transferred back to Interior when President Harding took office. Albert Fall was appointed by President Harding as the Secretary of the Interior, and fall became a central actor in the subsequent imbroglio over Teapot Dome. To the apprehension of conservationists, rights to the oil at Elk Hills were leased to Edward Doheny who was head of the Pan-American Petroleum and Transport Company. The Elk Hills reserve was leased through competitive bidding. Oil rights at Teapot Dome, however, were surreptitiously leased on a sole source basis to the business interests of Harry F. Sinclair, president of Mammoth Oil Company. The Senate obtained a copy of the Sinclair lease and an accompanying explanation that competitive bidding was not used due to naval preparedness and national defense. In defending his leasing of the Teapot Dome oil reserve, Albert Fall called on "national security." During the time while Hall was involved in leasing oil reserves to Sinclair Hall's personal finances were transformed from poverty to riches. The Senate conducted a protracted investigation that involved hundreds of witnesses. One of the most colorful witnesses was a real estate dealer and former train robber named Al Jennings. Jennings claimed that he accompanied Jake Hamon, a former Secretary of the Interior, to the 1920 Republican convention. Jennings claimed that Hamon told him he had paid one million dollars to secure the nomination of Harding as president.

In March of 1924 Sinclair was indicted for contempt of the Senate for his refusal to answer questions concerning his 1920 campaign contributions. After unsuccessfully appealing his conviction to the Supreme Court, Sinclair served a three-month prison term. He also served a six-month term for conspiracy. The Supreme Court also decided, unanimously, that the lease of the oil reserves was illegal. The Supreme Court subsequently declared that the oil reserves lease was the product of a Fall–Sinclair conspiracy. Albert Fall was the first cabinet member to be convicted of a major crime while serving in office. He was convicted of bribery, fined $100,000, and sentenced to one year in prison.

MODERN DAY CONTRACTING CORRUPTION

Readers might conclude that the long history of contract corruption in the United States resulting in the ruination of careers, personal finances, reputations, family lives, and losses of freedom would dissuade government contracting professionals from seeking or accepting ill-gotten rewards and that corporate representatives would repudiate any inclination to dispense gratuities in exchange for the award of contracts. Financial gains and personal entertainment for government officials and career enhancements for corporate executives eventually become colossal liabilities once one's criminal acts are discovered. Rogue government contracting professionals and corporate representatives who are considering participation in schemes involving an exchange of contracts for gratuities at the taxpayers' and their employers' expense are cautioned to first assess their organizational and personal ethics credos. The long-term consequences for corrupt government officials and company representatives repeatedly outweigh any short-term rewards by a monumental margin. Examples of such grim consequences are cited in this chapter.

CORRUPTION VERSUS INCOMPETENCE

Contract fraud investigated by investigatory agencies, such as the FBI, is predictably concluded with results commensurate to the crime, such as perpetrators pleading guilty or being found guilty during a court trial for their criminal violations and then being fined, imprisoned, or both. Apparent misdeeds discovered by the Government Accountability Office (GAO) oftentimes name individuals who have apparently committed crimes. The audits performed by the GAO are commendable, but apparently fall short of referring unethical public servants to investigatory agencies for possible prosecution. Internal offices of inspector generals (OIGs) seem, more understandably, reluctant to charge employees with illegal acts. The GAO and OIGs tend to address apparent contracting fraud problems more in the vein of administrative failures or incompetence. An example of this trend was found in a memorandum from the Office of Inspector General for the United States Department of State and the Broadcasting Board of Governors (Brown, 2014). This March 20th, 2014 memorandum described facts, excerpts provided below, discovered during an investigation into the closeout of contract files. A reading of the following excerpts from the report would lead most readers to conclude that corruption, rather than mere incompetence, exists in the State Department's handling of contracts.

> A recent OIG audit of the closeout process for contracts supporting the U.S. Mission in Iraq revealed that contracting officials were unable to provide 33 of 115 contract files requested in accordance with the audit sampling plan. The value of the contracts in the 33 missing files totaled $2.1 billion. Forty-eight of the 82 contract files received did not contain all of the documentation required by FAR [Federal Acquisition Regulation] 4.8. The value of the contracts in the 48 incomplete files totaled an additional $2.1 billion.

The State Department OIG report included the following findings of serious deficiencies that appear to warrant referral to investigatory agencies:

> In the case of work undertaken by the OIG's Office of Investigations, one investigation revealed that a contract file did not contain documentation the spouse of a contractor employee performing as a Contract Specialist for the contract. This contract was valued at $52 million.
>
> In another investigation, OIG found that a CO [contracting officer] falsified Government technical review information and provided the contractor with contract pricing information. The related contract file was not properly maintained and for a period of time was hidden by the CO. This contract was valued at $100 million. In a third investigation, OIG found that a COR [contracting officer's representative] allowed the payment of $792,782 to a contractor even though the contract file did not contain documents to support the payment.

The March 20th, 2014 State Department memorandum, mentioned earlier, does not name the employees who are responsible for the transgressions, and the memorandum's nominal subject line reads "Management Alert (Contract File Management Deficiencies)." The response to the memorandum predictably promises administrative reforms. To the State Department's credit, however, the names of individuals responsible for the contract file deficiencies were requested from the State Department OIG.

Readers might expect that, in rare instances, contract files might be lost or that they occasionally have missing documentation. The extent of missing files and documentation described in the above excerpt from the OIG's memorandum, however, would likely lead inquiring individuals to suspect that the extent of the missing documentation was not the result of incompetence, but of purposeful disposal of documentation for more nefarious reasons.

These deficiencies appear to far exceed the relative inconsequence of incompetence, and should be worthy of referral to the proper agency for investigation into possible criminal activity. Similar cases that were pursued vigorously by investigatory agencies, as well as less penetrating investigations that occurred during various stages of the contracting cycle, are presented below to serve as examples of the consequences suffered by government acquisition professionals and defense contractor representatives who participate in contract fraud.

CORRUPTION FROM PROCUREMENT PLANNING

The extreme nature of improprieties that are possible in the earliest stages of the contracting cycle is exemplified by the Air Force's air refueling tanker procurement that began in 2001 (U.S. Department of Defense, 2005). Although the $23.5 billion Air Force Boeing KC-767A tanker program met the criteria for a competitive procurement, Air Force officials sought and received approval to lease the tankers from Boeing. In December of 2003 the Deputy Secretary of Defense requested the DoD Inspector General (IG) to perform an audit of the acquisition of the Boeing KC-767A. In that audit request the Deputy Secretary asked the IG if the Air Force should or should not proceed with the tanker lease program. The response from the IG is below:

> it is our independent judgment that the Air Force used an inappropriate procurement strategy and demonstrated neither best business practices nor prudent acquisition procedures to provide sufficient accountability for the expenditure of $23.5 billion for the KC-767A tanker program. We identified five statutory provisions that have not yet been satisfied relating to: commercial items; testing (two statutes); cost-plus-a-percentage-of-cost system of contracting; and leases. Therefore, DoD should not proceed with the program until it resolves the issues pertaining to the procurement strategy, acquisition procedures, and statutory requirements.

Both the Air Force and Boeing have performed commendably while protecting the national security of the United States. The actions of rogue employees from both entities, however, resulted in an extensive delay in replacing the aged Air Force tanker refueling fleet and increased costs associated with the delay. The IG report determined that Darlene Druyun [the then Principal Deputy Assistant Secretary of the Air Force (Acquisition and Management)] guided the Air Force and that Mr. Michael Sears (the then Chief Financial Officer for Boeing) led Boeing in this aborted endeavor. A list of outcomes resulting from the investigation of this matter is provided below:

- Ms. Druyun recused herself from negotiating with Boeing, retired from the Air Force, and assumed an executive position with Boeing.
- Boeing agreed to pay $565 million in civil claims and $50 million as a penalty for its part in this matter.

- Ms. Druyun pled guilty to favoring Boeing while negotiating numerous contracts, including the air refueling tanker lease, because she felt indebted for jobs that Boeing gave her, her daughter, and her son-in-law. She was sentenced to nine months in prison, seven months in a halfway house, and fined $5,000.
- Mr. Sears pled guilty and was sentenced to four months in prison, two years probation, and fined $250,000 for helping Ms Druyun, while she was employed by the Air Force, to obtain an executive position with Boeing.
- Soon after Mr. Sears and Ms. Druyun were fired from Boeing, the Boeing Chief Executive Officer resigned.

The Air Force began to proceed with replacement of the air refueling fleet through a competitive procurement. The competitive procurement was plagued by protests. Contracts were awarded for procurement of replacement aircraft for the air refueling tankers; however, this was not until about ten years after the Air Force's initial approval to replace the aged fleet.

CORRUPTION DURING THE REQUEST FOR PROPOSALS

The U.S. Army Corps of Engineers prepared an RFP in connection with a planned contract for permanent canal closures and pumps at or near Lake Pontchartrain, Louisiana. Three of the competing contractors protested the award of the contract to CBY Design Builders, and the information on this procurement is based on the resulting GAO report (U.S. Government Accountability Office, 2011). The protests were based on discrepancies between the solicitation and the manner in which the proposals were evaluated as well as other matters. The RFP indicated, "non-price factors, combined, were significantly more important than price." Provisions of the RFP, as amended, also advised prospective contractors that "the best value technique known as 'Build to Budget' applied to this procurement" and the $650 million original budgeted amount was increased to $700 million. Prospective contractors were also advised that offers exceeding the budgeted amount would be eliminated without further consideration. The amended RFP also included the statement:

> In this competition, we expect our solutions to utilize the full budget available and not focus on providing a low bid design. Attempts to offer lower priced technical solutions may be determined non-competitive and result in elimination accordingly.

Prior to submittal of the proposals, a high level official of the Corps of Engineers who was responsible for the procurement advised the company selected for contract award that it would be to its benefit to, despite the provisions of the RFP as amended, to propose a price lower than the budgeted amount. The company selected for contract award was also planning to employ the Corps official who provided the advice regarding the advantage to proposing a price below the budgeted amount. In making the contractor selection announcement, the Army Corps of Engineers source selection authority (SSA) concluded that evaluated strengths of Bechtel and PCCP "do not support a $25M premium." This statement by the SSA is indicative of the Corps evaluation of proposals contrary to the provisions of the RFP. In sustaining the protests, the GAO stated, among other recommendations, that the agency should amend the RFP with respect to the build-to-budget concept and advise all competing contractors that lower priced offers would be accepted. One other GAO recommendation was that the Corps investigates the awardee's potential organizational conflict of interest (OCI) and, if it determines that the awardee has an impermissible OCI, determines how that conflict can be mitigated.

CORRUPTION FROM PREPARATION OF CONTRACTOR PROPOSALS

Corruption instigated by a government contractor during the preparation of proposals is illustrated through a discussion of the federal government's suspension of Litton Industries (Cushman, 1986). Northrop Grumman subsequently acquired Litton Industries. The decision to suspend the entire corporation, ranked as the military's nineteenth-largest supplier, was based on violations by one small division with approximately $25 million in annual sales. At the time of the suspension, Litton's Ingalls Shipbuilding had submitted a sealed bid, in competition with three other shipbuilding companies, for the purchase of 3 major ships with an estimated price of approximately $1 billion each. The suspension resulted in a dilemma regarding the justification for suspending all corporate divisions when the corruption was centered within one small division.[1] The military relied heavily on Litton but there were concerns that small businesses were not being treated fairly when their businesses were suspended in their entirety while large corporations might merely have one small division suspended. The entire corporation was suspended and the military thoroughly reviewed operations at each Litton division and reinstated their ability to compete for government contracts on an individual division basis.

The corruption involved collaboration between a Litton vice president of finance and the materials manager at Litton's Clifton Precision, Special Devices Division. The fraud was committed by Litton representatives obtaining blank bid forms from suppliers, completing bids supposedly submitted by those suppliers but with inflated prices, and then using the phony bids to substantiate the inflated costs used to support prices charged to the military. The prices were reportedly inflated from about 200 to approximately 400 percent. The former Litton Clifton Precision vice president of finance was sentenced to one year in prison and fined $10,000, while the former materials manager was sentenced to five years probation and fined $10,000.

EVALUATION OF CONTRACTOR PROPOSALS

The GAO sustained a protest from Solers, Inc. in the matter of the selection of Booz Allen Hamilton, Inc. (BAH) for award of a task order. Along with one other reason for protesting the selection of BAH, Solers took exception to the award of a cost reimbursement contract when the RFP specified a fixed price contract, and a flawed evaluation of Solers' past performance and technical approaches. With respect to BAH offering a cost reimbursement arrangement, BAH based its pricing on government-site and contractor-site rates, performing significantly more work at the government site than contemplated in the solicitation, and those higher rates may need to be applied if the government space proposed by BAH was not available. Regarding past performance, Solers argued that its score should be higher and BAH's score should be lower. GAO sustained Solers' protest regarding past performance because the agency's record of the proposal evaluation was inadequate to determine the adequacy of past performance. With respect to Solers' complaint regarding the technical evaluation, it claimed that the agency misunderstood the number of engineers that BAH proposed. GAO concurred with Solers' contention and also sustained the protest based on a flawed technical evaluation. Although one might consider the agency's errors to result from incompetence, the one-sided nature of the errors suggests that there may have been some bias in favor of BAH.

MISLEADING NEGOTIATIONS

One is likely to believe that a government negotiator who misleads a contractor negotiator by encouraging a cost or price increase resulting in that company's competitor being awarded the contract is likely acting out of nefarious reasons. One case illustrating this scenario was documented in a GAO decision (U.S. Government Accountability Office, 2012). The RFP was issued by the Department of Health and Human Services, Centers for Medicare and Medicaid Services (CMS), to provide its Financial Management Systems Group with technical and program management support services. Three contractors in the competitive range were competing for the contract that was to be awarded based on a best value basis wherein the combined technical evaluation factors were weighed approximately the same as price. The value of orders expected to be placed during the five-year contract was estimated between $6 million and $50 million. The CMS negotiator advised Signature Consulting Group that its number of full time equivalents (FTEs) was understated for a certain category of work. In response to this advice, Signature increased the number of FTEs and increased its proposed cost accordingly for that category of work. The categories of work, increase in the number of FTEs, and the original and revised costs were all redacted from the GAO decision.

CMS selected Tantus Technologies, Inc. based on its having the highest technical score and the lowest price. Both Signature and SeKON protested he selection of Tantus based on the technical and cost evaluation. Signature also based its protest on CMS' misleading discussions that resulted in Signature increasing the FTEs proposed for one category of work. SeKON also based its protest on an alleged Tantus Technologies OCI. GAO determined that CMS misled Signature by directing it to increase its FTEs based on the following facts:

- CMS assigned 461 of a possible 500 points to Signature's managerial and operational approach (which included staffing) to this work category.
- CMS identified eight strengths in Signature's proposal.
- Signature was presently performing this category of work.
- No concerns for Signature's staffing for this work element were documented as a result of Signature's oral presentation.

The facts presented in GAO's documentation of its decision in sustaining the protest due to CMS' misleading negotiations may not appear to represent a mere incidence of incompetence, but could suggest more nefarious reasons for misleading the contractor.

CORRUPTION IN THE AWARD OF THE CONTRACT

At the time of his arrest for steering government contracts to collaborating contractors in exchange for over $30 million in bribe and kickbacks, a former U.S. Army Corps of Engineers manager named Kerry F. Khan, the ringleader for a band of other corrupt public officials, was conspiring to award a $1 billion contract in exchange for money and other benefits (U.S. Attorney's Office, 2013). As of the U.S Attorney's Office July 11th, 2013 press release, 15 people and one company, including Khan's family, friends, and colleagues, pled guilty to what was referred to as "the largest domestic bribery and bid-rigging scheme in the history of federal contracting cases." Other individuals arrested along with Khan were Michael A. Alexander, a former program manager for the U.S. Army Corps of Engineers, businessman Harold F. Babb, and Khan's son, Lee A. Khan. In addition to the over 19-year prison sentence, the judge ordered Mr. Khan to pay:

> $32.5 million in restitution to the U.S. Army Corps of Engineers. The judge also entered a forfeiture money judgment against Khan for $11,082,687 and forfeited to the United States more than $.13 million in bank account funds; 13 properties in Virginia, Florida, and West Virginia; and a 2011 GMC Yukon Denali truck. Khan had previously forfeited over $700,000 in bank account funds and four luxury automobiles.

The following extracts from the FBI's press release describe how the scheme worked:

> According to a statement of offense signed by Khan, in or around 2006, he and Alexander agreed to work together to obtain government contracts for corrupt contractors who would reward them with bribes. Among others, Khan and Alexander worked with Babb on a scheme to use EyakTek as a vehicle for channeling contracts awarded by the Army Corps of Engineers. EyakTek, in turn, hired Nova Datacom and other sub-contractors that submitted fraudulently inflated or fictitious quotes for equipment and services. As directed by Khan and Alexander, the sub-contractors kicked back a significant portion of the payments to them as bribes for keeping the money flowing their way from the Army Corps of Engineers.
>
> Khan and the others attempted to obtain more than $30 million through the bribery scheme, primarily through the submission of fraudulently inflated invoices to the government, according to the statement of offense. In most cases, the corrupt companies provided the equipment and services legitimately included in the contracts, but also billed for inflated and fictitious equipment and services. Khan referred to the fraudulently inflated amounts as "overhead." Khan, Alexander, and the contractors agreed to split the "overhead."

In another case involving the corrupt award of government contracts, former Detroit Mayor Kwame Kilpatrick, along with his father and a city contractor, were convicted on racketeering, extortion, bribery, fraud, and tax charges. An extract from the FBI media release announcing the conviction is repeated below to illustrate the extent of the corruption and brazen disregard for the law exhibited by these individuals:

Bribery/Extortion Involving Other Public Contracts and Investments

Further evidence showed that during Kwame Kilpatrick's tenure as mayor, he and Bernard Kilpatrick solicited and accepted payments and property valued at over $1 million from persons seeking business with the city or its General Retirement System or police and fire pension funds. Included in this bribery/extortion scheme were the following:

- Karl Kado paid Kwame Kilpatrick and Bernard Kilpatrick approximately a quarter-million dollars in cash for favorable treatment with respect to his contracts for cleaning and electrical services at Cobo Hall.
- Jon Rutherford provided money and campaign-related payments totaling over $300,000 on behalf of Kwame and Bernard Kilpatrick in return for Kwame Kilpatrick's support of Rutherford's waterfront casino development plan.
- Tony Soave provided free private jet service and other benefits to Kwame and Bernard Kilpatrick worth over $300,000, so that he would not be harmed with respect to his business interests with the city.

- Marc Andre Cunningham paid Bernard Kilpatrick a portion of his commission on a pension fund consulting deal from a venture capital firm (totaling at least $15,000) for Kwame Kilpatrick's support of Cunningham's firm getting the pension fund money.

The *New York Times* article announcing the 28-year sentence for former Mayor Kwame Kilpatrick included the fact that he apologized for his actions and that prosecutors stated that the scandal helped accelerate Detroit's entrance into bankruptcy (Yaccino, 2013).

CORRUPTION IN CONTRACT ADMINISTRATION

Although different players are normally involved in bribery, extortion, and kickback schemes after the contract has been awarded, in the contract administration phase of the procurement cycle, such nefarious activities continue to be pursued assiduously. The U.S. Navy issued a press release containing a statement by Rear Admiral John F. Kirby, Navy Chief of Information, announcing the suspension of access to classified information for Vice Admiral Ted Branch, director of Naval Intelligence, and Rear Admiral Bruce Loveless, Director of Intelligence Operations (U.S. Navy News Service, 2013). The two admirals were also placed on leave. As alarming as this announcement relating to a contract administration corruption scandal is, there are other significant developments signifying this as one of the most alarming and nefarious corruption scandals ever. The decision to suspend access to classified material for the two admirals stemmed from a Naval Criminal Investigative Service (NCIS) investigation of improper and illegal relations with the CEO of Glenn Defense Marine, Mr. Leonard Francis. The press release stressed the fact that the admirals retained their rank and security clearances, which the announcement concerns allegations and neither officer has been charged with crimes or violations, and there was not any unauthorized release of classified information. It is surmised, however, that the denial of a breach of classified information pertained solely to the two admirals. A *Washington Post* story indicated that Mr. Francis was arrested for bribing other Navy officers with prostitutes and cash in exchange for classified or privileged information (Whitlock, 2013). The *Washington Post* story indicated that, also in connection with this case, an NCIS agent and two Navy commanders have been arrested and that a captain was relieved of command of his ship.

The *Washington Post* story indicated that the two Navy commanders informed Mr. Francis, also known as "Fat Leonard" by naval personnel because of his girth, of ship and submarine movements. The Navy commanders called Mr. Francis either "Lion King" or "Big Bro" in e-mails they exchanged, while Mr. Francis referred to the commanders as "bro" or "brudda." Some of the e-mails from Mr. Francis allegedly contained photographs of call girls he planned to set the commanders up with. The movement of the naval vessels was apparently important to Mr. Francis, a Malaysian citizen, so that he might allegedly steer aircraft carriers and other naval vessels to certain ports where his company could overcharge the Navy for tugboats, fuel, and sewage disposal. The NCIS agent, John B. Beliveau II, was charged with providing Mr. Francis with sensitive law enforcement files so that Fat Leonard might avoid charges.

Despite deplorable service provided the Navy by the contractor, Glenn Defense Marine Asia, it continued to be rewarded with government contracts. The Philippine Senate publicly excoriated the contractor after discovering that it had illegally dumped untreated sewage from U.S. Navy vessels into protected waters near Subic Bay (Whitlock, 2013). Another incident occurred at the port of Brisbane, Australia when the USS *George Washington* arrived in port and the approximately 5,000 sailors aboard could not disembark because the contractor could not locate a gangway. One week after the incident in Australia, Glenn Defense Marine Asia was awarded a $1 million sole source contract to provide port services in Malaysia.

RECOMMENDATIONS TO ALLEVIATE CORRUPTION

Despite the extensive history of devastated families, despoiled lives, and debased careers resulting from contract corruption scandals involving corrupt government contractor representatives enriching nefarious public servants and fleecing taxpayers to obtain favored contractor status, public servants and corporate officials continue to participate in these self-destructive activities. While all citizens may not be enticed to read, listen to, or watch every media account concerning government contract corruption, one would expect individuals involved in government procurement, whether from the public or private sector, to be captivated by tragic media stories regarding others in their profession. Why these public servants and contractor representatives continue to become embroiled in such schemes, in view of the continuing media coverage of investigations and trials, is enigmatic. The numerous examples cited earlier represent merely a small sample of the seemingly infinite stream of tales concerning public servants being bribed to provide corrupt contractors opportunities for bilking the government. In the hope of stemming irrational participation in corrupt schemes that risk personal ruination in return for relatively miniscule rewards, recommendations are offered to government agencies, government contractors, and individuals participating in government procurement.

Government Agencies

Code of Ethics: Government agencies which do not have written ethics guidelines are urged to establish a code of ethics. Government agencies with existing ethical guidelines are encouraged to review and revise their existing code of ethics. National nonprofit procurement associations that may provide guidance in developing a code of ethics for government agencies are listed below:

- National Contract Management Association (NCMA)
- National Institute of Governmental Purchasing (NIGP)
- National Association of Educational Procurement (NAEP)
- National Association of State Procurement Officials (NASPO).

Gratuity Limitations

While it may appear visionary to establish a zero-tolerance gratuity policy, disciplining employees for accepting inexpensive gifts such as coffee mugs, calendars, and ballpoint pens is imprudent. Such disciplinary actions would appear frivolous. The most common limit for the federal employees for unsolicited gifts is an aggregate market value of $20 or less per source per occasion, provided the aggregate amount from any one person shall not exceed $50 in a calendar year (U.S. Government Printing Office, 2015). The annual limitation on the value of gifts that may be accepted is crucial. Failure to include an annual limitation minimizes the limitation on the acceptability of occasional gifts.

Financial Disclosures

Making initial employment, annual, and employment termination financial disclosures by government employees in a position of trust is a common practice for government agencies. Such disclosures typically indicate the amounts and sources for funds, gifts received, and stock ownership during the reporting period. In addition to the standard disclosures, the recommendation here is that employees and consultants involved in procurement activities make financial disclosures regarding prospective contractors for upcoming acquisition efforts.

Contractor Certifications

Requiring contractors to provide certifications regarding the absence of conflicts of interest and restrictions against providing gratuities to government representatives helps to reinforce the fact that gift giving exceeding the acceptable value threshold is illegal and will jeopardize the contractors' prospects for being awarded government contracts. Obtaining contractor certifications is a prevalent practice and is highly recommended for agencies that have yet to incorporate certification forms in their solicitations. Once an agency adopts such a certification requirement, their solicitation documents should be modified to require that properly completed certifications shall accompany contractor proposals, bids, and quotations.

Determine Penalties for Fraudulent Award of Government Contracts

Penalties for the infraction of laws against fraudulent acts to steer contracts to favored contractors are certainly in place for public servants as well as for government contractors in all federal, state, and local jurisdictions. It is apropos at this point of the commentary on penalties for contract fraud to repeat the fact that the FBI frequently takes the lead in prosecuting state and local public corruption cases. It is, therefore, prudent to become aware of federal penalties for such crimes.

Cases prosecuted by the FBI generally result in appropriately significant penalties regardless of the perpetrator being a federal, state, or local agency public servant. When cases are resolved at the state or local level, however, penalties are inconsistent and not necessarily appropriate for the offense. Ethics violation penalties imposed by states and local government agencies may result in high level government officials merely being asked to retire early for committing serious infractions while lower level public servants may be prosecuted in court for less serious violations such as the inappropriate acceptance of a gift card. It is, therefore, recommended that states and local government agencies establish standards requiring appropriate, consistent penalties for punishing unethical public servants.

Communicate Ethics Guidelines and Penalties to Public Servants and Government Contractors

The frequency, manner, and effectiveness of communicating guidelines and penalties for ethical violations to individuals and entities in both the public and private sectors vary considerably between various government agencies. Public servants are oftentimes placed in positions of responsibility for selecting contractors and meeting with prospective contractors with little or no training on ethics guidelines or laws prohibiting favoritism in selecting contractors. Just as public servants oftentimes lack an understanding of the applicable government contract laws, private sector employees are oftentimes ignorant of the threats to their employment, finances, reputation, and actual freedom should they reward public employees in return for preferential treatment in the award of contracts.

Communicating guidelines and penalties to public servants can be accomplished through training as well as through the requirement to provide financial disclosures and certifications. Ethics training for newly assigned government employees who will interact with government contractors is essential. Within weeks of his initial assignment in the acquisition field, this chapter's author was offered an opportunity to name whatever entertainment he preferred at the expense of the government contractor under contract for his project. Although he had not yet received ethics training in any form, and despite the offer amounting to considerably less value than the notorious cases described elsewhere in this chapter, the offer seemed unethical. He refused that offer and forever doubted the integrity of the contractor. Had initial training in ethics been administered, he would likely have heard of the need to report the attempted bribe to his supervisor. Government employees newly assigned to positions in the acquisition field who received less generous gratuity offers, or who might have been tempted by the offer mentioned here, or possibly more generous offers, could likely have bumbled into long-term illegal relationship that would eventually lead to the tragedies discussed earlier in this chapter. Periodic employee training in ethics is essential to reinforce the initial training and to maintain government employees' attention to the illegality of accepting certain gratuities. Yet another momentous occasion for providing ethics training to public servants is when they are assigned to an ad hoc source selection team. Incorporating refresher ethics training into their briefing upon assignment to a team responsible for selecting a contractor or contractors for specific products or services is essential because their initial team assignment coincides with the greatest potential for being approached for special consideration by prospective contractors. Requesting a financial disclosure, as discussed earlier in this section, as it relates specifically to the upcoming acquisition, is strongly recommended.

When communicating the government's ethics rules and policies to public servants, it is recommended that employees be advised that low value gratuities are permitted merely because it is not feasible to enforce zero-tolerance gratuity rules, and that individuals are encouraged to establish their own personal zero-tolerance program.

Communicating the government's expectations of contractors is an entirely different challenge. If government sends communications to its suppliers on an annual basis, such communications provide an appropriate opportunity to advise or remind suppliers and prospective suppliers of the restrictions against and penalties for providing government employees with gratuities. There is also a fitting opportunity to communicate the government's rules regarding ethics and conflicts of interest along with solicitations transmitted to prospective contractors. The certification forms included in solicitations, which are required to be completed and returned by prospective suppliers, along with their proposals, bids, or quotations, also serve to communicate the government's ethics policies to its suppliers.

Avoidance of Contracting Processes That Contribute to Contract Fraud

The issue raised in Chapter 4, Contract Process, with respect to cryptic results from proposal evaluation teams illustrates a flawed process that contributes to procurement fraud. Cryptic proposal evaluation results empower the official responsible for selecting the successful contractor to select his or her most favored contractor. Receipt of such inconclusive results from the proposal evaluation team provides the source selection authority with justification for selecting one of two or more competing contractors.

Table 9.1
Actual Coast Guard Proposal Evaluation Results

Concept Design	Bollinger	Eastern	Bath Iron Works	Huntington Ingalls	VT Halter Marine
Soundness of Design	Superior	Superior	Superior	Superior	Superior
Mission Effectiveness	Superior	Superior	Superior	Superior	Superior
Design Approach	Superior	Superior	Superior	Superior	Superior
Organizational Management	Satisfactory	Satisfactory	Satisfactory	Satisfactory	Satisfactory
Production Capability	Satisfactory	Satisfactory	Satisfactory	Satisfactory	Satisfactory
Past Performance	Satisfactory	Superior	Satisfactory	Marginal	Marginal
Price	$21,950,000	$21,975,000	$21,400,000	$22,000,000	$22,000,000

When the individual with authority to award the contract has such cryptic information, the procurement process is subject to corruption. Such cryptic results from an actual proposal evaluation team are illustrated in Table 9.1, Actual Coast Guard Proposal Evaluation Results (U.S. Government Accountability Office, 2014).

To demonstrate the capacity for the recommended process for evaluating proposals to identify the best value proposal, the Coast Guard's results were adjusted by approximating a numerical weighing of the factors and converting the scoring from adjectival to numeric. The numerical weights are depicted in the second column, labeled "Factor Weights," in Table 9.2, Adjusted Coast Guard Proposal Evaluation Results. Although the factor weights approximate the significance of the factors according to the decision narrative (repeated below from the GAO decision), the description of the significance of the proposal evaluation factors for this adjustment is subject to interpretation.

> Offerors were informed that the Phase I contracts would be awarded on a best-value basis, considering, in descending order of importance: concept design, . . . design approach, organizational management, production capability, past performance, small business/Department of Homeland Security mentor-protégé participation, and price. . . . All non-price factors, when combined, were significantly more important than price. . . . Offerors also were informed that any proposal offering a price for Phase I exceeding $22 million would be rejected.

The weighed scores for the "Soundness of Design" subfactor through the "Past Performance" factor were all calculated with the formula, introduced in Chapter 4,

Table 9.2

Adjusted Coast Guard Proposal Evaluation Results

Concept Design	Factor Weights	Bollinger Raw	Bollinger Wtd	Eastern Raw	Eastern Wtd	Bath Iron Works Raw	Bath Iron Works Wtd	Huntington Ingalls Raw	Huntington Ingalls Wtd	VT Halter Marine Raw	VT Halter Marine Wtd
Soundness of Design	20	95	20	95	20	95	20	95	20	95	20
Mission Effectiveness	20	95	20	95	20	95	20	95	20	95	20
Design Approach	35	95	35	95	35	95	35	95	35	95	35
Organizational Management	30	85	30	85	30	85	30	85	30	85	30
Production Capability	25	85	25	85	25	85	25	85	25	85	25
Past Performance	20	82	17.3	95	20	88	18.5	75	15.8	75	15.8
Price (In Mil USD)	30	21.95	29.3	21.975	29.2	21.4	30.0	22.0	29.2	22.0	29.2
COMBINED SCORES			**176.6**		**179.2**		**178.5**		**175.0**		**175.0**

Raw and Weighed (Wtd) Scores

Contract Process, for subjective criteria where high numbers are favorable: S = R(W/HR). The weighed score for Evaluated Price was calculated with the formula for objective criteria where low values are favorable to the government: S = HO-(V-L)/(HO/W).

The variable names in the two formulas represent:

HO = Highest observed value

HR = Highest assigned subjective rating

L = Lowest observed value

R = Actual subjective rating

S = Weighed score

V = Observed value

W = Criterion weight.

If the procurement planning team had assigned numerical values to the factor weights rather than the relative values taken from the narrative in the GAO decision, the values could have varied somewhat from the values used in Table 9.2 example. The scores assigned to the evaluation factors would also likely have varied from those used in Table 9.2. The use of adjectival scoring of the factors and subfactors requires tied scores for all proposals meeting the criteria for each adjective. Had the proposal rating scheme provided a range of numerical scores, e.g. 91–100 for Superior, the proposal evaluation team would likely have assigned different scores to reflect perceived differences in the quality of proposals that meet the criteria for a Superior rating. If the team determined that all the proposals should be rated Superior for the Soundness of Design subfactor, for example, but that the team members could discern differences in the quality of the proposed solutions for each contractor, this subfactor could have received ratings ranging from 90 to 100, and every contractor could have received a different score. Although there are weaknesses to the example in Table 9.2 because it was impossible to determine the proposal evaluation team's discerned differences for all the factors and subfactors, this recalculation of the scoring of proposals does demonstrate the superiority of using numerical factor weighting, numerical factor scoring, and weighing of the factor scores. The COMBINED SCORE of 179.2 for Eastern clearly identifies this contractor as having submitted the proposal that represented the best value to the government. Had the government official making the final decision regarding contractor selection been presented with the results in Table 9.1, she or he could have justified award to two or three of the competing contractors. In this particular case, this was not a consideration because the Coast Guard intended to award the contract to the three contractors with the most favorable proposals. When presented with the results in Table 9.2, with numerical values representing the significance of the various factors and subfactors and with numerical scores representing the proposal scoring, the individual making the final decision regarding contract award would have a distinct indication of the contractor offering the best value to the government. Having a process that does not produce cryptic results, as shown in Table 9.1, but clearly defines the contractor offering the best value avoids the element of corruption introduced when the contractor selection official has the flexibility to award the contract to either one of the two or more competing contractors.

Working Lunches

If government agencies feel that important work can be accomplished during working lunches, yet are conflicted by their employees accepting free lunches from government contractors, it is recommended that the government establish working lunch budgets to permit government officials to reciprocate with corporate representatives by alternating the entities that pay for lunch.

GOVERNMENT CONTRACTORS

The discussion of recommendations for contractors is divided between meeting the minimal compliance standards and implementing ethical standards that exceed the minimum requirements. A government contractor's ethics policy that fails to meet the government's minimal compliance standards is unacceptable. While short-term gains may be achieved through the award of contracts through nefarious means, it is virtually assured that such criminal actions will inevitably be discovered. Entities and individuals likely to alert investigatory agencies concerning a defense contractor's illegal activities include:

- Contractor employees or former employees who seek monetary rewards through qui tam lawsuits. There were 752 qui tam lawsuits in fiscal year 2013. The government recovered $2.9 billion, and whistleblowers were paid a total of $345 million. The opportunity to share in the government's recovery of massive fines related to whistle blowing by employees or former employees is a significant inducement to report wrongdoing, leading to prosecution of corrupt contractor representatives and fines, debarment, or suspension of their employers.
- Concerned employees or former employees who feel obligated to report their employer's or past-employer's misdeeds without motivation for possible financial rewards.
- Competing contractors that have been unsuccessful in winning contracts when they were confident that they submitted the superior proposal, bid, or quotation.

Failure to meet the government's minimum ethical standards or to comply with the law with respect to gratuities and kickbacks is likely to result in severe financial penalties.

Companies tempted to consider violation of ethical restrictions are reminded of the $2.9 billion the government recovered in fiscal year 2013 through qui tam lawsuits. Failure to comply with government ethics rules can also result in suspension or debarment of government contractors, rendering it impossible to obtain new government contracts.

As an alternative to merely meeting the government's minimum ethics requirements, contractors might consider implementing a zero-tolerance approach to conducting business ethically with the government. Honest government officials will most certainly be offended by attempts to influence their decisions through the offering of money, vehicles, event tickets, sexual favors, vacations, or other gratuities. These same government officials may also be offended by the offering of gratuities that are valued below the threshold for acceptance. Token gifts are not likely to influence the decisions of government employees, and contractors who offer such gifts risk having them returned or having their reputation with customers damaged. It is, therefore, highly recommended that government contractors consider implementation of a zero-tolerance policy with respect to the furnishing of gratuities to government officials.

Regardless of whether government contractors elect to meet the government's minimal ethical standards or implement a zero-tolerance policy, it is imperative to train employees and stress the importance of compliance with corporate policy and penalties for noncompliance. It is also recommended that government customers be informed when contractors implement a zero-tolerance policy towards the giving of gratuities. Possible mediums for communicating ethics policies to customers and potential customers include incorporating such policies in advertising programs and publications, in proposals, bids, and quotations submitted to the government, and during presentations made in conjunction with proposals, bids, and quotations.

INDIVIDUALS

Just as with government contractors, it is imperative that individual public and private persons comply strictly with minimum government ethics laws and policies. Individuals who are tempted to circumvent ethics laws are reminded of the ruined careers, fines, imprisonment, and suicides that have caused severe impacts on individuals evading these rules.

Individual public and private persons are encouraged to adopt personal zero-tolerance ethics practices. Establishing and practicing a zero-tolerance policy for public employees is not a difficult task. The offer of gratuities from contractors may merely be politely rejected. Once it becomes known that public officials do not accept gratuities of any value, it is likely that future such offers will not be proffered. It may not be quite that simple for private sector employees to withhold the offering of token value gratuities to public officials. This is especially true when her or his private sector employer has established a policy that includes the offering of such gratuities. When there are conflicts between the private sector employee and her or his employer, a frank discussion of the gratuity policy is appropriate. When arguing for a company zero-tolerance gratuity program, individuals are encouraged to employ the rationale used in this chapter to support their position.

CONCLUSIONS

Gratuities offered in exchange for the hope for, or perhaps the promise of, favorable treatment of government contractors by public servants have existed since historical times. When the value of such gratuities exceeds the acceptance threshold established by government, laws are broken and individuals as well as business entities are subject to severe penalties. Despite seemingly ceaseless media coverage of tragedies resulting from kickbacks and similar schemes procurement fraud prevails to the present date.

From the perceptive of elected and executive level government officials, to middle managers, and extending downward to those serving in foxholes, citizens might expect public servants dealing directly or indirectly with private sector entities to refrain from accepting favors of any value from contractors.[2] Government representatives who direct, manage, or supervise subordinates might also expect that their employees will refuse to accept favors of any value from corporations. Enforcement of such zero tolerance edicts, however, will likely prove impractical to impossible. Consider, for example, the impracticality of disciplining an otherwise valuable employee for accepting a cup of coffee or an inexpensive ballpoint pen from a supplier. The preeminent result of this dilemma is the establishment of rules, or laws, by virtually every government entity to place a monetary limit on the value of and frequency for acceptance of gratuities by public servants. This seemingly illogical establishment of permission to accept gifts from contractors they deal with is likely confusing to the multitude of honest, dedicated government officials and employees. Adding to this confusion is that despite rules prohibiting the acceptance of valuable gratuities, incidents reminiscent of historical ethical imbroglios persists to the present time. Perhaps initial employment and follow-on periodic training in ethics should emphasize the fact that employees are encouraged to establish a personal zero-tolerance gift acceptance policy. Perhaps, for some employees, the mere act of informing subordinates that the agency is opposed to the acceptance of gratuities of any value will be effective. After informing those participating in ethics training that the agency discourages acceptance of all gifts, it might be explained that "acceptable" limits are placed on the receipt of contractor gratuities merely due to the impossibility of prosecuting employees for accepting token value gratuities. The effectivity of ethics training will likely be enhanced by including an explanation of the annual disclosure of income and gifts, and the fact that such disclosures are available for review by the public. Public servants who are periodically reminded that it is necessary to list all the gifts they accept, regardless of value, that gifts must be reported and that gift disclosures are made public will likely consider the consequences before acceptance of gifts either above or below the acceptable value threshold. Ethics trainees should also be advised that a tactic to render a public servant entrapped in a cycle of favors for gifts is for a contractor to initiate the gift giving with low value gratuities and to increase the value over time until the value of the gifts exceeds the acceptable threshold. Reciprocity may not be sought by contractors until after the public employee has compromised her or his ethical behavior by violating the agency's ethics rules. Such a multifaceted approach to ethics training is expected to help curtail future criminal acts.

While there may be cases wherein such nefarious acts were condoned at the highest levels of corporate structures, it is illogical to establish policies including the defrauding of their government customers to encourage profitability. Litton Systems, Inc. corporate-wide suspension discussed earlier in this chapter, clearly illustrates a case wherein two company executives colluded to increase the corporation's profitability solely to enhance their personal professional standing while violating the corporation's policies for conformance to government standards of conduct and the law.

KEY POINTS

- Contract corruption occurred during the early history of the United States and continues vigorously to the present.
- The FBI is the lead investigatory agency for contract corruption at the federal, state, and local government levels.
- Corruption is present during virtually all phases of the contracting process and at all levels of government.
- Proposal evaluation techniques that clearly identify the contractor offering the best value curtail the introduction of corruption permitted when proposal evaluation results are cryptic thus permitting the source selection authority to justify contract award to either of two or more contractors.
- Although it's impractical for government to enforce a zero-tolerance policy regarding gratuities, individual contracting professionals are encouraged to adopt their own personal policy to decline the offer of any gifts from contractors.

NOTES

1. The account of the suspension of Litton Systems, Inc. is based partially on the personal experience of the author of this chapter who was an employee of Litton Electron Devices Division at the time of the suspension.

2. The term "foxholes" should not be taken literally. In this instance, the reference is made to the contracts professionals who are directly involved in preparing solicitations, evaluating proposals, negotiating contract provisions, as well as awarding and managing contracts.

REFERENCES

Brown, N. P., OIG/AUD; Gershman, Anna S., OIG/INV; and Peterson, Robert, OIG/ISP; Memo subject "Management Alert (Contract File Management Deficiencies)," addressed to Patrick F. Kennedy and Joyce A. Barr, March 20, 2014.

Cushman, J.H. Jr. (1986, July 17) Litton Barred from Military Bidding, *The New York Times*.

Diner, H. (1975). Teapot Dome 1924. Schlesinger, Arthur M. and Bruns, Roger (Ed.), *Congress Investigates 1792–1974*, pp. 199–217. New York, NY: Chelsea House Publishers.

Federal Acquisition Regulation § 16.102(c).

Musicus, R. J. (1944) Cost-Plus-a-Percentage-of-Cost System of Contracting, *St. John's Law Review*, 19(1). Retrieved from http://scholarship.law.stjohns.edu/lawreview/vol19/iss1/3.

The New York Times, (1862, February 6) GOVERNMENT CONTRACTS; THE FRAUDS OF THE CONTRACTORS, Full and Authentic Digest of the Report of the Van Wyck Investigating Committee, Frauds in Army Supplies—Frauds in Navy Supplies—Frauds in the Purchase of Arms, in the Purchase and Charter of Vessels, in Horses and Wagons, in Cattle &c. The Northern Traitors and their Deeds THE STEAMER CATALINE, TESTIMONY IN REFERENCE TO HIDES, TALLOW AND CATTLE. EXAMINATION BY MR.STEELE. TESTIMONY IN REFERENCE TO THE PURCHASE OF HORSES AND WAGONS IN NEW-YORK. THE TESTIMONY IN RELATION TO THE PURCHASE OF ARMS. THE PURCHASE OF VESSELS AND NAVY SUPPLIES. TESTIMONY OF B.F. WOOLSEY. THE PURCHASE OF THE STARS AND STRIPES. TESTIMONY OF MR. W.W. BENEDICT. TESTIMONY OF MR. C.S. BUSHNELL. CRITICISMS BY THE COMMITTEE FURTHER TESTIMONY OF B.F. WOOLSEY. THE COMMITTEE ON GEORGE D. MORGAN. TESTIMONY IN REFERENCE TO THE PURCHASE OF ARMY SUPPLIES. PURCHASES OF HORSES AND MULES.

U.S. Attorney's Office (2013, July 11) [Press Release] Former U.S. Army Corps of Engineers Manager Sentenced to More Than 19 Years in Prison in $30 Million Bribery and Kickback Scheme.

U.S. Department of Defense, Office of the Inspector General of the Department of Defense, (2005, May 13) Management Accountability Review of the Boeing KC-767A Tanker Program, Report No. OIG-2004-171.

U.S. Federal Bureau of Investigation (2013, July 19) Cheating in Contracts: A $30 Million Case of Corruption, *News Stories*. Retrieved from http://www.fbi.gov/news/stories/2013/july/a-30-million-case-of-corruption.

U.S. Federal Bureau of Investigation (2013, December 20) [Press Release] Justice Department Recovers $3.8 Billion from False Claims Act Cases in Fiscal Year 2013.

U.S. Federal Bureau of Investigation (2014, June 17) Public Corruption Update: FBI Continues Efforts to Root Out Crooked Officials. Retrieved from http://www.fbi.gov/news/stories/2014/june/public-corruption-update/public-corruption-update.

U.S. Government Accountability Office (2011, April 6) Solers, Inc., File numbers B-404032.3 and B-404032-4.

U.S. Government Accountability Office (2011, August 4) PCCP Constructors, JV; Bechtel Infrastructure Corporation, File numbers B-405036, B-405036.2, B-405036.3, B-405036.4, B-405036.5, and B-405036.6.

U.S. Government Accountability Office (2012, January 17) SeKON Enterprise, Inc., Signature Consulting Group, File numbers B-405921 and B405921.2.

U.S. Government Accountability Office (2014, June 2) Huntington Ingalls Industries, Inc.; VT Halter Marine, Inc., File numbers B-409541, B-409541.2, B-409541.3, B-409541.4, and B-B-409541.5.

U.S. Government Printing Office, 5 CFR § 2635.204, Exceptions.

U.S. Navy News Service (2013, November 8) U.S. Navy Admirals Investigated by NCIS,: Story Number: NNS131108-37.

Whitlock, C. (2013, November 8) Two admirals face probe in Navy bribery scheme, *Washington Post*. Retrieved from http://www.washingtonpost.com/world/national-security/two-admirals-face-probe-in-navy-bribery-scheme/2013/11/08/d2d063a-48d8-11e3-bf0c-cebf37c6f484.

Whitlock, C. (2013, December 4) Navy fraud case prosecutors: Contractor got more work despite poor performance, *Washington Post*. Retrieved from http://www.washingtonpost.com/world/national-security/contractor-bilked-navy-in-excess-of-20million-prosecutors-say-in-court-filing/2013/12/04/b3f0f86a-56b2-11e3-835d-e7173847c7cc_story.html.

Yaccino, S. (2013, October 10) Kwame M. Kilpatrick, Former Detroit Mayor, Sentenced to 28 Years in Corruption Case, *The New York Times*. Retrieved from http://www.nytimes.com/2013/10/11/us/former-detroit-mayor-kwame-kilpatrick-sentencing.html?_r=0.

10

Impact of Contracting on Managing Government Organizations

Stephen B. Gordon

INTRODUCTION

This chapter examines the current role of contracting in the management of governmental organizations and how the contribution of contracting could be improved if elected officials and senior administrators understood how best practice contracting could support enterprise strategic goals. The chapter also looks at the complex and dynamic environment of public sector contracting and suggests steps that leaders in governmental organizations can and should take to transform this area of activity from a routine function into a powerful management tool. The challenges that must be addressed to effect such transformations are discussed. A proper understanding of best practice contracting is essential in an era of networked governance (Salamon, 2000).

Unlike private sector organizations, where the value of strategic contracting has long been acknowledged, contracting in public sector organizations has not been widely perceived or used as a strategic tool (Allair & Leenders, 2005; Bloom & Nardone, 1984; Snider & Rendon, 2007).[1] For the most part, neither the elected or appointed leaders of governmental organizations nor anyone else has paid much attention to contracting except when things have gone badly wrong (Snider & Rendon, 2007, 332).[2] The dramatically increased use of contracting beginning during the 1960s as a means for hiring nonprofits to provide human services (Salamon, 2002, 319–320) and the emergence during the 1980s of contracting as an instrument for privatizing traditionally public services constituted rare departures from the traditionally more prevalent view of contracting in governmental organizations as an activity of lesser importance than "budgeting, human resources management, [or] strategic planning" (Snider & Rendon, p.232). Leaders and others in public sector organizations generally have regarded contracting as a tedious, routine, bureaucratic, and tactical set of activities—a pain that must be endured for the sake of obtaining the materiel, services, systems, and infrastructure needed to operate and deliver services. Similarly, governmental contracting officials (and especially those who work for the U.S. federal government) often have been stereotyped (and in many but not all instances, unfairly) as unmotivated, risk-averse technocrats focused more on making it through the day, to the next pay check, and to retirement, than on supporting organizational excellence.[3]

Several reasons underscore the importance of meaningfully involving[4] contracting programs and contracting officials in the management of public organizations. First, as was mentioned in the opening paragraph of this chapter, the increasing reality of networked (or blended) governance, with its heavy reliance on contracts with for-profit and nonprofit contractors to produce public services, demands that governmental organizations have the best practicable contracting programs in place (Salamon, 2000). Second, the responsiveness and cost-effectiveness of the contracting function directly impacts the ability of governmental organizations to achieve their missions and goals. After all, departments and programs in these entities depend on the contracting function to supply the materiel, services, systems, and infrastructure they must have to achieve their goals; and how well they achieve their goals, in turn, directly impacts the achievement of enterprise goals (Allair & Leenders, 2005). Third, the significant amounts of money spent through contracts by governmental organizations[5] and the potential controllability of this money[6] justify leveraging the contracting function to squeeze available dollars for all the value they can provide. Opportunities to drive enterprise-wide efficiencies and service improvements through the importation and application of best practices, the use of technology, and the sharing of ideas, insights, and experiences within the organization comprise a fourth compelling reason. After all, the contracting unit, no matter where it is located on the organization chart, possesses in-depth, real-time knowledge of what is happening throughout the organization. Fifth, as Eimicke and Cohen have noted:

> [C]ontract management is more complex than internal management. It requires all the functions of effective internal management with the additional requirement of managing the interoganizational relationships required to get work done by "outsiders." *The management capacity needs are high, but so too is the potential payoff.* (Cohen & Eimicke, 2008 [Emphasis added])

The list of "twenty key problems created by government contracting" developed by Eimicke and Cohen are shown in Figure 10.1.[7]

Despite these and other strong justifications, most governmental organizations are only now beginning to use contracting as a tool for providing maximum support for enterprise goals. This emerging trend must be accelerated, but more widespread use of best practice strategic contracting in governmental organizations faces many obstacles, not the least among them being the politics within and external to public sector organizations.[8]

Figure 10.1 **Twenty Problems Created by Government Contracting**

Problems related to Letting Contracts	1. Flawed Request for Proposal (RFP) and/or contract language 2. Overly bureaucratic contracting procedures resulting in delays and high contracting cost 3. Too few bidders and/or contractor monopolies
Communication Issues	4. Poor communication between government and contractor management 5. Poor communication between government and contractor staff 6. Inadequate direction from government to contractors
Contractor Internal Management Issues	7. Contractors that give an agency's work a low priority 8. Insufficient contractor staffing, training, equipment, and facilities 9. Poor contractor management
Government Contract Management Issues	10. Underestimating or overestimating resource needs for contractor-performed tasks 11. Insufficient or sufficient profits 12. Inappropriate or outmoded performance measures and insufficient systems 13. Incomplete methods for auditing performance reporting 14. Inadequate methods for incorporating performance data into government and contractor decision making 15. Misdirected or inadequate contractor incentive provisions
Environmental or External Issues	16. Political opposition to contracting 17. Political interference in contractor selection or management 18. Conflict of interest issues 19. Union opposition to contracting 20. Media and political attention to contractor failures

Source: Created by author using content from Cohen and Eimicke, 2008, pp. 125–127.

Leaders in governmental entities can use contracting as a strategic tool to enhance the management of their organizations by providing their contracting programs with capable and motivated leadership and staff,[9] hierarchical status, organizational voice, technology, resources, and consistent internal political backing, all of which are essential for excellence in public contracting. Assuring that the contracting workforce is as capable and motivated as it can be requires many things, including carefully selecting individuals to fill contracting positions, assuring that these individuals have the education and training they need to succeed in strategic contracting roles, and creating an appropriate system of incentives, rewards, and recognition. However, leaders in many public sector organizations appear to remain unconvinced that the potential benefits of a best-practice strategic contracting program justify changing how they allocate their time, attention, and resources. So, instead of moving quickly to upgrade their contracting programs, these leaders continue to focus their time, attention, resources, and political capital on the services and other outputs that citizens and other stakeholders see. In so doing, they completely overlook the obvious fact that poor contracting can cripple the quality and responsiveness of all services and outputs, thereby impeding the achievement of most if not all enterprise strategic goals.

Among the many contributions that contracting used as a strategic tool can make include:

- Stretching the purchasing power of, and optimizing the value obtained for, every dollar spent through contracts;
- Reducing the total costs associated with acquiring and using materiel, services, systems, and infrastructure—both simple and complex;[10]
- Identifying and exploiting opportunities to eliminate waste and generate revenue;[11]
- Mitigating risks for elected officials, senior administrators, clients, and other stakeholders—economic, political, reputational, and other;
- Doing a better job of managing and responding to the needs of clients, customers, and other stakeholders—both internal and external;
- Driving efficiencies and other improvements in the methods and processes that are used to supply needed materiel, services, systems, and infrastructure;
- Initiating and managing decisions processes for determining whether individual requirements for materiel, services, systems, and infrastructure should be "made" (that is, produced in-house) or "bought" (that is, produced by a third-party contractor).

Capable and properly resourced, equipped, and funded contract managers who have the backing of the policymakers and senior administrators can make these contributions reality by:

- Planning contracts as they should be planned;
- Forming contracts as they should be formed;
- Administering contracts as they should be administered;
- Ensuring full understanding of contract requirements and how those requirements can be fulfilled as responsively, timely, economically, efficiently, and cost-effectively as possible;
- Developing and sustaining working relationships with end-users, transaction processors,[12] and others in client departments and programs, built on shared mutual goals, common courtesy,[13] communication, and cooperation;[14]
- Engaging in more timely and richer communication with potential suppliers and contractors, if justified by the dollar value and risk of the requirement to be fulfilled, well in advance of a solicitation being published, an order being issued, or a contract being formed;
- Cultivating and sustaining productive relationships with suppliers and contractors within the boundaries of legal and ethical constraints;
- Leveraging technology and productive relationships among contracting officials, client officials, and other functional areas within the organization (including the financial and information technology units) to identify opportunities for improvement.

The goals of this chapter include enabling the reader to:

- Describe the traditional perception of contracting in public organizations;
- Discuss factors that have shaped how contracting in public organizations traditionally has been used and viewed;
- Sell the benefits of strategic (as opposed to tactical) contracting to elected officials and other decision-makers in public organizations;
- Install and sustain strategic contracting as a tool in a public organization.

Enabling the reader to achieve these goals will require understanding of:

- The meaning and scope of public contracting;
- The history and environment of contracting in the public sector;
- The potential for procurement to be a strategic tool in public organizations.

One limitation that must be stated is that the details of how contracting is, could, and should be structured and executed naturally vary among the different levels and types of public organizations. Among the more significant and obvious factors that differentiate how contracting is structured and executed from one governmental organization to another are level of government, specific mission(s), size, complexity, and political and organizational culture.[15]

This chapter does not address in any depth core contracting processes, contractor monitoring and auditing, or performance-based contracting, which are addressed in other chapters in this book.

THE MEANING AND SCOPE OF PUBLIC CONTRACTING

Public contracting comprises the authority, capacity, competencies, expertise, hard skills, soft skills, structure, culture, tools, decisions and actions required to supply materiel, systems, services, and infrastructure to the departments, programs, and individuals that do the work of public organizations.[16] For reasons discussed in this chapter, governmental contracting is typically more challenging than buying or ordering for personal consumption or in support of profit-making enterprises. As the reader will learn (if the reader does not already know), governmental contracting officials must deal with most of the issues faced by their counterparts in private sector supply management plus many more challenges that are unique to public sector contracting.

Public organizations, like all organizations, contract for materiel, systems, services and infrastructure, or at least some of these things. *Materiel* encompasses a broad range of tangible and relatively simple items, including supplies, goods, and equipment. In some cases, materiel can be procured in the commercial marketplace. In other cases, it must be custom-made or built to conform to non-commercial requirements. Public organizations at the federal, state, and local levels all buy materiel and the majority of that materiel is the same or similar to what is available in the commercial marketplace. *Systems* are more complex than materiel, because they integrate both tangible and intangible elements (for example, hardware and software) to fulfill a public organization's requirement to address a problem or exploit an opportunity. Governmental organizations at all three levels also contract for many of the same systems, including information technology (IT) systems, and many of those systems also are identical or similar to what is available in the commercial marketplace. Weapons systems procured by the military services are an obvious exception. The cost-effective and timely procurement of IT systems has been a very real challenge for federal, state, and local organizations. *Services* contracted by public sector organizations range from the most routine, housekeeping requirements such as janitorial or grounds maintenance services to requirements for highly complex services to ensure the proper functioning and reliability of very costly technology solutions. Human services such as foster care, day care, home health care, and meals-on-wheels are among the most challenging requirements for which public entities contract. Contracting for infrastructure encompasses entering into business relationships with contractors to deliver roads, streets, highways, bridges, tunnels, buildings, and facilities to support the missions of governmental organizations.

A particular governmental organization, depending on its mission, size, and other characteristics, may only have to contract for materiel and services on a small scale. Another public organization may have to contract for materiel, services, systems, and infrastructure on a grand scale. One public sector entity may be able to meet its needs in the commercial marketplace, while another may have to have its needs custom designed and built (or delivered, in the case of services).

Further, what contracting is called differs among public organizations. The term "acquisition" with a lower-case "a" is used widely within the federal government to refer to contracting, yet there are procurement officers and contracting officers to be found aplenty in agencies at that level of government. "Acquisition" with an upper case "A" as used at the federal level comprises all the actions that must be taken to fulfill an end-user's need for materiel, services, systems, or infrastructure from conceptualization to disposal and sometimes beyond.[17] State and local government organizations tend to refer to contracting as procurement or purchasing. Their contracting offices and programs also get involved in acquisition with a lower case "a" and an upper case "A," but the term acquisition, regardless of the case of the first letter in the word, is not used at the state and local levels.

THE HISTORY AND ENVIRONMENT OF CONTRACTING IN THE PUBLIC SECTOR

Schapper, Malta, and Gilbert (2006) have provided this description of the environment of public contracting in both developed countries such as the U.S. and developing countries:

Public procurement frameworks in developed and developing countries alike are [recognized] as being [characterized] by an unstable tension between the public expectations of transparency and accountability, and of efficiency and effectiveness of resource management . . .

This conformance—performance tension, manifest throughout a complex procurement environment, [has been] further [destabilized] by conflicting stakeholder interests at the political, business, community and management levels and exacerbated by competing claims between executives, lawyers, technologists and politicians for lead roles in this arena.

Public expectations of transparency and accountability in governmental contracting are embodied in statutes, ordinances, regulations, and other policies created at every level of government. These policies specify what public contracting officials must do, may do, and cannot do. Most policies relating to governmental contracting have been established though standard legislative and rule-making processes. However, courts and quasi-judicial agencies, boards, and other bodies have also made their contributions to the body of law that controls how public entities do their contracting.

The Federal Acquisition Regulation (FAR) "provides uniform acquisition policies and procedures for use by all executive agencies of the United States government" (Defense Procurement and Acquisition Policy web portal located at http://www.acq.osd.mil/dpap/dars/far.html). Found in Title 48, "Federal Acquisition Regulations System," of the U.S. Code of Federal Regulations, the intent of the FAR is to provide for the achievement of several often-competing goals in and through the federal government

Figure 10.2 **The Environment of Governmental Contracting**

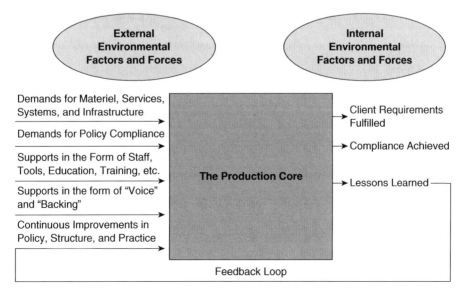

executive branch's acquisition process. Paragraphs (a) and (b) of FAR Section 1.102, "Statement of Guiding Principles for the Federal Acquisition System," state:

a. The vision for the Federal Acquisition System is to deliver, on a timely basis, the best value product or service to the customer, while maintaining the public's trust and fulfilling public policy objectives. Participants in the acquisition process should work together as a team and should be empowered to make decisions within their area of responsibility.

b. The Federal Acquisition System will—

1. Satisfy the customer in terms of cost, quality, and timeliness of the delivered product or service by, for example—

    i. Maximizing the use of commercial products and services;
    ii. Using contractors who have a track record of successful past performance or who demonstrate a current superior ability to perform; and
    iii. Promoting competition.

2. Minimize administrative operating costs;
3. Conduct business with integrity, fairness, and openness; and
4. Fulfill public policy objectives.

Both the Department of Defense (DoD) and the National Aeronautics and Space Administration (NASA) have their own supplements to the FAR. The former supplement, the Defense Acquisition Regulation Supplement (DFARS), is found at http://www.acq.osd.mil/dpap/dars/dfarspgi/current/. The latter supplement, the simply-named NASA FAR Supplement, is found at http://www.hq.nasa.gov/office/procurement/regs/nfstoc.htm.

The categories of procurement policy addressed in the FAR include:

- Improper Business Practices and Conflicts of Interest
- Administrative Matters
- Publicizing Contract Actions
- Competition Requirements
- Acquisition Planning
- Required Sources of Supplies and Services
- Contractor Qualifications
- Market Research
- Describing Agency Needs
- Acquisition of Commercial Items
- Simplified Acquisition Procedures
- Sealed Bidding
- Contracting by Negotiation
- Types of Contracts
- Special Contracting Methods

- Emergency Acquisitions
- Small Business Programs
- Application of Labor Laws to Government Acquisitions
- Environment, Water, and Energy Efficiency, Renewable Energy Technologies, Occupational Safety, and Drug-Free Workplace
- Protection of Privacy and Freedom of Information
- Foreign Acquisition
- Other Socioeconomic Programs
- Patents, Data, and Copyrights
- Bonds and Insurance
- Taxes
- Cost Accounting Standards Administration
- Contract Cost Principles and Procedures
- Contract
- Protests, Disputes, and Appeals
- Major System Acquisition
- Research and Development Contracting
- Construction and Architect-Engineer Contracts
- Service Contracting
- Federal Supply Schedule Contracting
- Acquisition of Information Technology
- Acquisition of Utility Services
- Contract Administration and Audit Services
- Contract Modifications
- Subcontracting Policies and Procedures
- Government Property
- Quality Assurance
- Transportation
- Value Engineering
- Termination of Contracts
- Extraordinary Contractual Actions and the Safety Act
- Use of Government Sources by Contractors
- Solicitation Provisions and Contract Clauses and
- Forms.

(http://www.acquisition.gov/far/, PDF Format, FEDERAL ACQUISITION REGULATION, General Structure and Subparts)

Although a plain reading of the introductory portion of the FAR would indicate that a federal acquisition official can exercise discretion when interpreting and applying the FAR, whether this is truly the case remains a source of debate and contention within the federal acquisition community.[18]

All fifty states also have their own procurement codes or acts, which comprise the core of the state's body of contracting policy. As is the case at the federal level, these codes and acts are supplemented by regulations and other policies, including those created by courts and quasi-judicial agencies, boards, and commissions. Each of the state procurement codes reflects, to a greater or lesser degree, provisions of the American Bar Association's *Model Procurement Code for State and Local Government* (hereafter, the MPC). Never intended to be a uniform code, the *MPC* was designed as a "smorgasbord," as one of the drafters said during the initial developmental process, for state policymakers to adapt in order to plug the gaps in or otherwise improve their existing procurement policies. First published in 1979, the *MPC* has been updated and supplemented several times. One contrarian, commenting on the incorporation of a large amount of MPC content into a comprehensive revision of Maryland's procurement code in 1980, referred to the new Maryland procurement code as the "lawyers relief act,"[19] Like the FAR, the MPC addresses numerous categories of contracting policy and is very detailed and comprehensive.[20] For additional information about the procurement policies, processes, and procedures of the individual state governments (see the *Guide to State Governments: A 50-State Primer on Purchasing Laws, Processes, and Procedures*).[21]

At the local government level, procurement policies vary as to who creates them and who is responsible for executing them. Larger local governments generally operate under charters or other forms of independent authority granted to them by state governments. Thus, they are able to formulate their own contracting policies, or at least most of their contracting policies. Smaller local governments, on the other hand, generally operate directly under the requirements of state government contracting policy and the oversight of state legislatures. Some larger local governments such as the Metropolitan Government of Nashville and Davidson County (in Tennessee) and the City of Alexandria, Virginia, adapted and included in their contracting policies significant portions of the *MPC* and the *Recommended Regulations to the Model Procurement Code*, which were developed soon after the development of the original MPC documents. Several other local governments—large, medium-sized, and small—have adapted some or all of the *Model Procurement Ordinance*, a condensed version of the full MPC.

The very detailed and comprehensive policies that regulate contracting by governmental entities at all three levels of government prescribe in detail how contractors are to be selected, and require public sector organizations and their contractors to support the achievement of multiple and sometimes competing goals. Clearly, having to comply with these policies complicates the task of providing end-users with needed goods and services. However, mitigating corruption and assuring fair play—primary goals of procurement policy in the United States—have been a priority for policymakers for nearly a century and a half.

Beginning at the national level during the American Civil War, policymakers have put in place a framework of laws, court decisions, and administrative rulings that have succeeded in mitigating fraud, waste, and abuse and promoting openness in public contracting, but this same framework has also impeded the ability of contracting programs and officials to provide the best possible support for the strategic goals of public enterprises.[22] The emphasis on control, sometimes implemented to the extreme by public contracting officials, whom some argue have placed a greater emphasis on gatekeeping and self-interest than on providing support for departmental, programmatic, and enterprise goals, has frustrated many elected officials, managers and supervisors, front-line managers and staff, and other stakeholders in governmental organizations. It has also contributed to public outcries and reputational damage for public sector organizations and their leaders when governmental contracting officials, seeking to fulfill twenty-first-century requirements, have been unable to address stakeholder needs in a timely manner or well as a result of being compelled to use straight-jacketed nineteenth-century methods and procedures formulated when the environment was simpler and less dynamic. As one respected authority noted in a late twentieth-century critique of the "system" that regulates federal government contracting: "When we design organizations based on rules, we guard against disaster, but [we do so] at the cost of stifling excellence" (Kelman, 1990). Compliance with policy is essential, but strategically minded public contracting officials (as well as elected officials and senior administrators) have a professional obligation to seek changes in policy that can optimize, as well as possible, the values of both process integrity and maximum practicable support for the mission, vision, and goals of the public enterprise.

The undesirable consequences of compliance-based, very comprehensive, and detailed legal frameworks for public contracting have included delays in administrative offices, line departments, and end-users (hereafter, "clients") obtaining needed goods and services well, cost-effectively, and in a timely manner. Several factors in addition to those previously mentioned have exacerbated the effects of the legal framework, including:

- The inability or unwillingness of public contracting officials to work with their clients to properly plan, form, and administer contracts or to seek policy changes within the legal framework that would improve the support they can provide for client goals.
- Unwillingness by some clients to work with contracting staff to ensure the timeliness and cost-effective fulfillment of their needs, including for example, by not involving the contracting staff early in the planning phase for a contract for a complex requirement. Just as bad if not worse, some client departments have been known to send requisitions for the procurement of a complex requirement to the contracting office at the last moment and then throw the contracting office under the bus when an elected official or senior administrator inquired about the status of the requisition by responding that the requisition is "in the contracting office."

- Bidders exploiting loopholes in the legal framework by engaging in such unethical practices as submitting unrealistically low bids with the intent of making up the difference (and more) through contractor-generated change orders planned prior to the submission of their bids.
- Contracting officials making it easy for bidders to exploit loopholes in the legal framework when the contracting officials are not as diligent in performing their duties and responsibilities as well as they should. An example is when a contracting official—as a result of being unwilling or unable (for a variety of reasons, some of which could be legitimate)[23] fails to perform such basic but essential tasks as assuring that specifications or scopes of work are competitive before a solicitation is issued, questioning why a bid is much lower than one might reasonably expect, or assuring through adequate vetting that a bidder is qualified to be awarded a contract, much less, perform a contract.
- A tendency by some governmental contracting officials—conditioned by legal requirements for equitable treatment of all parties, transparency, and due process, by pressure from above to "just get it done," and by the very real potential for protests, litigation, and political intervention—to opt to "take the easy way out" by not taking reasonable risks that could result in achieving the best deal for their clients and serving the best interests of all stakeholders (Kelman in Salamon, 2002).[24] An example is when a public contracting official, knowing that he or she could get a better deal by awarding a contract on a total cost or best value basis opts instead to go with a traditional low-bid award, even when there are no compelling reasons (which there very possibly could be) for doing so.[25]
- A second tendency by at least some governmental contracting officials, related to their perception that serving as a gatekeeper is their primary role, is to restrict the discretion of their clients[26] and/or to communicate and otherwise interact poorly (or not at all) with individuals in offices and departments that are on the receiving end of what the contracting officers are doing or should be doing. In the worst cases, the relationships between contracting officials and individuals whose goals they should support can be accurately described as adversarial.
- Inefficiencies and ill-will created by frustrated client staff that intentionally circumvent legalistic bureaucratic contracting "systems" in public organizations to obtain the materiel, services, systems, and infrastructure they need to discharge their duties and responsibilities on a timely, cost-effective basis.[27]
- Delays in client needs being met resulting from "aggrieved" bidders and contractors being legally entitled to challenge contracting actions and decisions, regardless of the merit of their challenge, typically with no fear of retribution.[28]

Other factors that have hampered the ability of contracting to provide optimal support for the strategic goals of public sector organizations include:

- A seeming lack of awareness or recognition by elected officials and senior appointed managers of the value that contracting—if properly staffed, resourced, and authorized—could add to mission attainment;[29]
- Limited direct access—formal or informal—in many public sector organizations by top contracting officials to inner policy-making and decision-making circles, due to such positions typically being separated by one or more levels from the position of the chief executive officer;[30]
- Limited analysis of contracting data to drive continuous improvement and often unawareness by senior administrators that this data could be mined and analyzed to gain valuable strategic intelligence;
- Limited use of professional certification or even a minimum of a bachelor's degree as a standard for hiring and promoting contracting officials;
- Lower salaries paid to contracting officials than to employees in other comparable lines of work, such as accounting and budgeting: these two functions arguably lacking in the same level of complexity as public contracting but enjoying a higher level of prestige than contracting;
- Meddling by elected officials and senior level appointed officials in the technical aspects of contracting;[31]
- Newer contracting officials often being pushed rapidly upward into positions that require more experience and expertise than they possess; and
- Legally mandated methods and procedures, such as those required when contracting for information technology, which are out of date and ineffectual.

Policymakers added to the challenges public sector contracting officials face when, during the 1930s, they began the practice of using governmental contracting as a vehicle for implementing a variety of socioeconomic policies unrelated to meeting needs of agencies and programs for materiel, systems, services, and infrastructure (Page, 1980). Through statutes, executive orders, codes, ordinances, and regulations, policymakers began to require their own procurement programs to conform to various "non-needs-related"[32] policies in the planning, formation, and administration of contracts and those procurement programs. At the same time, they also began to require the recipients of the contracts they award to comply with policy mandates, which, depending on the level of government at which the public contracting program operates, may include any combination of federal, state, and local government contracts.

Among the non-needs-related policies with which federal agencies and recipients of federal grants and contracts must comply are policies designed to achieve socioeconomic objectives. Examples of such policies include those related to:

- Non-discrimination;
- Equal employment opportunity;

- Working conditions;
- Employee rights;
- Payment of workers;
- Hiring of illegal labor;
- Environmental protection; and
- Required or preferred use of certain classes of businesses, such as minority-owned, female-owned, disabled-owned businesses, veteran-owned businesses, and service-disabled-owned businesses, as contractors, consultants, sub-contractors, sub-consultants, and suppliers.

A "Matrix of [Federal] Socioeconomic Programs and Their Applicability—Current through FAC 01–12" can be viewed at www.acquisition.gov. Policymakers at the state and local levels also require their own contract programs and the recipients of contracts and contracts within their political jurisdictions to comply with many of the same types of non-needs-related policies as the federal government. In addition, state and local policymakers also require the contracting programs of their jurisdictions and the recipients of contracts and grants from their jurisdictions to comply with non-needs-related socioeconomic requirements included as conditions of contracts or contracts awarded to them. Examples of policies that a local government procurement program is required to enforce can be viewed at http://www.nashville.gov/Finance/Procurement/Purchasing/Standard-PO-terms-and-Conditions.aspx.

While it is clearly the prerogative of policymakers to seek to effect non-needs-related public policy through contracting, this practice can impact the management of public organizations in various ways, including:

- Placing an additional administrative burden on contracting offices that already may be stretched to their capacity, thereby further impacting their abilities to meet client needs for materiel and services responsively and cost-effectively;
- Further reducing any available time contracting officials might have to engage in research and other activities that could provide strategic support for client and enterprise goals;
- Reducing competition and thereby increasing the prices paid for materiel, services, systems, and infrastructure;
- Potentially degrading the quality of material, services, systems, or infrastructure purchased.

A controversial, high-profile, but ultimately unsuccessful attempt by policymakers at the national level to use the contracting function to enforce non-needs-related public policy was made law by Section 511 of the Tax Increase Prevention and Reconciliation Act of 2005 (P.L. 109–222). Section 511, entitled "Imposition of Withholding on Certain Payments Made by Government Entities," required:

3% withholding on payments for goods and services to contractors made by all branches of the federal government and its agencies and all units of state and local governments, including counties and parishes. Local governments with less than $100 million of annual expenditures were excluded from the withholding requirement. The section also imposed information reporting requirements on payments that [were] subject to withholding. (Bickley, 2011)

As noted in a Congressional Research Service (CRS) report published in late 2011:

Substantial opposition developed to this withholding provision. Critics argued that the public and private compliance costs were unacceptable, existing IRS enforcement tools were adequate, and privacy would be reduced. The American Recovery and Reinvestment Act of 2009 (P.L. 111–5) delayed the implementation of the withholding provision until January 1, 2012. On May 5, 2011, the IRS issued regulations that further delayed the implementation of the withholding provision until January 1, 2013. (Bickley, 2011)

Ultimately, the 3 percent withholding provisions were repealed when "President Obama signed H.R. 674 (P.L. 112–56), *3% Withholding Repeal and Job Creation Act of 2011*" (Bickley, 2011).

Policymakers in many jurisdictions also require governmental contracting departments and officials to give advantages in stipulated situations to:

- Bidders who fall into specified demographic categories, such as minority business owners, female business owners, disabled business owners, veteran business owners, and disabled veteran business owners.
- Bidders that are located within specified jurisdictional areas, such as the United States (the Buy America policy), the particular state of which the policy makers are officials (in-state vendor preferences), and the particular local government whose citizens are served by such policy makers (local vendor preferences).

Finally, an additional strand of complexity (and perhaps the most obvious one) is that public procurement is a "business activity [that must be] conducted in a political environment" (Page, 1980, p.7). This reality presents at least a couple of challenges. Contracting officials clearly should and must provide support for the legitimate strategic goals of public enterprises, no matter whether they personally agree with the political principles those goals embody. On the other hand, they must be careful not to be sucked into participating in or tolerating illegal or unethical contracting actions through which elected or other officials might seek private gain or improper advantage for themselves or others.

There are some ways in which politics can affect public contracting decisions at the national level over which public contracting officials have very little control. One of those ways is the manner in which Congress frequently distributes the supply chains for major weapons across the nation, posing major challenges for economy, efficiency, and effectiveness, but shielding the particular program from cancellation. Another is the ability of large corporations to influence the authorization and funding of major weapons and other programs, especially in the wake of the Supreme Court's decision in *Citizens United vs. FEC* (taftlaw.com, 2012).

Professor Steven Kelman has observed that corruption in governmental contracting in the United States has, with a few exceptions at the local level, "basically disappeared from the agenda." However, as Kelman also has noted, "interest group politics remains a potent source of pressure shaping how governmental contracting in the U.S. is used." According to this former head of the Office of Federal Procurement Policy:

> Among those with stakes in the outcomes, trade associations representing governmental contractors, unions representing governmental employees, and, often, organizations representing values or interests that could be represented through governmental contracting are well organized. (Kelman in Salamon, 2000)[33]

THE POTENTIAL FOR PUBLIC CONTRACTING TO BECOME A STRATEGIC TOOL

Academic experts, consultants, and leading-edge public contracting professionals have begun to encourage public contracting officials in the twenty-first century to transition from "bidding and bashing" to a more relationship-based approach that is focused on "the goals of what the acquisition is trying to accomplish" rather than only on buying what departments, clients, and end-users tell them they need. (Lawther & Martin, 2004). Put another way, these parties are calling on governmental contracting officials to get themselves and their programs more integrated into the strategic management of public organizations—to become advisors, partners, and contributors inside the leadership team—to gain the "voice" and impact many governmental contracting officials and programs do not currently have.

In a white paper published online for organizational leaders in the public and private sector in New Zealand, a global consulting firm noted:

It is our point of view that [a] procurement function should:

1. Have a detailed spend map across your entire organization, updated quarterly.
2. Be a driver of sustainable savings (when, where, why, and how) across the organization.
3. Be engaged with the wider organization to understand how procurement can reduce costs across the value chain.

4. Ensure that value is realized through contract management and supplier relationship management frameworks, which are operationalized.
5. Be delivering procurement within an operating model that connects commercial and technical capability to drive optimal client outcomes. (Ernst & Young, 2014)

Writing in an article published in the December/January 2015 issue of *GOVERNMENT PROCUREMENT* magazine, Mike Richart, the deputy secretary for procurement for the commonwealth of Pennsylvania explains what the headline of the article described as the "five fields key to becoming a strategic [public contracting] agency." Those five key fields, which the author said kept coming up in his discussions with "several state and city [chief contracting officers] and consultants," are:

- Position
- Planning
- Processes
- People
- Technology. (Richart, 2014 December 2)

POSITION

With regard to the first key field, Richart, while recognizing that most public sector contracting officials do not report directly to the chief executive officer, asserted that the "place of procurement is critical" because "an executive-led position coupled with a center-led structure[34] is a significant tool for the enterprise." The author gave several reasons to support his assertion, including the importance of having:

- The authority to manage the "spend" of the enterprise for everything that must be acquired through contracts (i.e., to determine and execute the strategies for procuring all needed materiel, services, systems, and infrastructure);
- The access to provide "essential input into legislation that affects [contracting]";
- "Appropriate authority to independently develop and implement policy";
- The "opportunity to have a voice in discussions at the beginning," which he describes as the most critical point," because that is "when the procurement team can add value" (Richart, 2014).

Following up on the last point, the author added:

> When involved early, an effective procurement team can help reduc[e] cycle times, ensure appropriate [contracting] vehicles (RFP, IFB, cooperative contracts) are used, and because of its knowledge of the marketplace, identify and develop a supply base and provide ideas on reducing costs. (Richart, 2014)

PLANNING

In his discussion of what he describes as the second key field, Mr. Richart observes that if the Chief Contracting Officer is a member of the senior leadership team, he or she has the ability to provide direct, unfiltered input on the front end of the development of the organization's enterprise strategic plan. The strategic planning process, he states, is one of those critical conversations referred to in the previous point about position on the organization chart. The author offers NIGP's Public Procurement Practice for Strategic Procurement Planning as a useful starting point. That practice can viewed at http://principlesandpractices.org/wp-content/uploads/2013/04/StrategicProcurementPlanning.pdf.

PROCESSES

With regard to what he asserts is the third key field, Richart describes a "Vision Map" developed by NIGP and solution provider SciQuest: a "valuable [provider] of information about transforming a [public organization's contracting program] from tactical to strategic. He tells how one of the "tenets" of this vision map "addresses processes to help a [public organization's procurement program] evolve from a tactical 'processing center' to a 'service center,' with the goal of the [contracting] team to ultimately become consultants and advisers rather than 'worker bees.'" The author continues by pointing out that:

> This type of transformation is foundational to becoming strategic, but to do this, the organization's processes, including business processes, policies and procedures, business tools and technology must be evaluated, changed if necessary, and benchmarked to manage ongoing performance.[35]

PEOPLE

Pennsylvania's chief procurement officer leads off the discussion of his fourth "key field" by noting: "People are an organization's best assets." He continues by saying:

> Knowledgeable, well-trained resources are the lifeblood of any organization, and they are essential to a strategic transformation. To that end training and professional development must be key components of the transformation plan in order to achieve and maintain an efficient and effective workforce.

"Skill assessment," the author points out, "is a vital first step." Weaknesses, he notes, can best be addressed "through a structured training and professional development program."

Unlike most public procurement officials in years past, today's public procurement officials must possess a wide variety of competencies, including knowledge, skills, and abilities related to strategic management, network management, and communicating and working well with people within and beyond their entities.

Technology

In his discussion of his fifth and final "key field," Richart points out that "[t]hrough using the right tools, governmental procurement organizations have made significant advances in reducing or eliminating tactical processes through automation, increased transparency and bidding efficiencies for suppliers." He describes the valuable role that electronic procurement systems and spend analysis[36] have played in transforming state government procurement organizations from tactical to strategic roles.

The Pennsylvania procurement chief reminds the reader in the last sentence of his article that "no [procurement program] can achieve the [status of a recognized supporter of enterprise mission] without an appropriate position in the enterprise." This chapter continues with a discussion of other keys to contracting obtaining "an appropriate position in the enterprise."

The Commissioner of General Services for the State of Georgia had explained in an earlier magazine article why and how "Georgia's efforts to transform how government manages its supply and demand chain reveal the need for new procurement processes, technologies and skills." The author pointed out that, in order for public organizations to transform their contracting programs from tactical to strategic functions, the people involved in contracting must have:

- Strategic sourcing expertise
- Negotiation expertise
- Project management skills
- Change management experience.

He added: "these are only some of the many new skills that will increasingly be seen as crucial attributes in government's efforts to change its approach to procurement" (Douglas, 2009, p.32).

KEY POINTS

- Convince elected officials and senior administrators of the benefits of strategic contracting for public organizations;
- Persuading the senior administrator that implementing and sustaining a strategic contracting program requires that the chief contracting officer report directly to her/his position;
- Developing, adopting, and implementing a strategic plan for the contracting program[37] that aligns with the mission, vision, and goals of the organization as a whole

and the individual missions, visions, and goals of the departments and programs within the organization;
- Developing and securing the adoption of a budget for the contracting program that will provide all the necessary ingredients for success;[38]
- Creating an appropriate organizational structure that will support the success of the program;
- Designing, installing, and using processes that will support contracting program goals;[39]
- Formulating standards for employment that will assure a contracting workforce whose members possess the demonstrated willingness and ability to perform at the required level of excellence;[40]
- In the spirit of management guru Jim Collins, "getting the wrong people off the bus" [41] and putting the "right people are in the right seats on the bus, doing the right things" (Collins);
- Developing learning, performance, and retention plans for each participant to-be in the strategic contracting program;[42]
- Incorporating the necessary competency requirements into those learning and performance plans, including requirements for knowledge, skills, and abilities related to strategic management, network management, and communicating and working well with people inside and external to the public entity;
- Implementing and, as necessary, adjusting those learning, performance, and retention plans;
- Doing everything reasonable and practicable to retain top-performing staff;
- Recognizing that it will sometimes be necessary to replace top-performing staff as well as staff that do not perform at the required level;
- Installing enabling mechanisms and incentives for participants in contracting programs, including contractors, to exceed the minimally expected and required standards of excellence;
- Using technology and analytics to identify and exploit opportunities to improve processes, create efficiencies, drive down costs, and stretch the buying power of available dollars;
- Adopting and adapting best practices from other organizations;
- Continuously monitoring and improving the strategic contracting program.

NOTES

1. Procurement practitioner and adjunct instructor of procurement Darin Matthews noted in a journal article published a decade ago (2005) that several barriers stood in the way of the contracting function and contracting officials being viewed as significant to the management of governmental organizations. The three barriers Matthews cited were the lack of discretion public contracting officials are able to exercise (and therefore demonstrate their competency) due to having to operate within

an extraordinarily comprehensive and detailed legal framework, continuing ethical breaches in governmental contracting (but not all committed by governmental contracting officials) that cast this area of activity (and those involved in it) in a negative public light, and the absence, with few exceptions, of courses and degree programs in public sector contracting at the university level. Matthews questioned whether public sector contracting officials were able to take on the responsibility of leading and implement strategic contracting. The National Association of State Procurement Officials and the National Association of Chief Administrators, in a more recently published white paper for state chief administrators (NASPO and NASCO, 2005), note that the large and steady number of retirements of Baby Boomers underscores the need for more offerings in governmental procurement and contract management at the college and university level.

2. The multiple contracting failures associated with the federal government's response to the Hurricane Katrina catastrophe called an enormous amount of unwanted attention to defects in federal government contract management and program management. Numerous U.S. General Accountability Office (GAO) reports address those failures. Contracting by state and local governments during Hurricane Katrina was not without its issues either. See, for example, Atkinson and Sapat (2012). Moreover, recurring instances of corruption at all three levels of government continue to draw attention to public sector contracting in an unwanted way.

3. As Professor Steven Kelman of Harvard University has noted about contracting officials at the federal level, "In government, the source of unique knowledge and expertise of contracting officers is the regulations. [Contracting officials] are evaluated by how few regulatory violations they allow or how few 'waves' the procurement causes. Because exercise of discretion generates the congressional investigations and media stories, contracting officials tend to be safe rather than sorry. Given their lack of program responsibility for what is procured, [contracting officials have little to compensate them for taking risks" (Kelman, 1990, 26).

4. "Meaningful involvement" of contracting and contracting officials in the management of municipal governments, one type of public organization, is discussed in Schiele (2005).

5. Although the percentage of funds spent by governmental organizations through contracts for materiel, services, systems, and infrastructure, the generally agreed percentage of total budget contract expenditures comprise is in the 25 to 35 percent range. In some public organizations, the percentage total budget is lower; in others, it is higher.

6. "Controllability," as used in this context, refers to the ability to save money or avoid costs. The common informal budgeting rule in many public sector organizations of "spend it or lose it" militates against any money truly being saved by an organization obtaining the best possible contract pricing. It would be comforting to taxpayers to believe that money saved in one area is diverted to another area of need, but whether is true is not proven.

7. Although this list appears in a book about contracting for services in the context of blended or networked government, it is applicable to contracting by public sector organizations for any requirement: materiel, services, systems or infrastructure.

8. There can also be internal pressures, sometimes coupled with external interests, to maintain the traditional status and roles of contracting in public organizations. For example, a client of the contracting function that reports directly to the senior administrator may prefer to maintain the informal control it has (the legal authority of the contracting agent to award contracts and resolve contracting issues notwithstanding) over contracting decisions and the accompanying flexibility and lessened accountability. An individual contractor or industry that benefits from the informal control and flexibility may be very supportive of that high-level client's preference.

9. Cohen and Eimicke observe that there are many "obstacles that public managers must overcome to be better contract managers" (122), noting that "the new era of privatization requires a substantial increase in the sophistication and managerial skills of government managers" (123). In an article in a magazine published for North American public works directors by their professional

association, Professor Cliff McCue (2013, August 26) asks how public contracting officials themselves view their role in the present era. He concludes: "Businesslike utilitarians and resigned custodians are the two most commonly assumed roles."

10. "Total costs" include administrative, life cycle, and opportunity costs. Persuading policymakers to spend more money on the front end to achieve the best long-term deal for a public organization can be a tough sell when the anticipated "life" of what is being purchased exceeds an elected official's expected tenure in her/his current office.

11. There are plenty of opportunities in most public organizations to eliminate waste and generate revenue through improved contracting. However, one must note that not all acts of waste are unintentional or unprotected. Elected officials are fond of saying that governments should be run like businesses, but their decisions and actions are not always consistent with their words.

12. Transaction processors are the staff members of client departments and programs who interface directly with contracting staff on behalf of those departments and programs and the managers and end-users within them. Staff members who perform in the role of transaction processors typically will not have those two words in their official or unofficial job title. They may be for example, fiscal officers or administrative service officers. "Transactions processors" is a position title the author first encountered while working in the corporate procurement unit at the World Bank.

13. Due to the typical placement of the contracting unit on the organizational chart in governmental organizations, some clients appear to operate under the assumption that the contracting department (or whatever it might be called in particular entity), regardless of its workload and capacity, should drop everything to meet their needs immediately, even when the item to be procured is complex, the client had plenty of opportunities to plan and schedule the contracting action with the contracting department, the contracting unit is seeing the specifications or scope of work for the first time, and the "need by" date is close at hand.

14. Developing an effective working relationship requires engaging in "rich" communication and interaction—ideally, through face-to-face meetings, or if that is not practicable, through communication through Skype or other similar technologies. The number and dispersion of staff in large, complex organizations, and an increasing reliance on contractor personnel as team members, can pose obvious challenges to building effective working relationships.

15. In an article about the response of state and local governments to the effects of Hurricane Katrina, the authors noted the role of culture in governmental contracting. See Atkinson and Sapat (2012).

16. The author's list adds to the excellent list developed by two academic experts in an article printed in 2009. The two academic experts noted that "three dimensions that are critical to an appropriate understanding of public [contracting's ability to contribute strategically to the achievement of a public organization's mission]." The three dimensions they listed were "authority for action"; "the right organizational matrix to deliver what is wanted and needed"; and [understanding] exactly what is to be done, and what specific actions are to be taken" (Prier and McCue, 362). A recent KPMG report noted: "An increased focus on developing 'soft' procurement skills and relationships with business customers would allow Procurement to move up the value chain" (KPMG, 2012, 42).

17. The Defense Acquisition University defines "Acquisition" with a big "A" as "The conceptualization, initiation, design, development, test, contracting, production, deployment, logistics support (LS), modification, and disposal of weapons and other systems, supplies, or services (including construction) to satisfy DoD needs, intended for use in, or in support of, military missions" (Hagan, 2009 November, B-1).

18. See, for example, Vernon J. Edwards, "FAR Knowledge: The Key to Creativity and Inspiration—A Counterpoint to Mr. Stan Soloway's Article, 'Rethinking the Workforce Dilemma,'" *Contract Management*, February 2015, 21–27. Mr. Edwards states in his article that "Contrary to popular belief, the FAR is not all that prescriptive or descriptive."

19. As is pointed out in the section "Brief Overview and History of Procurement in Maryland" in the *Review of Maryland's Procurement Policies and Structures* published by that state's Department of Legislative Services, Office of Policy Analysis, in November 2014, "[The State of Maryland's] procurement law is codified as Division II of the State Finance and Procurement article of the Maryland Annotated Code. It traces its roots, in part, to the resignation of Vice President and former Maryland Governor Spiro T. Agnew, which was prompted by the revelation that, while Governor, he had taken kickbacks and bribes from State contractors. However, it was not until the enactment of Chapter 775 of 1980 that the State adopted a version of the American Bar Association's Model Procurement Code as Maryland's comprehensive procurement statute."

20. The strong involvement of the American Bar Association and numerous professional and industry association representing contractors to public sector organizations in the funding, development, and promotion for adoption of the MPC is indicative of a reality that cannot be overlooked. The professional associations representing the public sector contracting community—including NIGP, NASPO, and NCMA—were invited by the ABA to participate and did participate actively in the drafting process, but they did not serve in any leadership roles. Following the release of the original MPC document in 1979, both NIGP and NASPO went on record as endorsing the MPC, but noted that their endorsement did not include agreement with the special provisions in the model code that granted waivers from standard competition requirements in the selection of construction-related services and "professional" services.

21. This guide was published by the American Bar Association Section of Public Contract Law in 2011.

22. Public contracting in what is now the United States can be traced to the outsourcing of printing by the early settlements and colonies. Although the contracting practices employed to supply the Continental Army were known to have been corrupt, contracting by public organizations in the early days of the nation did not draw any significant attention from policymakers until the latter part of the nineteenth century, when President Abraham Lincoln, frustrated by the shoddy goods that were being supplied to Union soldiers, put in place laws at the national level that became the foundation of public contracting as we now know it. These early laws required competitive bidding and quality assurance among other things. Over the next few decades, state and local governments, whose procurement processes also were riddled by corruption, enacted laws requiring competitive bidding and often very burdensome controls for the purchasing of goods and services for public purposes. The central intent of these laws was to promote integrity in public contracting, even if integrity was ensured at the cost of best value or responsiveness to end-user requirements (Page, 1980, 2–7).

23. Many public sector contracting departments are not staffed or equipped with the technology they need to fulfill the needs of their clients responsively, efficiently, or economically. As has been alluded to previously, a department or program that provides services visible to the public and valued by the public is more likely to secure funding when resources are scarce than a department or program, such as contracting, that operates out of sight.

24. Sadly, politicians often succeed in exercising influence on public sector contracting decisions and actions (see, for example, Goldman et al., 2013).

25. The potential for contracting officials to provide maximum practicable support for a public enterprise's goals frequently gets blocked in the milieu of hierarchical status, professional biases, and internal and external politics, especially when public sector contracting officials opt to take a conservative path in order to avoid the grief they might incur by taking more risky actions to secure the best deal.

26. As Steven Kelman has commented about federal contracting officers, "While there are exceptions, in general contracting officers often try to reduce the exercise of discretion by the technical or program people, partly through their role as guardians of the regulatory process. As the ones who almost always know the regulations better than the technical or program people, they advise these

others about how to proceed.... They insist on reviewing and signing documents—although their ability to spot, for example, restrictive specifications is limited by their deficiencies in the knowledge of computers" (Kelman, 1990, 25). Desires to avoid protests and litigation further contribute to federal contracting officials tendencies to want to avoid risks, regardless of the impact of such behavior on organizational goals.

27. As one of the author's mentors told the author many years ago, when the author was the director of procurement for a large local government, "If you don't figure out a legal way for a client to get what it needs when it needs it, the client will figure out her or his own way, and that way may or may not be legal or ethical."

28. It is no secret that bidders and proposers on governmental contracts, possibly acting with the full intent to game the system, sometimes file protests for seemingly no other reason than to deny or delay awards to competitors or to gain another opportunity to win the contract.

29. Whatever the reason(s), contracting offices and officials typically are not positioned appropriately on the organizational chart, resourced, allowed, enabled, or invited to contribute directly to organizational success—even when they are willing, able, and eager to do so (Page, 1980, 1–2 and Kelman in Salamon, 2000, 282). One possible (and simple and obvious) explanation is that senior administrators in public organizations believe that contracting is a compliance-based, transactional set of activities of no strategic consequence, unless someone in the contracting department makes a serious error of commission or omission in the performance of her or his duties and responsibilities. Related to that possible explanation is the commonly-held perception that contracting is at best an area of technical specialization in which pretty much anyone can perform adequately with sufficient training, regardless of their educational or other credentials. The viewpoints associated with both of these possible explanations are invalid.

30. The separation of the top contracting officer's position by one or more levels on the organization chart from the c-suite can stifle and filter the flow of information, intelligence, insights, and institutional knowledge that could be used to improve the management of the organization. Placement of the top contracting officer under the chief financial officer, in particular, can exacerbate the stifling and filtering effects because finance officials tend to highly value process and control and to view contracting as a transactional and compliance activity.

31. Justice often prevails when this happens, as it did in the case of former New Orleans mayor Ray Nagin. See, for example, the television news story at http://www.wwltv.com/story/news/local/nagin-trial/2014/09/03/14561762/.

32. "Non-needs-related" public policies are those policies not related to the functional, design, output, or outcome related need of management, supervisors, staff and service deliverers in a public organization for materiel, services, systems, and infrastructure.

33. See also (Goldman et al., 2013).

34. As defined by a senior-level private sector contracting official, "Center-led procurement (CLP) is a procurement model that suits the needs of the business unit and the special characteristics of specific goods and services categories. CLP applies different purchasing models including centralized shared-service, decentralized, and hybrid buying, depending on what is being bought, who needs it, and where it will be used.... Buying is executed where and how it makes the most sense, while the [central contracting unit] contributes structure, expertise, and measurement to the process" (Stephens, 2005, 1).

35. Professor Rene Rendon of the Naval Postgraduate School has noted that "[r]ecent studies have shown that organizations with established and mature contract management processes are able to generate millions of dollars in additional savings and have a distinct competitive advantage over their competitors." Rendon points out that "[l]eading organizations conduct an assessment of their contract management process maturity through the use of the Contract Management Maturity Model (CMMM)." He cites several advantages of conducting a maturity model assessment,

including insights into "which contract management key process areas need to be improved" and which programs require the most attention and "a roadmap of additional needed training and education for improving the organization's contract management process capability. "The CMMM© consists of five levels of maturity ranging from an ad hoc level (Level 1), to a basic, disciplined process capability (Level 2), to a fully established and institutionalized processes capability (Level 3), to a level characterized by processes integrated with other corporate processes resulting in synergistic corporate benefits (Level 4), and finally, to a level in which processes focused on continuous improvement and adoption of lessons learned and best practices (Level 5)." For details, see (Rendon, 2007).

36. For an excellent discussion of the benefits of spend analyses for public contracting programs, see (Bevis, 2012).

37. The word "program" is used intentionally because successful strategic contracting in a public organization requires the buy-in, participation, coordination, and cooperation of staff throughout the organization, regardless of their program or department—not just the staff in the contracting department.

38. The required ingredients that must be funded include all that is necessary to intake, develop, and retain the "right" human assets and the required technology, technology services, and technology support.

39. Professor Rene Rendon of the Naval Postgraduate School has commented, "Both individual competence as well as organizational process capability are needed for success in DoD contracting. Perhaps a balanced emphasis on both individual competence and organizational process capability will help to alleviate the problems of policy without practice, corruption by incompetence, and acquisition malpractice in DoD contracting" (Rendon, 2013).

40. Standards for hiring and evaluating the performance of contracting officers in public organizations must include *required personal traits* (for example, demonstrated commitments to excellence and ethical conduct), required soft competencies (for example, strong interpersonal and communications skills), *required core competencies in public contracting*, and *a wide variety of other required competencies*, including analytical skills and expertise in such disciplines as financial management and information technology. There should also be requirements for professional certification through international certifying bodies such as the Universal Public Procurement Certification Council (UPPCC) and the National Contract Management Association (NCMA), especially for positions at the journeyman and master levels. The catastrophe experienced by the Obama administration when attempting to launch the healthcare.gov web portal for the Affordable Care Act and similar glitch-ridden attempted launches at the state level comes to mind immediately in the context of required competencies. See, for example, the blog "Obamacare Website Problems" at http://www.huffingtonpost.com/news/obamacare-website-problems/.

41. This could be accomplished with relative ease in a private, for-profit organization, but in a public sector organization replacing a "wrong" employee with the "right" employee can be very difficult and in some instances impossible. Unless the chief contracting officer has the full support of the administration to terminate or transfer an employee who is not capable of performing her or his role in a strategic contracting program, or unless the chief contracting officer has an unlimited budget, he or she may have to figure out a workaround or two. Even if the chief contracting officer is successful in moving the less than desirable employee out of the contracting program, he or she then will face the daunting challenge of hiring a person with the needed competencies through a civil service system that likely will make it difficult for that "right" person for the job to make the short list.

42. The right training is a must, but it is not enough, especially if does not create and improve the softer competencies and create and improve competencies in contracting and other important functional areas. Staff development plans must include requirements for education as well as training.

REFERENCES

Allair, L. & Leenders, M. (2005, March). How is procurement strategically important to an organization. *SUMMIT: Canada's Magazine on Public Sector Purchasing*, 10–11. Retrieved from http://www.summitconnects.com/Articles_Columns/PDF_Documents/200502_08.pdf.

Atkinson, C. L. & Sapat, A. K. (2012). After Katrina: Comparisons of post-disaster public procurement approaches and outcomes in the New Orleans area. *Journal of Public Procurement 12*(3), 356–385.

Bevis, M. (2012 November). Harnessing the power of money. Reprinted from *Public Management*. Retrieved from http://webapps.icma.org/pm/9410/public/cover.cfm?title=Harnessing+the+Power+of+Money&subtitle&ahttp://webapps.icma.org/pm/9410/public/cover.cfm.

Bickley, J. M. (2011). *Tax gap: Should the 3% withholding requirement on payments to contractors by government be repealed?* Congressional Research Service [Report] 7–5700, R41924, December 16, 2011. Retrieved from http://www.fas.org/sgp/crs/misc/R41924.pdf.

Bloom, H., & Nardone, J. M. (1984). Organizational level of the purchasing function. *Journal of Purchasing and Materials Management, 20*(2), 14–17.

CIPS and NIGP (2012). Public procurement practice: strategic procurement planning. Retrieved at http://principlesandpractices.org/wp-content/uploads/2013/04/StrategicProcurementPlanning.pdf.

Cohen, D. (2014, May 7). Obamacare website problems: The glitches of outsourcing IT services. *The Huffington Post*. Retrieved from http://www.huffingtonpost.com/news/obamacare-website-problems/.

Cohen, S. & Eimicke, W. (2008). *The responsible contract manager: Protecting the public interest in an outsourced world*. Washington, DC: Georgetown University Press.

Cooper, P. J. (2003). *Governing by contract: Challenges and opportunities for public managers*. Washington, DC: CQ Press.

Copeland, M. J. (2011). *Guide to state government: A 50 state primer on purchasing laws, processes, and procedures*. Chicago, IL: ABA Book Publishing.

Department of Justice (U.S.), Office of Public Affairs (2015, January 15). Defense contractor and its CEO plead guilty to corruption conspiracy involving "Scores of Navy Officials" [Press release]. Retrieved from http://www.justice.gov/opa/pr/defense-contractor-and-its-ceo-plead-guilty-corruption-conspiracy-involving-scores-navy.

Department of Legislative Services, Office of Policy Analysis, Annapolis, Maryland (2014 November). *Review of Maryland's Procurement Policies and Structures* [Government report]. Retrieved from http://mgaleg.maryland.gov/Pubs/BudgetFiscal/2014-Procurement-Structures-Policies-Practices.pdf.

Douglas, B. (2009). The rapidly changing nature of government procurement. [Reprint of an article originally published in *Supply and Demand Chain Executive*, March 2009]. Retrieved at http://www.sdcexec.com/article/10269459/the-rapidly-changing-nature-of-government-procurement.

Edwards, V. J. (February 2015). FAR knowledge: The key to creativity and inspiration—A counterpoint to Mr. Stan Soloway's article, "rethinking the workforce dilemma." *Contract Management*, 21–27.

Ernst & Young, Australia (2014). Five things: Getting the basics right in procurement [White paper]. Retrieved from http://www.ey.com/Publication/vwLUAssets/Five_things_-_Getting_the_basics_right_in_procurement/$FILE/Five_things_you_should_expect_from_procurement.pdf.

Goldman, E., Rocholl, J., & So J. (2013). Politically connected boards of directors and the allocation of procurement contracts. *Review of Finance, 17*(5), 1617–1633.

Gordon, S. B. (2012, November 9). Advancing and improving procurement and contract management in government. *PA Times*. Retrieved from http://patimes.org/improving-procurement-contract-management-government/.

Hagan, G. (2009 November). *Glossary of defense acquisition acronyms & terms* (13th ed.). Fort Belvoir, VA: Defense Acquisition University Press. Retrieved at http://www.dau.mil/pubscats/pubscats/13th_edition_glossary.pdf

KPMG International Cooperative (2012). *The power of procurement: A global survey of procurement functions* [Commercial report published electronically]. Retrieved from http://www.kpmg.com/US/en/IssuesAndInsights/ArticlesPublications/Documents/the-power-of-procurement-a-global-survey-of-procurement-functions.pdf.

Kelman, S. (1990). *Procurement and public management: The fear of discretion and the quality of government performance*. Washington, DC: The AEI Press.

Kelman, S. (2002). Contracting. In L. M. Salamon, & V. E Odus (Eds.). *The tools of government: A guide to the new governance* (pp. 282–318). New York, NY: Oxford University Press.

Lawther, W. L. C. & Lawrence L. M. (2004). Public procurement partnerships. In K.V. Thai, A. Araujo, R. Y. Carter, G. Callendar, D. Drabkin, R. Grimm, K. Jensen, R. E. Lloyd, C. McCue & J. Telgen (Eds.) *Challenges in public procurement: An international perspective* (Vol. 3), (pp. 159–178). Boca Raton, FL: PRAcademics Press.

Matthews, D. (2005). Strategic procurement in the public sector: A mask for financial and administrative policy. *Journal of Public Procurement, 5*(3), 388–399.

McCue, C. (2013, August 26). The ever-changing role of the procurement professional. *Government Procurement*. Retrieved from http://americancityandcounty.com/government-procurement/ever-changing-role-procurement-professional.

McKevitt, D., Davis, P., Woldring, R., Smith, K., Flynn, A.& McEvoy, E. (2012). An exploration of management competencies in public sector procurement. *Journal of Public Procurement, 12*(3), 333–355.

National Association of State Procurement Officers and National Association of Chief Administrators (2012). Working Together: Procurement as a Partner [White paper published electronically]. Retrieved from http://www.nasca.org/dnn/Portals/21/NASCA_NASPO_Working_Together-Procurement_As_Partners.pdf.

Page, Harry Robert (1980). *Public purchasing and materials management*. Lexington, MA: DC Heath and Company.

Prier, Eric, and McCue, C. P. (2009). The implications of a muddled definition of public procurement. *Journal of Public Procurement, 9*(3/4), 326–370.

Rendon, R. G. (2007). *Best practices in contract management*. Paper presented at the 92nd Annual International Supply Management Conference. Las Vegas, NV. Retrieved from http://www.ism.ws/files/Pubs/Proceedings/GGRendon.pdf.

Rendon, Rene (2013, January 22). The current state of defense contracting. *PA Times Online*. Retrieved from http://patimes.org/current-state-defense-contracting/.

Richart, M. (2014, December 2 2014). Moving from tactical to strategic: Five fields to becoming a strategic procurement agency. Reprinted from *GOVERNMENT PROCUREMENT*. Retrieved from http://americancityandcounty.com/purchasing-procurement/moving-tactical-strategic.

Salamon, L. M., ed. (2002). *The tools of government: A guide to the new governance*. New York, NY: Oxford University Press.

Salamon, L. M. and Odus, V. E. (2002). *The tools of government: A guide to the new governance*. New York, NY: Oxford University Press.

Schapper, P. R., Malta, J. V. & Gilbert, D. L. (2006). An analytical framework for the management and reform of public procurement, *Journal of Public Procurement, 6*(1/2), 1–26.

Schiele, J. J. (2005). Improving organizational effectiveness through meaningful involvement of municipal purchasing departments—case studies from Ontario Canada. *Journal of Public Procurement, 5*(2), 145–163.

Snider, K. F., and Rendon R. G. (2007). Public procurement: Public administration and public service perspectives. *Journal of Public Affairs Education, 18*(2), 327–348. Retrieved from http://www.naspaa.org/jpaemessenger/Article/VOL18-2/07_SniderRendon.pdf.

Stephens, D. (2005 February 3). Strategic view: Why center-led purchasing is gaining in purchasing popularity. Reprinted from *Purchasing*. Retrieved from http://www.nilior.com/pdfs/purchasing_mag_center_led_proc.pdf.

Taftlaw.com (2012). Contractor campaign contributions post-*Citizens United*. *Taft/news & views*. June 1, 2012. Retrieved from http://www.taftlaw.com/news/publications/detail/952-contractor-campaign-contributions-post-citizens-united.

11

Contracting in State and Local Governments

Donna T. Ginter

The amount of spending associated with state and local governments is astounding, and with volume comes complexity. No longer is the activity in procurement a clerical task, but instead one that is dynamic, complex and subject to constant change. While pinpointing exact figures for spending is difficult,[1] it was estimated that spending for state and local jurisdictions approached almost $1.5 trillion in 2007. Projecting a similar growth percentage from the 1997 of an estimate of $750 billion[2] forward to 2014, spending is estimated to be close to $2 trillion.

Procurement at the state and local level is also the focus of many reform efforts and the entry point for public policy implementation in the areas of economic development, sustainability as well as social responsibility. Buying activity occurring at this level can be defined as contracting initiated by states, counties (boroughs and parishes), cities (towns), school districts, public colleges and universities, as well as special taxing districts. Other specialized jurisdictions fall into this grouping, such as airport authorities, utilities and transit agencies.

It has often been said that the main difference between private sector and public sector acquisition is the environments in which they operate. Both are grounded in the establishment of an effective buyer-seller relationship and the mutuality of trust that enables the relationship to grow and prosper. Each utilizes similar processes quotes, formal solicitations, evaluation committees and award protocol; however, the consideration for special circumstances such as local preference, federal regulations and politics in general tend to make the public sector more challenging for the procurement professional.

Similarities can be drawn between that of federal procurement agencies to that of their state and local counterparts. Most often, the approach to acquisition in these subdivisions of government is decentralized, with the main focus of the procurement department being that of oversight and coordination across units. Cooperative procurements are widely utilized across the state and local spectrum, especially where small jurisdictions can gain from the economy of scale offered through a large consortium. In fact, most of the innovative approaches in procurement come from the state and local sector due to their ability to quickly change process and procedure without the need to coordinate across multiple agencies and divisions.

HISTORY OF STATE AND LOCAL PROCUREMENT

Public sector procurement began in municipalities with the first declaration of a central procurement function by the City of Chicago, Illinois in 1898, followed closely by Philadelphia, Pennsylvania in 1903.[3] This movement continued throughout the early 1900s and continues to this day as municipalities and special taxing districts continue to form throughout this country. States began to organize their procurement function in the early 1900s, with Oklahoma being the first to establish a board to centrally procure items for all state divisions and agencies,[4] and, as a result, centralization has become the standard that most public agencies follow when establishing procurement departments. Arguments have been made over time that centralization is not the best approach for governments to manage acquisition activities, in that it can prove to be inflexible and un-responsive to user's needs. What can be stated is that governments rarely have truly centralized or decentralized procurement functions. The hybrid structure is most often implemented— one that is mindful of the policies of the entity, but is designed to facilitate the needs of the institution through best value, efficiency of process and strong customer service. As state agencies gain autonomy, the relationship to and enforcement by the state procurement office becomes more and more difficult. In fact, in most states, higher education is treated as a separate entity to the state offices with its own procurement guidelines. Undoubtedly, the debate as to the virtue of centralized vs. decentralized procurement structures among practitioners and researchers will continue, as there is no one-size-fits-all right answer.

THE ABA 2000 MODEL PROCUREMENT CODE FOR STATE AND LOCAL GOVERNMENTS

As the procurement function matured over the course of time, the concept of a uniform approach to structure and process was espoused by the American Bar Association and further refined in their *2000 Model Procurement Code for State and Local Governments*.[5] Along with the standardized approach to procurement procedures, came a shift from process driven transactions to spend analysis and oversight by the procurement staff. The need to stretch tax dollars shifted award considerations from lowest price to best overall value for the entity, taking into account useful life, operating expenses and sustainability. The Model Procurement Code has been widely accepted as the reference for state and local agencies and if not fully incorporated to an entity's procurement policy, its structure and impact is easily identifiable in codes and manuals.

GOALS AND OBJECTIVES OF STATE AND LOCAL PROCUREMENTS

As in the private sector, the goal of public procurement is to get the best good or service through competition, at the best price and quality, in a timely manner, while mitigating risk to the entity and achieving the socio-economic goals set by law. The greatest difference between the two is that the money saved in the public sector is not measured in profit and then paid out in dividends to stockholders. Strategic and effective sourcing at the state and local level is measured in the ability to maximize the value of tax dollars—and thereby allow for the addition of new programs or expansion of existing programs while remaining constant in assessments. The true balancing act comes in the management of each of these competing areas so as not to trade one in favor of another. Most often, purchasing agents must compromise on quality to achieve a cost consideration, accept a later-than-desired delivery in exchange for a lower price, or, in the worst case, accept a great deal of risk in order to keep costs at a minimum. In the absence of competition, it is easy to identify that increased cost and risk fall to the buyer; however, quality remains constant. The introduction of socio-economic goals often results in increased costs; however, it is widely held that intrinsic benefits can be identified by spending dollars locally or with underutilized businesses. The main line of thought here is that by spending more with small business, you create more jobs and potential sources of supply, thereby potentially increasing competition.[6]

COMPETITION REQUIREMENTS

The very basic tenet of any procurement organization, whether private or public, is that competition should always be sought for goods and services. In the public sector, the perception is that everyone should have an opportunity to compete for tax dollars, and the taxpayer deserves to receive the best benefit possible from those expenditures. Competition also eliminates the appearance of impropriety through favoritism by infusing transparency and integrity into the procurement process. It must be noted that there are certain components of public governance that remain exempt from the need to compete when acquiring goods and services, but these are very limited in scope. Most often, these exemptions are related to the health, welfare, and safety of the public, contracts tied to other governmental agencies, expert witnesses, one of a kind artwork, etc. A review of any of the 50 states' enabling legislation on procurement will reveal a list of items that are exempt from competition, with the flow-down of those provisions found within the subdivisions of government within that state/commonwealth. In each case where an exemption exists, the chief procurement officer, whose sole judgment shall determine the allowance for the exception, must grant the exemption.

SMALL DOLLAR PROCUREMENTS

It is safe to say that, in all entities, there exists a threshold by which the value of the procurement beneath that price does not require competition. This threshold is known as the single-quote or micro purchase threshold. These low dollar non-compete thresholds vary by location and size of agency, and are often identified to be paid on procurement cards whenever possible.

BEST PRACTICES IN PUBLIC PROCUREMENT

Procurement Cards

In the early 2000s, the use of procurement cards by governments moved from best practice to current practice.[7] Card use continues to grow across the spectrum through greater adoption by entities as well as through innovative use resulting in revenue generation. Procurement cards can be defined as corporate credit cards that allow for goods and services to be procured outside of the traditional purchase order.

At the state and local levels of government, the procurement card account is paid centrally for all cards on a regularly scheduled basis, such as weekly or monthly. This differs from the federal government's approach to procurement cards, as federal cards are an extension of the government's credit to cardholders, but the responsibility for payment is borne by the cardholder from personal funds. The cardholder from the government then seeks reimbursement. The majority of card programs in place in the public sector include some form of rebate on spend, which varies by the speed in which payments are made. The faster the payment (i.e. 4–7 days vs. 30 days) from the date of the transaction, the higher the rebate paid to the entity.[8] Procurement cards are thought to be beneficial to governmental units for a variety of reasons:[9]

- Transactional cost savings—the level of effort to reconcile a procurement card charge vs. a traditional requisition to PO, invoice to payment translated to dollars is $90 for PO to $20 for a procurement card, or $70 per transaction;
- Simplification of the procurement process in cycle time and approval processes;
- As delegation of authority is facilitated by card use, manpower requirements are reduced in traditional Procurement and Accounts Payable roles;
- Cycle time is reduced by 68 percent as well as a corresponding 31 percent reduction in the number of suppliers paid by Accounts Payable;
- Data availability is increased for other purposes such as spend analysis and negotiation purposes; and
- Cash advances reduce the requirement for petty cash.

On average, the single purchase threshold, or the amount allowed to be charged on a card on one transaction is limited to $2,500 as a default within jurisdictions. This amount represents procurement delegation to end users for needed purchases. It also represents the threshold at which it has been determined that procurement staff has no "value-add" to the purchasing process. Value-add is defined as work that is performed on a given procurement that results in supplemental benefit or savings to the entity.

COOPERATIVES AND GROUP PURCHASING ORGANIZATIONS IN PUBLIC PROCUREMENT

Cooperative procurement is one of many best practices in public procurement. According to the NIGP Public Procurement Dictionary of Terms,[10] cooperative procurement (purchasing) or consortium is defined as:

1. The action taken when two or more entities combine their requirements to obtain advantages of volume purchase including administrative savings and other benefits.
2. A variety of arrangements whereby two or more public procurement units purchase form the same supplier or multiple suppliers using a single Invitation for Bids or Request for Proposals.
3. Cooperative procurement efforts may result in contracts that other entities may "piggyback." Piggybacking is when a large entity enters into an agreement and the terms and conditions are extended to another, often smaller entity by the supplier.

Group purchasing is best exemplified at the state level of government. State procurement organizations identify goods and services that are common to its agencies and political subdivisions, and the resulting contracts represent the best pricing available. These contracts are advantageous to small agencies because the volume buy that the state agreement represents far surpasses that of what an individual agency would spend on an annual basis. The National Association of State Procurement Officials (NASPO) firmly endorses the use of state agreements as cooperative agreements for the entire state's buying organizations. NASPO, however, does not endorse the use of any or all other types of cooperatives and this has been a point of contention between other professional organizations such as the American Association of State Colleges and Universities (AASCU) as well as the Association of School Business Officers (ASBO). States commonly require their agencies and subdivisions to procure commodities that are under state contracts or manufactured by state industries (Prisons and Blind as an example) without extensive review and request for exemption. Mandates such as these are often seen as conflicting with the true premise of free and open competition, especially when another cooperative offers the same good or service at a lower price.

NASPO endorses the use of cooperative purchasing by states; however that use should consider the following factors:

- Avoid circumvention of state rules through the use of cooperatives. Cooperatives that substantially follow the state's processes should be used, not ones that are far more relaxed.
- Pricing tied to volume is often lost when jurisdictions "piggy-back" or join cooperatives after the contract has been awarded. Cost-savings may be great for the

late-joining entity, but are lost to the agencies that were part of the original solicitation thus becoming a windfall for vendors.
- Beware of pricing traps—selecting a cooperative because it offers the vendor of choice does not necessarily mean that pricing will be preferential to that agency. Large cooperatives are comprised of many small entities that are disbursed across a geographical region. Increased costs may be imbedded to accommodate increased logistical considerations, whereas a state contract may be more preferential.
- Keep in mind that large cooperatives severely restrict the ability for small and disadvantaged businesses to participate in the solicitation. This mere fact may work against local goals for inclusion of these business classifications by the entity. Often, local governments are called upon to un-bundle large procurements in order to meet economic development and inclusion goals. Cooperatives, by their very justification for existence, work against allowing small businesses to participate.

The following list represents a sampling of cooperatives available for use by state and local governmental units:

- Educational & Institutional Cooperative Service, Inc. (E&I)
- Houston-Galveston Area Council Cooperative Purchasing Program (H-GAC)
- Midwest Multi-State Contracting Alliance for Pharmacy (MMCAP)
- National Intergovernmental Purchasing Alliance (National IPA)
- National Joint Powers Alliance (NJPA)
- U.S. Communities Government Purchasing Alliance (US Communities)
- U.S. General Services Administration (GSA)
- Western States Contracting Alliance (WSCA)
- Baltimore Regional Cooperative Purchasing Council (BRCPAC).

Expenditures in 2014 associated with use of the above contracts are estimated to be in the hundreds of billions,[11] which indicates their widespread use. Cooperatives are a very useful tool for procurement officials to ensure that they receive effective, best-value solutions for their constituency. Volume purchases, when aggregated, offer deep price breaks. For the lead agency hosting the contract, cooperatives also offer a revenue source to offset the cost of administration. Most often, there is an administrative fee paid by supplier under contract (usually a percentage or fraction thereof) for each dollar spent against the agreement. This can be a very beneficial offering to large agencies that manage the agreements as it can often offset the overall department's cost to the entity. The mere thought of Procurement as a revenue source is a paradigm shift for most acquisition professionals—the thought would be to return the excess in fees to reduce the price of the goods being purchased. To have rebates accrue for the benefit of one group and not all is often debated.

CONSIDERING THE ENVIRONMENT IN WHICH PUBLIC PROCUREMENT FUNCTIONS

Over the last quarter century or more, there has been a trend at the federal level to pass more and more activities on to the state and local jurisdictions, in some case with funding and others without. A focus on acquisition reform through the National Performance Review sought to cut the bureaucratic red tape in procurement with little success. The paperwork reduction act, while effective at its onset in reducing documentation requirements, was effectively overshadowed by increased socio-economic considerations when making federal awards. The flow-down of executive orders and federal regulations on pass-through funding imposes supplemental terms and requirements on to small and often understaffed local governments. While in most cases jurisdictions were happy to gain more autonomy over programs and to have an influx of operating revenue, the administrative burden of accounting for program operation came without funding, thus causing an overtaxed staff to be stretched even further.

Inclusion of public policy objectives within state and local procurement such as the Buy American Act, Fly America Act, and living wage, as well as efforts to include disadvantaged businesses, create a greater reliance on the acquisition efforts of the entity to bring about change.

There remains a strong sense of pride among Americans and with the introduction of foreign policy initiatives such as NAFTA and WTO-GPA international trade agreements. State and local governments find themselves conflicted. Historically, local tax dollars were spent within the confines of the borders of United States, only reaching out to other countries for high-tech solutions for rail, energy, or research equipment. The need to comply with federal requirements for trade adds another layer of consideration and effort, which may in some cases conflict with local codes and state statutes, illustrating the need for savvy purchasing agents to know the "color of the money," as well as any flow-down terms that come along with the funding.

Not only is the public procurement system affected by external environmental forces, it is affected also by competing internal influences. At any given time, the three branches of the legislative sector, departmental conflict, and/or funding constraints impact the process. Added to these influences are socio-economic considerations, market fluctuations, sustainability factors, as well as legal considerations and the ability to accomplish the buy of an item at the best price, best delivery, and best quality. Furthermore, the buy of an item can come in over budget, behind schedule, and modified to meet a requirement other than its original purpose.

POLITICAL CONSIDERATIONS IN STATE AND LOCAL PROCUREMENT

State and local governments have long set policies that include favorable clauses for disadvantaged businesses and local businesses, as well as other instruments to encourage economic development within their jurisdiction. In a 2011 survey of jurisdictions in Georgia, North Carolina and South Carolina, over 50 percent of the governmental units had some form of local preference laws in place.[12] The efforts, while well intentioned, come with great scrutiny from both sides of the issue. Strong defenders of spending dollars locally to build small business and improve the economy find solace in preference laws that allow these businesses to compete against larger, non-local businesses.

Those in favor of local preference programs cite the positives of such efforts as:

- Boost in economic activity for the locality through:
  - Employment increases
  - Tax revenue is increased.
- Local economy benefits by keeping the spend of tax dollars within the area.
- Local businesses are given a competitive advantage in the procurement process.
- When local knowledge is needed, preference easily eliminates the non-familiar our outside vendor.

The arguments against local preference include:

- Limitations on the tenets of procurement: fair and open competition.
- Effect on competition:
  - Creates inefficiencies (distortions) in the markets; not purchasing from most efficient source;
  - Discourages competition and reduces the pool of competing bidders;
  - May impeded creativity by providing a competitive advantage for a location versus a pure advantage for innovative solutions or lower cost goods.
- Effect on prices
  - Higher prices are paid to local companies when a preference is in place and all other considerations are equal—this increased cost is then passed on to the taxpayers.

In a position paper, the Virginia Association of Governmental Purchasing (VAGP) provides a good understanding of how preference laws are justified for local governments:[13]

> The intended goal of local procurement preferences is to achieve a socioeconomic goal for the locality. There are a variety of techniques that legislative bodies have enacted to establish local procurement preferences, ranging from percentage thresholds to an absolute requirement. The matter has been reviewed by state and federal courts, which have generally upheld the statutes if crafted in a manner that

relates to the state's interest. There is a body of economic research that suggests that local procurement preferences create a multiplier effect to the benefit of the local economy. However, local procurement preferences are not easily reconciled with the basic principles of public procurement of free and open competition.

Virginia is a Dillion Rule state. The Dillion Rule is used in interpreting state law when there is a question of whether or not a local government has certain authority. The Dillion Rule provides that municipalities only have those authorities that are expressly granted by statute, those necessarily or fairly implied from expressly granted authority, and those that are essential and indispensable. Virginia procurement practices are governed by the Virginia Public Procurement Act (VPPA). Section 2.2–4328 0f the VPPA expressly allows a local preference in the case of a tie bid.

Local preference procedures come in varied forms - they can be described as easily as "tie bids go to the local business," while in some jurisdictions the local business is offered the opportunity to match the price of the non-local low bidder. In some areas of the country, the preference for a local business reflects a willingness to pay up to 14 percent more for a good or service.[14] Opponents to any sort of preference program are especially prevalent where large municipalities can be found on bordering states. While preference towards local business would seem to be a good thing as described by the VAGP, companies that bid on contracts across state lines find that they have preferences used against them, when in fact a majority of their workforce comes from the very geographic location issuing the solicitation. Inverse preference can be found across most state's procurement policies. Here is the State of Nevada's approach to inverse preference:

NRS 333.336 INVERSE PREFERENCE IMPOSED ON CERTAIN BIDDERS RESIDENT OUTSIDE STATE OF NEVADA

For the purpose of awarding a contract pursuant to this chapter, if a person who submits a bid or proposal:

- Is a resident of a state other than the State of Nevada; and
- That other state, with respect to contracts awarded by that other state or agencies of that other state, applies to bidders or contractors who are residents of that state a preference which is not afforded to bidders or contractors who are residents of the State of Nevada, the person or entity responsible for awarding the contract pursuant to this chapter shall, insofar as is practicable, increase the person's bid or proposal by an amount that is substantially equivalent to the preference that the other state of which the person is a resident denies to bidders or contractors who are residents of the State of Nevada.

This practice has come to the attention of several large professional associations such as the NASPO and the Associated General Contractors of America (AGC), the nation's largest consortium of the construction industry. For NASPO, preference laws interfere with free trade, discourage open competition, and increase the cost of government. NASPO sees preference laws as complex, confusing to vendors, and fraught with increased costs to the administration of the State. In an effort to prohibit or limit the use of any preference in contracting, AGC has established a strong lobby in Washington to work towards ending any form of favoritism in an effort to focus on true competition in procurement. This effort to limit preference extends not only to local preferences, but to a variety of programs, that, if not effectively monitored, could lead to fraud waste and abuse.[15]

SUSTAINABILITY AT THE STATE AND LOCAL LEVEL OF PROCUREMENT

First, let's define sustainability. Encompassing far more than "green purchasing," sustainable procurement takes into consideration supplemental components of goods and services when making procurement decisions in an effort to reduce the environmental impact or "footprint" left behind after consumption. These considerations include:

- Raw materials needed for manufacture, packaging and delivery;
- Energy consumption and emissions resultant from the manufacturing process;
- Total cost of ownership to include supplies and materials needed to operate the good or provide the service; and
- Disposal impact.

Procurement must be cognizant of not only of sustainable products; they must also consider a supplier's sustainability practices as a whole. In addition to the above considerations, the following should be included as part of the overall supplier selection:

- Supplier's social practices such as safety, health and diversity; as well as
- Supplier's environmental practices/impact.

Fortunately for procurement professionals, there are third parties that certify products and conduct independent evaluations of suppliers to which procurement can turn to for assistance. Inclusion of certifications as well as requirements from groups such as the Environmental Protection Agency and Forestry Service Council, as well as the Department of Agriculture, can be advantageous in meeting agency goals.

Of all the discussion that surrounds sustainable procurement, perhaps the evaluation of life-cycle costs vs. initial costs is the most contentious.[16] Green products in most markets cost more than their virgin (non-recycled content) equivalents. When considering the full life-cycle cost of virgin over recycled, proponents for life-cycle evaluation believe that the production costs are only a mere fraction of the overall cost to society. When considering the true costs, use, maintenance, and disposal must be considered. For procurement, the evaluation of sustainable "buys" will require a more in-depth reveal of the hidden costs of the good or service, thus requiring more planning in the development of solicitation documents.

As state and local acquisitions move towards more of a policy implementation role through sustainability and local preference, procurement has moved from transactional to transformational as a facilitator for social reform. Politicians have identified that the procurement function can be utilized to affect efficient use of tax dollars in creating markets and to drive technology innovation.

THE ROLE OF STATES AND LOCAL GOVERNMENTS IN CREATING MARKETS

Similar to that of their federal counterparts, the tremendous purchasing power of state and local procurement can drive change and create markets for new product innovation. Promotion of new ideas and technology by state and locals is fed through:

- Investment in research and development; and
- By becoming early adopters through procurement of early market or prototype technology.

The federal government is a prime example of how this behavior can work. Vehicle use and production was well into high gear prior to the late 1950s. A few manufacturers, both domestically as well as internationally, offered seat belts as an option on new car purchases. At the same time, many groups such as the American Medical Association lobbied car manufacturers to add seat belts as one of several safety features and standards needed in automobile production. The newly built highway system afforded high-speed travel, resulting in an increase in vehicular fatalities. While all this sparked interest in automobile safety, the cost of design, testing, and production was prohibitive to manufacturing industry.

In the 1960s, he federal government took a firm stance on highway safety though establishing standards for safety in vehicles.[17] Soon thereafter, states required manufacturers within their borders to incorporate safety features. While many manufacturers offered seat belts as optional equipment or after-market items, the first automobile manufacturer to include seat belts as a standard offering was Studebaker in 1963. In 1966, the Highway Safety Act and National Traffic and Motor Vehicle Safety Act were passed, and the federal government's order for new vehicles specified standard equipment that included front and back seat belts in each car. This paved the way for consumer vehicles to come with seat belts as standard equipment. By 1974, three-point harnesses had become the norm for safety belts.

With regard to sustainability, state and local governments have a role to play in market creation for recycled products. Using office supplies as an example, in its acquisition plan, a consortium or group purchasing organization of several state and local governments can issue a solicitation that specifies a large need for 30 percent recycled content paper. This demand can drive pricing down through the creation of a market for such products. This, indeed, happened not only by state and locals, but also through a mandate that required that business be only transacted with the federal government on 30 percent recycled paper.

Now more than ever, it is important to understand all the aspects of the procurement process while recognizing the importance of the acquisition function in establishing environmental and sustainable policies and practices. Governmental leaders have been called upon to advance the sustainable agenda for this country, and they are counting on procurement professionals to exercise sound judgment in soliciting, evaluating, and implementing sustainable procurement practices for their jurisdictions.

PUBLIC INSTITUTIONS OF HIGHER EDUCATION

An interesting subject for study is that of public colleges and universities and their oversight by the central procurement office of the state. Depending on the state and its statutes, higher education may or may not be subject to the same procurement laws as the balance of the state subdivisions of government. Two large professional associations, the AASCU as well as the National Association of Education Procurement (NAEP), lobby for greater autonomy in higher education and, as such, have worked to secure exemptions from broad-reaching procurement mandates. In many states, such as Virginia, Georgia and Florida, The Board of Regents or Trustees have established a separate set of procurement rules for university systems.

In response to the call for greater autonomy, the NASPO offers an equal defense of central procurement authority for all state procurements.[18] While it is true that central procurement operations generate savings for all size agencies within a state, large institutions and systems such as those found in higher-ed may be large enough and specialized enough to warrant their own policies and procedures in an effort to streamline processes resulting in savings of time and money.[19] Adding to this thought is the fact that compliance with state procurement requirements often adds time and paperwork delays that would be avoided through autonomy.[20] While it may be true that public colleges and universities have complex research agendas and specialized requirements that cannot be found in other divisions state agencies, true independence as sought by these lobbies is inconsistent with the intent of a cooperative approach to procurement by a State.

Removing the volume of higher-ed from commonly purchased items may translate to increased prices for all participants. While no conclusive determination has been made as to the pros and cons of allowing a separate set of rules for higher education, the arguments posed by both side have merit. Reform in the higher-ed sector will continue, not because of its unique positioning, but because reform in procurement as a whole is much needed and on-going.

PROCUREMENT ETHICS IN STATE AND LOCAL GOVERNMENT

If you are a practicing professional in public procurement, there is a very good chance that, during the course of your career, be it a mere 6 months or even after 30 years, you have been exposed to a code of ethics that governs your procurement outlook and actions. Ethical violations can be found in all professions and procurement is not exempt from its newsworthy events. Public scrutiny is ever present when spending tax dollars. Procurement professionals must always be mindful of their fiduciary responsibility in the expenditure of public dollars along with the requirement to maintain the public trust. According to a 2014 survey by Gallup, Americans trust local government more that state government, continuing a trend that began in the late 1990s.[21] The reason for this difference can be tied to economic downturns and their effects on state budgets. When money is tight, spending is scrutinized at a higher level.

Governmental entities adhere to a state code or municipal code that governs the behavior of those acting as agents for the jurisdiction. Most often there is also a corresponding Supplier Code of Ethics that governs the relationship between the vendor community and the governmental body to which it contracts. No matter whether you are looking at the Government in the Sunshine Legislation from the State of Florida, The Universal Public Procurement Certification Council (UPPCC) (Appendix A) or the National Institute Governmental Procurement's Code of Ethics, (Appendix B) there are cornerstones of business principles that will appear in any sort of guide to the proper behavior of procurement professionals, that being loyalty, impartiality and honesty.[22] In acting on behalf of an agency, practitioners must:

- Believe in the work that they are doing and respect the trust that the entity has placed in them to act in its best interest;
- Any and all actions taken should be in a manner that would preclude any question of impropriety in order to preserve the public's trust and respect;
- Recognize that any action taken should not ever result in personal benefit to the individual;
- In cases where a conflict of interest, even if it is perceived and none exists, the procurement professional should recuse themselves from any further involvement in the procurement process.

Procurement certifications carry with them an adherence to a set of ethical standards. Across esteemed business certifications such as Certified Internal Auditor, Certified

Public Accountant, and Project Management Professional, the requirement for an individual to comply with an appropriate set of standards, along with behavioral indicators and competencies, gives the profession a great deal of credibility and validity.

Ethical behavior in public procurement can be influenced by a variety of factors; salesmanship,[23] competition, politics as well as regulation. In the cases of ethical violations found most often in procurement regardless of public or private sector, federal or state and local, the employee has received some sort of personal gain as a result of the discharge of their duties.[24]

PUBLIC PROCUREMENT AS A PROFESSION

No discussion on procurement would be complete without a compare and contrast of training and certification of the federal workforce vs. that of the state and local procurement workforce. If you become an CS1102 or contracting officer for the federal government, you must obtain a Federal Acquisition Certification in Contracting (FAC-C) at one of three levels, I, II or III.[25] Attainment of the FAC-C certification requires the successful completion of a curriculum of classes designed to ensure knowledge and specific competencies have been delivered to the acquisition workforce. The levels are progressive and more complex than the other, reflecting a more specialized set of skills in order to demonstrate knowledge of the acquisition requirements and process at each level. A federal contracting officer is not granted authority to contract on behalf of the government until which time they hold a warrant, and a warrant is not awarded until the FAC-C is achieved. Each agency has the ability to determine who receives the certification for their agency.

A few states, such as Florida, Virginia, Texas and Massachusetts, have created their own certifications for procurement professionals. The curriculum for each state varies and is grounded in the standards of procurement established by the Unified Public Procurement Certification Council[26] with supplemental training on state specific requirements and policy.

Procurement at the local level reflects a myriad of approaches to training and education of the workforce, as well as a paucity of certification requirements in order to bind the entity contractually.

For decades, both the NASPO and the National Institute for Governmental Procurement (NIGP) have worked to elevate the profession through collaborative efforts with similar associations such as the National Association of Counties (NACO), National Contract Management Association (NCMA), National League of Cities (NLC), National Conference of Mayors (NCM), International City/County Managers Association (ICMA), and others. Through enhanced educational offerings and investment in scholarly research and publications such as the *Journal of Public Procurement*, as well as other reference books, these organizations have sought to give the certifications held by public procurement professionals the same recognition and credence as that of the Certified Public Accountant, Certified Internal Auditor, and Project Management Professional. Each of the aforementioned certifications is grounded in an established body of knowledge with associated competencies and behavioral indicators. Further, a review of curricula at most institutions of higher education reflect offerings in accounting, auditing, and program management but nothing on public procurement.

SUMMARY

Procurement in the public sector is complex and requires a blend the understanding of a variety of disciplines such as law, economics, sociology, political science, and accounting. The successful procurement official will be able to understand and communicate effectively with a variety of groups and will be able to translate policy and procedure to effectuate the delivery of goods and services to their constituents. The greying of the workforce over the last 10 years and into the next decade will put an undue burden on entities to find, train, and hold on to an acquisition team that will move the jurisdiction forward. Competition will be strong for the available resources, and until which time the higher-ed sector recognizes procurement as a profession and not just a career, we will fail to have college graduates knowledgeable of the theories and practices of acquisition. State and local governments will need to rely on their own budgets for training, as the dedication of certification resources is scarce in comparison to the federal outlook for acquisition reform.

Procurement is no longer the clerical process of yesteryear. It has developed into an integrated science comprised of strategy and predictive analytics to identify what will be needed when and how it is best procured. It requires an educated, trained, and savvy professional that is able to translate requirements to action, combined with the ability to navigate the waters of bureaucracy, arriving at the end product of goods or services that meet the demands of the taxpaying public.

KEY POINTS

- Spending on state and local government contracts has grown significantly in recent years in terms of total dollars and the areas where contracting is used for service delivery, and represents a significant portion of public sector contract expenditures.
- State and local sector procurement is very rules-based (while these rules vary among different jurisdictions) and procedure-driven, often at the expense of innovation. Competition is the basis for award, with fairness and transparency being the basic tenants of the profession. In the private sector, however, decisions and management of the acquisition process is more relationship based with its suppliers thus working in concert to drive new products and efficiencies. Procurement

enjoys a more strategic role in the corporate sector, often sitting at the table with the CEO and his/her c-suite team. Because strategic sourcing plays such a key role in the manufacturing process and overall bottom-line of a company, procurement enjoys a more esteemed corporate position than that of their state and local governmental counterparts.

- There is little difference between the private and public sector with regard to their approach to procurement process. The environment that the public sector operates in requires much more transparency and consideration for fairness and equity in contracting, as everyone should have the opportunity to vie for business that is generated from tax dollars.
- Competition is the basis for all procurements. It is the vehicle that provides the taxpayer with assurance that the best value is attained in a contract for a good or service. Each governmental jurisdiction sets the limits for a variety of dollar thresholds that dictate what procurement process should be followed.
- Procurement cards facilitate low-dollar buys, allow for the quick purchase of items, and have lower transaction costs than the typical requisition to purchase order process. In order to streamline procurements and empower end users, most entities have set thresholds where no competition is required. Most often, this threshold matches that of the single purchase threshold for procurement cards.
- A Purchasing Cooperative allows its members, regardless of size, the ability to enjoy the pricing of a large volume contract. Small entities enjoy the same pricing for goods and services as that of their large counterparts, thus allowing them to do more with a dollar than if they hosted a solicitation by themselves.
- Public entities allow for the consideration of disadvantaged businesses to level the playing field to that of their large counterparts though preference laws, set-asides, and other programs identified to boost economic development with a variety of business classifications. In response to these preferences, some agencies have enacted inverse preferences on non-local bidders, which can at times have negative impacts on the same audience that the preference sought to provide.
- As with the private sector, sustainability and social responsibility areas are receiving greater and greater attention by governmental units. No longer is the lowest bid the approach for most procurement, but a more inclusive analysis of the overall cost of ownership and overall environmental impact of the good or service is taken prior to its purchase.
- The magnitude of the spending in the public sector can have a monumental impact on products and services. Governments can create a market for a product, can drive innovation through its specifications, and have a profound impact on society through its procurements.
- Ethics and professionalism are cornerstones of the procurement profession. Contracting officers carry with them the public's trust in each and every decision. It is

a responsibility that should weigh heavily in each decision made by procurement professional, to ensure that belief in the process and outcome remains steadfast in spite of politics and other socio-environmental factors.
- Procurement has grown over the years to be recognized as a profession rather than a clerical function. More and more the department is called on to strategize how spend can be controlled, reduced, and work for the agency not as a profit center, but more as a cost-savings area that will enable an expansion of services through the re-use of budgeted funds that become available for re-use due to negotiations and managed spend.

Appendix A

UPPCC CODE OF ETHICS

All UPPCC certificants as well as applicants and candidates for UPPCC certification must subscribe to the following ethical principles. Breaching this Code of Ethics will be just reason for revocation of UPPCC certification.

- I will seek or accept a position of employment only when fully in accord with the professional principles applicable thereto, and when confident of possessing the qualifications to serve under those principles to the advantage of my employer.
- I believe in the dignity and worth of the services rendered by my employment and the societal responsibilities assumed as a trusted public servant.
- I shall be governed by the highest ideals of honor and integrity in all public and personal relationships in order to merit the respect and inspire the confidence of my employer and the public served.
- I believe that personal aggrandizement or personal profit obtained through misuse of public or personal relationships is dishonest and intolerable.
- I will identify and eliminate participation of any individual in operational situations where a conflict of interest may be involved.
- I believe that individuals that possess UPPCC certification should at no time or under any circumstances accept directly or indirectly, gifts, gratuities or other things of value from suppliers, which might influence or appear to influence purchasing decisions.
- I will keep my governmental organization informed, through appropriate channels, on problems and progress of applicable operations by emphasizing the importance of the facts.
- I will handle all personnel matters on a merit basis. Politics, religion, ethnicity, gender and age carry no weight in personnel administration in the agency being directed or served.
- I shall not seek or dispense personal favors that are in conflict with my profession. I will handle each administrative problem objectively and empathetically without discrimination.
- I subscribe to and support the professional aims and objectives of the Universal Public Procurement Certification Council.

Appendix B

NIGP CODE OF ETHICS

The Institute believes, and it is a condition of membership, that the following ethical principles should govern the conduct of every person employed by a public sector procurement or materials management organization:

Seeks or accepts a position as head (or employee) only when fully in accord with the professional principles applicable thereto and when confident of possessing the qualifications to serve under those principles to the advantage of the employing organization.

- Believes in the dignity and worth of the service rendered by the organization, and the societal responsibilities assumed as a trusted public servant.
- Is governed by the highest ideals of honor and integrity in all public and personal relationships in order to merit the respect and inspire the confidence of the organization and the public being served.
- Believes that personal aggrandizement or personal profit obtained through misuse of public or personal relationships is dishonest and not tolerable.
- Identifies and eliminates participation of any individual in operational situations where a conflict of interest may be involved.
- Believes that members of the Institute and its staff should at no time, or under any circumstances, accept directly or indirectly, gifts, gratuities, or other things of value from suppliers, which might influence or appear to influence purchasing decisions.
- Keeps the governmental organization informed, through appropriate channels, on problems and progress of applicable operations by emphasizing the importance of the facts.
- Resists encroachment on control of personnel in order to preserve integrity as a professional manager.
- Handles all personnel matters on a merit basis, and in compliance with applicable laws prohibiting discrimination in employment on the basis of politics, religion, color, national origin, disability, gender, age, pregnancy and other protected characteristics.
- Seeks or dispenses no personal favors. Handles each administrative problem objectively and empathetically, without discrimination.
- Subscribes to and supports the professional aims and objectives of NIGP – The Institute for Public Procurement.

Appendix C

NJ TRANSIT CODE OF ETHICS FOR VENDORS

- No vendor shall either directly or indirectly pay, offer to pay, or agree to pay any fee, commission, compensation, gift, gratuity, or other thing of value of any kind to any NJ TRANSIT Board Member or employee or to any member of the immediate family, as defined by N.J.S.A. 52:13D–13i., of any such Board Member or employee, or to any partnership, firm, or corporation with which any such Board Member or employee is employed or associated, or in which (s)he has an interest within the meaning of N.J.S.A. 52:13D–13g.
- The solicitation of any fee, commission, compensation, gift, gratuity or other thing of value by an NJ TRANSIT Board Member or employee from any NJ TRANSIT vendor shall be reported in writing forthwith by the vendor to NJ TRANSIT's Senior Director, Corporate Affairs who shall comply with the Executive Order.
- Whether or not pursuant to employment, contract or other agreement, expressed or implied, no vendor may, directly or indirectly, undertake any private business, commercial or entrepreneurial relationship with, or sell any interest in such vendor to any NJ TRANSIT Board Member or employee having any duties or responsibilities in connection with the purchase, acquisition or sale of any property or services by or to NJ TRANSIT or with any person, firm or entity with which he is employed or associated or in which he has an interest within the meaning of N.J.S.A. 52:13D–13g. Any relationships subject to this provision shall be reported in writing forthwith to NJ Transit's Senior Director, Corporate Affairs who will consult with the Executive Commission on Ethical Standards and the Office of the Attorney General about further action. The Executive Commission may, upon application of the NJ TRANSIT Board Member or employee, grant a waiver of this restriction upon a finding that the present or proposed relationship does not present a potential, or actual appearance of a conflict of interest.
- No vendor shall influence, or attempt to influence or cause to be influenced, any NJ TRANSIT Board Member or employee in his official capacity in any manner which might tend to impair the objectivity or independence of judgment of any Board Member or employee.
- No vendor shall influence, or attempt to influence or cause to be influenced, any NJ TRANSIT Board Member or employee to use, or attempt to use, his official position in any manner to secure unwarranted privilege or advantage for the vendor or any other person.
- No vendor may offer any NJ TRANSIT Board Member, employee or family member any gift, payment, loan or other thing of value regardless of whether it might be reasonably inferred that such gift, payment, loan, service or other thing

of value was given or offered for the purpose of influencing the Board Member or employee in the discharge of his or her official duties. In addition, Board Members, employees or family members of NJ TRANSIT are not permitted to accept breakfasts, lunches, dinners, alcoholic beverages, tickets to entertainment and/or sporting events, wagers or other item or consideration which could be construed as having more than nominal value.

NOTE: NJ TRANSIT Board Members and employees may accept food or refreshments of relatively nominal monetary value provided during the course of a meeting, conference or other occasion where they are properly in attendance (for example, coffee, tea, danish, or soda served during a conference break) or made available to all attendees at a conference or seminar (for example, hospitality suites or conference meals). Acceptance of unsolicited advertising or promotional materials of nominal value (such as inexpensive pens, pencils, or calendars) is also permitted. Any questions as to what is or is not acceptable or what constitutes proper conduct for an NJ TRANSIT Board Member or employee and any solicitation of gifts, consideration or items of value by or on behalf of an NJ TRANSIT Board Member or employee should be referred to: Senior Director, Corporate Affairs NJ TRANSIT One Penn Plaza East Newark, NJ 07105-2246 (973) 491–7022

Failure of vendors to comply with this policy will subject them to debarment pursuant to N.J.A.C. 16:72–4.1.

NOTES

1. Conway, D. M. (2012) Sustainable Procurement Policies and Practices at the State and Local Government Level (April 15, 2012). *Greening Local Goverment* K. Hirokawa & P. Salkin, eds., 2012. pp. 43–49.

2. American Bar Assocation. (2000). *The 2000 Model Procurement Code for State and Local Governments*, p. 6. Chicago, IL: Author.

3. Thai, K.V. (2001) Public Procurement Re-examined. *Journal of Public Procurement*, (1)1, pp. 9–50.

4. Page, H.R. (1980). *Public Purchasing and Materials Management*. Lexington, MA: D. C. Heath and Company.

5. American Bar Association. (2000). *The 2000 Model Procurement Code for State and Local Governments*. Chicago, IL: Author.

6. Hefner, F. (1996). State Procurement Preferences; Evaluating their Economic Benefit. *The Journal of State Government*, 69(1), 33–38.

7. Palmer, R. & Gupta, M. (2005) *2005 Purchasing Card Benchmark Survey Report*, p. 6. St. Louis, MO: RPMG Research Corporation.

8. Fairfax County, Virginia, Procurement of Credit Card Services. http://www.fairfaxcounty.gov/cregister/ContractDetails.aspx?contractNumber=4400000261. Accessed July 12, 2014

9. Palmer, R. & Gupta, M. (2014) *2014 Purchasing Card Benchmark Survey Results* p. 77. St. Louis, MO: RPMG Research Corporation.

10. National Institute for Governmental Procurement. NIGP Public Procurement Dictionary of Terms. 2014. http://www.nigp.org/eweb/StartPage.aspx?Site=NIGP&webcode=pd-ep_online_dict. Accessed September 7, 2014.

11. Conservative estimate of annual spend across GSA Schedules, E & I, U.S. Communities, NJPA, State Contracts, WSCA agreements, National IPA, H-GAC, MMCAP et al.

12. Abutabenjeh, S. International Public Procurement Conference Proceedings. 2012. http://www.ippa.org/IPPC5/Proceedings/Part9/PAPER9-3.pdfExamination of the Economic Impact of State Procurement Preference Policies. Accessed September 16, 2014.

13. Virginia Association of Governmental Procurement. Local Preference Purchasing. 2013. http://vagp.org/_docs/legislative/LocalPreferencePurchasing072913.pdf. Accessed September 15, 2014.

14. District of Columbia Municipal Regulations Rule 27 Contract and Procurement; http://www.dcregs.dc.gov/Gateway/TitleHome.aspx?TitleNumber=27. Accessed July 23, 2014.

15. Associated General Contractors of America. Legislative Action Center. http://www.agc.org/topics. Accessed July 6, 2014.

16. Conway, D. M. (2012) Sustainable Procurement Policies and Practices at the State and Local Government Level (April 15, 2012). *Greening Local Goverment* K. Hirokawa & P. Salkin, eds., 2012. p. 46.

17. Amy, D.J. (2007) Government Is Good: An Unapologetic Defense of a Vital Institution. http://www.governmentisgood.com/articles.php?aid=13&print=1. Accessed July 24, 2014.

18. National Association of State Procurement Officials. Cooperation and Collaboration in State Higher Education Procurement: http://www.naspo.org/higherEdProcure.cfm. Accessed September 16, 2014.

19. American Association of State Colleges and Universities, National Association of Educational Procurement. Public College and University Procurement: A Survey of the State Regulatory Environment, Institutional Procurement Practices, and Efforts Toward Cost Containment (2010). http://www.aascu.org/uploadedFiles/AASCU/Content/Root/PolicyAndAdvocacy/PolicyPublications/aascunaepfinal(1).pdf. Accessed September 10, 2014.

20. American Association of State Colleges and Universities. http://www.aascu.org/map/PSSNRDetails.aspx?id=215. Accessed September 19, 2014.

21. American City & County. Americans Trust Local Government more that State. Prall, D. September 29, 2014; http://americancityandcounty.com/administration/americans-trust-local-government-more-state. Accessed October 1, 2014.

22. Thai, K.V. (2007). *Introduction to Public Procurement* (2nd edition); Herndon, VA: National Institute of Governmental Purchasing.

23. Farmer, D. (1985) *Purchasing Management Handbook;* London, England: Gower Publishing.

24. Palmer, R. J. & Gupta, M. (2007). Use and misuse of purchase cards by U.S. government employees: Examining costs, benefits, and an emerging control framework. *Public Contract Law Journal*, 36(2), 175–202.

25. Federal Acquisition Institute. Contracting FAC-C. http://www.fai.gov/drupal/certification/contracting-fac-c. Accessed September 15, 2014.

26. Calender, G., & Mattthews, D. (2000). Government purchasing: An evolving professions: *Journal of Public Budgeting, Accounting & Financial Management*, 12(2), 272–290.

Appendix A Unified Public Procurement Certification Council. Code of Ethics, 2014. http://uppcc.org/ethics/index.aspx. Accessed September 7, 2014.

Appendix B National Institute for Goevernmal Procurement. Code of Ethics, 2014. http://www.nigp.org/eweb/Dynamicpage.aspx?webkey=11cdf004-0883-4a24-a295-ddc7e4245cd6. Accessed September 7, 2014.

Appendix C New Jersey Transit Authority. NJT Code of Vendor Ethics. http://www.njtransit.com/tm/tm_servlet.srv?hdnPageAction=VendorEthicsTo. Accessed September 8, 2014.

REFERENCES

Hefner, F., & Blackwell, C. (1996). State Procurement Preferences: Evaluating their Economic Benefit. *The Journal of State Government*, 69(1), 33–38.

McCue, C., Buffington, K., & Howell, A. (2003). The Fraud/Red Tape Dilemma in Public Procurement: A Study of US State and Local Governments. *Public Procurement: International Cases and Commentary* edited by Louise Knight, Christine Harland, Jan Telgen, Khi V. Thai, Guy Callender, and Katy McKen, London: Routledge, pp. 247–263.

Qiao,Y.,Thai,K.V.,& Cummings, G. (2009). State and local procurement preferences; A survey. *Journal of Public Procurement*, 9(3 & 4), 371–410.

Thomas, A. G. (1919) *Principles of Government Purchasing;* New York, NY: D. Appleton and Company.

12

Implications for the Future of Government Contracting

Robert A. Shick

This chapter reviews the reasons why governments contract out for services and explores the persuasiveness of these arguments. The chapter then reviews the data relating to the growth of contracting, its effectiveness, and its probable future. Finally, the chapter ends with recommendations for the future.

The use of contracting by government is based on the idea that competition, through contractors bidding to provide services currently being supplied directly by government, can result in reduced costs and better quality. There are markets for many government services and private or nonprofit organizations are prepared to bid on them. There are, however, instances in which government looks to provide a service through a contractor where there are few or no existing providers in the private or nonprofit sectors, resulting in a few or no bidders. This can occur in less-populated geographic areas or where government can be the only provider of such services. This was true in the past for certain human services. In some instances, government can become the impetus for the private and nonprofit sectors to establish organizations or to expand their existing organizations to provide these directly delivered government services. In order to determine if there is a market to form the basis of competition, some in the field of government contracting suggest the use of the "yellow pages test," to determine whether a reasonable number of private or nonprofit service providers exist in a geographic area. Limited competition, under any circumstances, weakens the economic justification for the use of contracting to achieve governments' intended objectives.

Another concern regarding the efficacy of government contracting is the principal-agent problem. When government as the principal provides services directly, it can concentrate on the management of those services to achieve public objectives. However, when government uses an agent—a contractor—to deliver services, the interests of government and the contractor may not be aligned. In this situation, while contractors seek to meet the terms of their agreement with government, they may also promote their own interests, such as generating profit for private sector organizations. This can also be the case with nonprofit contractors, as they seek to increase their retained earnings, even though they are mission driven organizations, as is government. The government can mitigate the principal-agent problem by effectively designing contracts and monitoring and evaluating contractors.

While these concerns regarding contracting exist, political and philosophical values and economic conditions have propelled government into the continued use of contracting. One such political and philosophical value concerns the size and appropriate role of government in American society. This concern has been present since the founding of the country and the debate in drafting the American constitution. However, during the twentieth century, concerns about the role of government were overshadowed by events such as the Great Depression in the 1930s and the recognition of racial discrimination and urban poverty and decay in the 1960s, which resulted in an expanded role of government, with new government programs. This approach enlarged the presence of government in American society.

Concern for the size and the appropriate role of government was revived with the 1980 presidential election of Ronald Reagan, and his belief in the private sector as a source of innovation and improved performance, which he felt could be applied to the public sector. This change in direction coincided with new ideas about how to manage government more effectively, which was embodied by the Reinventing Government and the New Public Management movements, which encouraged the use of the private and nonprofit sectors of the economy to produce public services. In their book, *Reinventing Government: How the Entrepreneurial Spirit is Transforming the Public Sector,* David Osborne and Ted Gaebler argue that government bureaucracy, created a hundred years ago to combat official corruption, has outlived its usefulness. To remedy this, the authors advocate that governments become more market-and customer-driven. Within the field of public administration, a new approach for administering government was developed. The New Public Management movement, whose tenets for managing government are consistent in many ways with the ideas underlying the Reinventing Government movement, in promoting a change from bureaucratic to entrepreneurial government. Both of these approaches encouraged government to use the private and nonprofit sectors as a means to make government more efficient and effective. Donahue and Nye have referred to this prevalence of government contracting as "market-based governance."

The debate on the size and appropriate role of government continues to the present, as demonstrated by comments made by Scott Walker, Governor of Wisconsin and presidential candidate for 2016, who said, "I believe that smaller government is better government." This statement is not significantly different from Ronald Reagan's remark in his first inaugural address in 1981, when he said "Government is not a solution to our problem; government is the problem." President Barack Obama expressed the opposite perspective on government in a 2012 presidential debate, when he said "Government's first role is to keep people safe . . . I also believe that government has the capacity—the federal government has the capacity—to help open up opportunity and create ladders of opportunity, and to create frameworks where the American people can succeed."

From this long history, to the current statements and the continued vigorous debate on this issue, it is reasonable to anticipate that the role of government in American society will continue to be debated well into the future. The more government is believed to be, in the words of Ronald Reagan, "part of the problem," the more likely it will be that government will further pursue the other sectors of the economy to provide public services, and thereby reduce the size of government. On the other hand, if the opinions of Barack Obama and those in favor of an expanded role for government prevail, then the tide could turn regarding the use of contracting.

In addition to political and value concerns, economic conditions affect the level of government contracting, as a difficult financial environment causes governments to consider alternative mechanisms principally to control costs. In the belief that the "market" will contain costs and improve quality, and governments can avoid reductions or elimination of services and/or increased taxes, government will be encouraged to expand their use of contracting. Since 2008, economic conditions have been extremely challenging, which has been an important factor contributing to the increased use of contractors by government. Data from the Federal Reserve Board of Governors' Open Market Committee projects the growth of real GDP will be 2.1 to 3.1 percent in 2015, 2.2 to 3.0 percent for 2016, and 1.8 to 2.5 percent in the longer run. This projection of stable but modest growth is similar to the growth in real GDP over the last five years. GDP forms the basis of the health of the economy and has implications for government contracting. A robust economy is related to an increase in revenues at all levels of government, and can reduce the financial pressure on governments, and the use of contracts, as they are now perceived by many to reduce costs.

The budget deficit is another important indicator of the well being of the economy. The Congressional Budget Office predicts a similar stable position for the budget deficit in the near future, but maintains a more pessimistic outlook through 2025. "Under the assumption that current laws will generally remain unchanged, the budget deficit is projected to decline in 2016, to $455 billion, or 2.4 percent of GDP, and then to hold roughly steady relative to the size of the economy through 2018. The deficit in 2025 is projected to reach $1 trillion, or 3.8 percent of GDP, and cumulative deficits over the 2016–2025 period are projected to total $7.2 trillion." State and local governments, unlike the federal government, must enact balanced budgets and cannot have budgeted deficits. The continued budget deficit conditions at the national level will impact state and local governments in terms of reduced availability of financial support

As Weikart and Curry point out in previous chapters of this volume, contracting has been a part of the operation of American government since the American Revolution. The record of the use of government contracting over the last fifteen years shows that contracting has continually expanded. Since 2000, contracting for goods and services at the federal level grew from $276.9 billion to $518.4 billion, or 87 percent from 2000 to 2012, and the share of federal costs allocated to contracts also increased from 11 percent to 15 percent from 2000 to 2012. (CBO). In Chapter 11, Donna Ginter states that, while it is hard to pinpoint the exact figures for state and local government spending on contracts, it was estimated to be $1.5 trillion in 2007, and is projected, based on a similar projected growth rate from 1979 forward to 2014, to have been $2 trillion for the estimated 89,004 state, county, municipalities, townships, special districts, and independent school districts. These numbers show that the dollar value of contracts at the state and local level far exceed that of the federal level. At this point in time, contracting is clearly a critical element of the operations of virtually every agency at all levels of government and appears to be here to stay.

With contracting serving an expanded and more significant role in the public sector, an important question is whether government contracting is achieving its intended results of containing or reducing costs and maintaining or improving quality. Evidence-based research on this issue could form the basis of future decisions regarding the use of contracting versus government concentrating on improving its functioning. While there is not sufficient research to draw definitive conclusions, some academicians have addressed the question of the effectiveness of contracting as a strategy to restrain costs. A meta-analysis of the privatization of water distribution and solid waste collection services found no systematic support for lower costs with private production (Bel, Fageda, & Warner, 2010). Smirnova and Leland's review of the literature agrees with Bel, Fageda, and Warner on reserving judgment on the benefit of contracting. As they point out in Chapter 2, there is a growing body of literature indicating that contracting out may not produce desired savings (Miranda & Lerner, 1995; Brown, Potoski & Van Slyke, 2006). However, other research by Hodge suggests positive conclusions regarding the effectiveness of government contracting in the areas of garbage collection, cleaning, and maintenance in his meta-analysis from international data. Hodge's results suggest that contracting may achieve its goals for certain government provided services and not others.

Governments can influence the effectiveness of contracts by instituting greater oversight of contractors. In Chapter 7, McCue and Davison report that this oversight does not appear to be occurring, pointing out that governments have not always done a good job in establishing effective contract monitoring and evaluation plans to insure that they receive exactly what they intended. Without monitoring and evaluation data, it is difficult for government to determine not only if they received what was required under the terms of the contract, but also whether contracted service delivery is an improvement over government provided services in terms of costs and quality. Additional research into the effectiveness of government contracts is needed to determine whether there is evidence to support the government's use of the private and nonprofit sectors to control costs and improve quality of government services.

Elected officials and government administrators, fueled by the belief in the "market" and policies and philosophical values of the benefits of a smaller government, appear to continue to move forward with the expansion of government contracting, even though there seems to be a lack of clear evidence that its intended results will be realized. Considering the degree to which contracting has become entrenched in the delivery of services at all levels of government, the strong "smaller government is better government" movement and the new public management approach that emphasizes market-based solutions to the operation of government, it appears that the expansion of government contracting will continue unabated.

If trends in government contracting continue on their current trajectory, and government contracting continues to expand, the findings in this volume can form the bases of recommendations to guide elected officials and public administrators to be more effective in their use and management of government contracts, and to achieve contracting's intended results of reduced costs and increased quality. A summary of the most important recommendations of the authors to realize this end is provided here.

The recommendations follow the order of the parts of this volume: Government Contracting Theory, Issues in Government Contracting, and Government Contracting: Ethics, Management, and Governance. In the Government Contracting Theory section, the recommendations proceed with understanding the foundation for contracting, the decision process to determine whether government should provide a service directly or through a contractor, and then, once a decision to contract out a service is made, the critical steps to follow in implementing that decision.

Weikart begins Part I with her chapter on the political and economic philosophy and value considerations of contracting. She concludes that, while there is no agreement among Americans about the appropriate size and scope of government contracting, the public values of transparency, equity, protecting human capital, accountability, quality, and the recognition of unintended consequences are crucial and should be considered in contracting decisions. Weikart emphasizes that the more these public values can be included in the public debate, and can be framed as necessary for further contracting out, then the more Americans can have some assurance that service, whether delivered by government or by the private or nonprofit sectors, will be likely to achieve their intended results of reduced costs and improved quality.

Smirnova and Leland continue the theoretical discussion in their examination of the contracting decision, acknowledging that contracting represents a public management dilemma between the make (in-house provision) and buy (contract out) decision. They recommend completing an adequate analysis of all of the relevant costs and benefits of each method of service provision when making a decision to contract out a service. While efficiency and effectiveness should be the primary focus of the contracting decision, there should also be recognition that the political environment and actors will always play a role and be a factor in contracting out decisions.

Finally, in Part I, Curry, in his review of the contract process, explains that once the decision to contract out a service has been made, the steps in the contracting procedure, from contract planning to the contract audit and closeout, are now well defined and established, and include the responsibilities of both government and the contractor. He stresses that all phases of the contract process are important, but contract planning is especially critical and when well executed, significantly contributes to the success of the entire contracting effort. Providing the best value to government and taxpayers will also be greatly enhanced with the design and implementation of an effective contractor selection process, which clearly identifies the proposal offering the best value and helps to protect government and taxpayers from the possibility of not achieving the goals of contracting and minimizes the possibility of procurement fraud.

The Issues in Government Contracting section of the volume presents recommendations on specific topics in contracting that warrant close attention, as they are areas where government needs to make critical decisions, such as whether and when to use performance based contracts or public private partnerships, the unique characteristics of contracting with nonprofit organizations, and the role of monitoring and evaluating contracts.

Martin, who covers performance contracting, points out that while there is no universally agreed upon definition of performance based contracting, results are at the center of this type of contract. It is an umbrella term that includes many approaches that attempt to alter contractor behaviors, including focusing more on performance than process, or *how* contractors complete their work. Contractors are, thus, motivated to use new and innovative service delivery methods. This is accomplished through the use of performance specifications (outputs, quality, and outcomes), while attempting to minimize the use of design specifications. As such, performance based contracts have become the recommended and preferred method for government to acquire services. Performance based contracting can include monetary and non-monetary approaches as well as incentives and penalties.

Prentice and Brudney review contracting with nonprofit organizations and the important role they play in government contracting for human services. The authors argue that contracting with nonprofit organizations works best when these organizations have missions and goals that are aligned with those of government. An essential government task is to evaluate and check the meaning and priority accorded by nonprofit contractors to determine their consistency with government objectives. Prentice and Brudney recommend that government view contracting with nonprofit organizations not as an abdication of government authority, but as an opportunity to use its authority creatively, for example, through strategic contract design, monitoring, and evaluation, to achieve shared results. Government contracting with nonprofit organizations should not be concerned exclusively with paring public budgets. Rather, government contracting with nonprofit organizations is about working together to achieve effective and efficient services with committed partners, which are accountable to the public.

Public private partnerships, examined by Lawther, are another type of partnering arrangement, which present an alternative avenue for government to engage the private and nonprofit sectors to meet public goals. Public private partnerships are more complex relationships than contracting, and the author recommends that government officials need to carefully plan and implement these types of projects. Detailed examinations, such as benefit cost analysis, should be employed when considering a public private partnership. Due to the complexity of the process, public private partnerships require a flexible approach that maximizes negotiation among the parties to the public private partnership. Key contract issues include the choice of payment mechanisms and performance management systems.

McCue and Davison are concerned with the role of monitoring and evaluation of government contracts. They point out that governments have not always done a good job in establishing effective contract monitoring and evaluation plans nor implementing them. They emphasize that an effective contract monitoring and evaluation program will determine a contractor's performance, whether government is achieving its intended results through contracting, and if government should continue a contract relationship. McCue and Davison recommend that government develops a contract monitoring plan to establish a process, whether periodic or continuous, to measure and confirm contractor compliance with the terms, conditions, and requirements of a contract. A conflict resolution and corrective action process addressing how conflict and contract problems are to be resolved should also be components of this plan.

The Government Contracting: Ethics, Management, and Governance section examines each of these broad and different aspects of government contracting, and contracting in state and local government and implications for the future of government contracting, and offers recommendations that should enhance the success of government contracting endeavors.

Carboni explores how contracts are an increasingly important part of governance at all levels of government, particularly in policy implementation. She explains that it is essential for government administrators to accept and understand that with contracting, public managers are still responsible for ensuring the effective implementation of public policy, but that their role has shifted from managing service production to managing contract relationships. Contracts then become a tool of governance that structure formal interactions between government and its contractors. Carboni argues that contracts are not a proxy for effective government management, and public managers need to develop contract management strategies that are specific to service characteristics, contractor characteristics, and market conditions.

Curry examines ethics in contracting: an issue that receives a great deal of exposure, and can have a significant affect on how citizens perceive government. Contract corruption occurred throughout the early history of the United States and continues vigorously to the present. Unfortunately, opportunities for corruption are present during virtually all phases of the contracting process and in all levels of government. Curry recommends that contract proposal evaluation processes have clear criteria for identifying the contractor that provides the best value for government; this also helps to minimize the introduction of corruption, in contrast to proposal evaluation processes that are not clear, and are more cryptic. The latter situation permits a contract to be awarded to less qualified, and possibly more costly, contractors. The author acknowledges that although it is impractical for government to enforce a zero-tolerance policy regarding gratuities, rules regarding gratuities should be established and adhered to, and individual contracting professionals should be encouraged to adopt their own personal policy to decline the offer of gifts of any kind from contractors.

Gordon, who reviews the impact of contracting on managing government organizations, argues that it is critical to convince elected officials and senior administrators of the benefits of strategic contracting for public organizations. This includes developing, adopting, and implementing a strategic plan for contracting that aligns with the mission, vision, and goals of the government organization as a whole and the individual missions, visions, and goals of the departments and programs within that organization. Government organizations also need an organizational structure that will support the success of an effective contracting program. Gordon observes that government requires public managers who are contract professionals, and are knowledgeable and trained in this relatively new and growing government function. An indispensible component of this training is knowledge of network management, or managing by interacting with contractors, and communicating and working well with people inside and external to government.

Ginter examines contracting in state and local governments, and describes how rules for contracting vary among different jurisdictions, and are procedure driven, often at the expense of innovation. She reinforces the idea that competition is the basis for all procurements, and that it is the vehicle that provides the taxpayer with assurance that the best value is attained in a contract for a good or a service. State and local governments have instituted innovations, which Ginter supports, such as procurement cards that facilitate low-dollar buys, allowing for the quick purchase of items with lower transaction costs than the typical requisition to purchase order process. Other contract developments include purchasing cooperatives, which allow its members, regardless of size, the ability to enjoy the pricing of a large volume contract. In this situation, small entities enjoy the same pricing for goods and services as that of their large counterparts, thus allowing them to do more with a dollar than if they hosted a solicitation by themselves. Public entities also allow for the consideration of disadvantaged businesses to level the playing field to that of their large counterparts through preference laws, set-asides, and other programs identified to boost economic development with a variety of business classifications. She observes that, in response to these preferences, some agencies have enacted inverse preferences on non-local bidders, which can at times have negative impacts on the same audience that the preference sought to provide. As with the private sector, it is important to note that sustainability, as well as social responsibility, is receiving greater and greater attention by government. Ginter notes that the lowest bid is no longer the best approach for most procurements. Instead, she recommends a more inclusive analysis of the overall cost of ownership and overall environmental impact of the good or service is taken prior to its purchase.

This volume moves the field of government contracting forward, into a new phase, through the academic and practitioner knowledge that has been gained over the last three decades, and shared here. Contracting has played, and will continue to play, an important role in the delivery of public services at all levels of government as we move forward in the twenty-first century. For this reason, contracting should be considered a serious and important endeavor, one that significantly influences the effectiveness of government and the services that it provides.

The bases for government contracting are economic principles concerning the benefits of competition, and government actions should be aligned with these principles, especially in determining whether a market exists for a service considered to be contracted out.

The public's interest would be best served if political philosophy and values are not the driving force when making government contracting decisions, but rather the potential for achieving reduced costs and improved quality of services being delivered.

Judgments on the effectiveness of government should be evaluated in terms of meeting the needs of citizens, who are the payers for the services government provides. This can only be accomplished through government devoting the resources and employing professionals specifically trained in the skills required in contracting, and who can manage all of the elements of the contracting process. Effective monitoring and evaluation of contracts is particularly important, as this activity should yield the information required to determine if contracting achieved its intended goals.

Government officials should attempt to share best practices in the field in order to improve the contracting functions of all government entities at all levels of government. The academic community also needs to continue to pursue research in government contracting to determine its effectiveness and provide related valuable information that can be used by elected officials and government practitioners in their efforts to provide public services at the least cost and the highest quality.

REFERENCES

Bell, G., Fageda, X. & Warner, M. (2010). Is private production of public services cheaper than public production? A meta-regression analysis of solid waste and water services. *Journal of Policy Analysis and Management*, 29(3), 553–577.

Board of Governors of the Federal Reserve System Open Market Committee Meeting, March 2015. http://www.federalreserve.gov/monetarypolicy/files/fomcprojtabl20150318.pdf. Retrieved on September 9, 2015.

Brown, T. L., Potoski, M., & Van Slyke, D. M. (2006). Managing public service contracts: Aligning values, institutions, and markets. *Public Administration Review*, 66(3), 323–331.

Congress of the United States, Congressional Budget Office, Letter to the Honorable Chris Van Hollen, Federal Contracts and the Contracted Workforce, March 2015. https://www.cbo.gov/sites/default/files/114th-congress-2015-2016/reports/49931-FederalContracts.pdf. Retrieved on September 9, 2015.

Congress of the United States, Congressional Budget Office, Updated Budget Projections: 2015 to 2025, March 2015. https://www.cbo.gov/sites/default/files/114th-congress-2015-2016/reports/49973-UpdatedBudgetProjections_0.pdf. Retrieved September 9, 2015.

Conservative estimate of annual spend across GSA Schedules, E & I, U.S. Communities, NJPA, State Contracts, WSCA agreements, National IPA, H-GAC, MMCAP et al. http://gsablogs.gsa.gov/gsablog/2015/01/07/taking-category-management-government-wide/. Retrieved on September 9, 2015.

Donahue, J. D. & Nye Jr., J. S. (2002). *Market-based governance: Supply side, demand side, upside, and downside*. Washington, D.C.: Brookings Institution Press.

Hodge, G. (1998). Contracting public sector services: A meta-analytic perspective of the international evidence. *Australian Journal of Public Administration, 57*, 98–111.

Miranda, R. & Lerner, A. (1995). Bureaucracy, organizational redundancy, and the privatization of public services. *Public Administration Review*, 193–200.

Obama: Role of Government Is to 'Create Ladders of Opportunity' Susan Jones, CNSNEWS.Com, October 2014. http://cnsnews.com/news/article/obama-role-government-create-ladders-opportunity Retrieved on September 9, 2015.

Osborne, David and Gaebler, Ted. (2000). *Reinventing government: How the entrepreneurial spirit is transforming the public sector*. Easter Rutherford, NJ: Plume.

Reagan's First Inaugural: "Government is not the solution to our problem; government is the problem." Heritage.org. http://www.heritage.org/initiatives/first-principles/primary-sources/reagans-first-inaugural-government-is-not-the-solution-to-our-problem-government-is-the-problem?ac=1. Retrieved July 15, 2013.

United States Census Bureau, Newsroom Archive 2012 Census of Governments, August 2012. https://www.census.gov/newsroom/releases/archives/governments/cb12-161.html. Retrieved September 9, 2015.

Walker, S. (n.d.). BrainyQuote.com. Retrieved May 3, 2015, from BrainyQuote.com http://www.brainyquote.com/quotes/quotes/s/scottwalke440830.html Retrieved May 3, 2015.

About the Editor and Contributors

Jeffrey L. Brudney, Ph.D., is the Betty and Dan Cameron Family distinguished professor of Innovation in the Nonprofit Sector at the University of North Carolina Wilmington. Dr. Brudney is the Faculty Director of Quality Enhancement for Nonprofit Organizations (QENO), a university-community partnership to build the capacity of nonprofit organizations and increase philanthropy in southeastern North Carolina. The Urban Institute calls him "the foremost research expert on volunteer management programs and community volunteer centers in the United States." Dr. Brudney is the Editor in Chief of *Nonprofit and Voluntary Sector Quarterly*, the premier journal in nonprofit sector studies. He is the author of *Fostering Volunteer Programs in the Public Sector: Planning, Initiating, and Managing Voluntary Activities*, which received the John Grenzebach Award for Outstanding Research in Philanthropy for Education, and many other publications. Dr. Brudney serves on the United Nations Volunteers Programme Technical Advisory Board on the *State Of The World's Volunteerism Report*.

Julia L. Carboni (Ph.D. Management, University of Arizona) is an assistant professor in the School of Public and Environmental Affairs and the Lilly Family School of Philanthropy at Indiana University (IUPUI) where she teaches management courses. Her research focuses on collaborative, multi-sector governance arrangements designed to address large-scale social issues. She has expertise in alternative service delivery arrangements and network analysis. The empirical context for her work includes as anti-hunger coalitions, food system governance and juvenile justice rehabilitation systems. Dr. Carboni is active in several professional associations including the American Society for Public Administration, the Public Management Research Association, and the Association for Research on Nonprofit Organizations and Voluntary Action. She serves on the Board of Directors for the Indy Food Council and is an agency evaluator for the United Way of Central Indiana. Prior professional experience includes managing youth mentoring programs and fundraising.

William Sims Curry is president of WSC Consulting and consults on government contracting for government agencies and prime contractors. He has authored three books, numerous articles, and several research papers on government contracts. Curry presented papers on government contracts at the National Contract Management Association (NCMA) World Congress and for other professional associations. He taught college courses in materials management. Curry served as an Air Force systems procurement officer at a prime contractor's facility and in contracting directorates for two Air Force systems centers. He gained contracts experience while working for prime contractors on NASA's Hubble Space Telescope, DOE's Positron Electron Project, and numerous DoD programs. Curry's county government experience includes purchasing manager and general services director. He is an NCMA Fellow, CPCM, and served on NCMA's Professional Standards and Ethics Committee for four years. Curry earned a BS from Florida State University and an MBA from Ohio State University.

Bill Davison, CPPO, is the director of Purchasing for Stearns County Minnesota. He received his Masters in Contract Management from Florida Institute of Technology. His research examines the relationship between contract problems and contract types. He has presented the results of his research at several international conferences and is recognized as leading authority in public procurement.

Donna Ginter, Ph.D., is the executive director of procurement and travel services at the George Washington University. Dr. Ginter is a recognized expert in public procurement with more than 33 years in the field and has served as a procurement manager for city, county, school district and special taxing districts. Prior to joining GW, she served as the Director of the Federal Acquisition Institute as well as the Director of Research and Consulting for the National Institute of Governmental Purchasing. She holds a Ph.D. from the University of Central Florida in Public Affairs with a dissertation on the Socially Responsible Expenditure of Public Funds at the State and Local Levels of Government, an MBA from Southern New Hampshire University and a B.A. in Political Science from the University of New Hampshire. Donna is a Certified Purchasing Manager (C.P.M.), Certified Public Procurement Officer (CPPO) and a Certified Public Professional Buyer (CPPB).

Stephen B. Gordon, Ph.D., FNIGP, CPPO, is a professor of practice and the program director of the Graduate Certificate in public procurement and contract management (GCPPCM) at Old Dominion University (ODU). Prior to coming to ODU to stand up the GCPPCM, Dr. Gordon spent more than thirty-five years in the public procurement arena. Stephen is a past president of NIGP—the Institute for Public Procurement—and the recipient of NIGP's two highest individual awards. Advancing the strategic contribution of public procurement and contract management has been a primary focus of Dr. Gordon's career. Stephen is an academic adviser to the Universal Public Procurement Certification Council (UPPCC), a member of the editorial board of the *Journal of Public Procurement*, and a founding principal of ODU's Alliance for Procurement and Program Excellence (APPX). He was a member of the initial steering group of AGA's Intergovernmental Partnership for Management and Accountability.

Wendell C. Lawther is an associate professor in the School of Public Administration at the University of Central Florida (UCF). He received a BA from the University of Delaware and a PhD from Indiana University. His research interests include public private partnerships, transportation policy, and public procurement policy. He is the co–editor of the forthcoming book: *Private Financing of Public Transportation Infrastructure*, as well as the author/co-author of three books: *Privatizing Toll Operations; Capital Acquisitions;* and *Contracting for Construction Service*s. In addition to receiving grants from agencies such as the Florida Department of Transportation, he has published in journals such as *Public Works Management and Policy*, *Journal of Public Procurement*, and *Public Performance Management and Review*. Dr. Lawther has held numerous academic positions while at UCF, including Director, Ph.D. Program in Public Affairs; Chair, Department of Public Administration; and Associate Dean, College of Health and Public Affairs.

Suzanne Leland (PhD, University of Kansas) is a professor of political science and public administration at the University of North Carolina Charlotte and the director of the Gerald G. Fox MPA Program. Her research on urban politics and policy and alternative service delivery models appears in journals such as *Public Administration Review, American Review of Public Administration, Public Budgeting and Finance* and the *Journal of Urban Affairs.* She is the co-editor of two books on city-county consolidation.

Lawrence L. (Larry) Martin is a professor of public affairs at the University of Central Florida in Orlando. Dr. Martin holds the Ph.D. degree in political science from Arizona State University and the MBA degree in international business from the Thunderbird School of Global Management. Prior to his academic career, he worked for 15 years as a state and local government administrator. Dr. Martin's research interests include public procurement and contracting, state and local government, performance measurement and budgeting and financial management. His works have been published by the National Institute for Government Purchasing, the International City/County Management Association, the National League of Cities, the IBM Center for the Business of Government and others. Dr. Martin has consulted with numerous governmental and nonprofit organizations both domestically and internationally.

Clifford McCue received his Ph.D. in public administration from Florida International University. His research examines the intersection of professionalization and public administration, including examination of the social and institutional barriers to enhancing accountability, sustainability, and good governance in public procurement. He is recognized as one of the world's leading authorities on public procurement, and has received a number of national and international awards for his work in the field.

Christopher R. Prentice, Ph.D., is assistant professor in the Department of Public and International Affairs at the University of North Carolina Wilmington, where he teaches public and nonprofit management. Dr. Prentice is co-founder of UNCW's undergraduate Minor in Nonprofit Management and Leadership and founder of UNCW's chapter of Pi Alpha Alpha, the global honor society for public affairs and administration. His research focuses on government-nonprofit relations and nonprofit finance, and appears in *Nonprofit and Voluntary Sector Quarterly* and *Human Service Organizations: Management, Leadership, and Governance*. Active in the community, Dr. Prentice is a frequent advisor to community-based nonprofits. He is board Treasurer of the Blue Ribbon Commission on the Prevention of Youth Violence, a nonprofit organization that, in partnership with local government and nonprofits, provides programs to assist and benefit children in Wilmington's Youth Enrichment Zone so that they can lead safe, healthy, educated, and successful lives.

Robert A. Shick, Ph.D., is a visiting scholar at Rutgers University–Newark's School of Public Affairs and Administration (SPAA). He received his degree from New York University in Public Administration. Dr. Shick is a former faculty member and Director of the Executive Master in Public Administration Program at SPAA and a former faculty member at Long Island University. He has extensive experience in the public sector as a senior administrator in New York City government, working in contracting out of government services, financial and budget management, policy analysis, information technology, and intergovernmental and community relations. Dr. Shick's research interests and publications are in the areas of privatization and the contracting out of government services, nonprofit management, and organizational development. He serves on the editorial boards of the *Journal for Health and Human Services Administration* and the *Journal of Administrative Sciences*.

Olga Smirnova is associate professor of East Carolina University, MPA program, Political Science Department. Her research on performance measurements and governance has been published in the *Public Administration Review*, *Administration and Society*, *Journal of Public Transportation*, *Southeastern Geographer*, *Municipal Finance Journal*, and *North Carolina Geographer*. She also researches complex systems and cybercrimes and has published articles in journals such as *Global Crime and International Journal of Cybercriminology*.

Lynne Weikart, a retired associate professor from Baruch College School of Public Affairs, the City University of New York, received her Ph.D. from Columbia University in politics and education. She is now practitioner-in-residence at James Madison University for the Public Administration Program. Her current research focuses upon urban finance and resource allocation issues as well as financial management for nonprofits.

She is the author of three books: *Budget Tools, Follow the Money: Who Controls New York City's Mayors? and Budgeting and Financial Management for Nonprofits* as well as many articles in these areas. In 2001, Professor Weikart won the Luther Gulick Award for Outstanding Academic, New York Metropolitan Chapter of the American Society for Public Administration. Before her academic career, Professor Weikart held several high-level government positions as well as serving as the executive director of the nonprofit, City Project, a progressive fiscal think tank, which focused upon reforming NYC's resource allocation patterns.

Index

ABA *see* American Bar Association
acceptable quality level (AQL) 67
acceptance 121–122, 123, 131, 133
access 17, 18
accountability 13, 17, 18, 180–181, 230; due diligence 103; Federal Funding Accountability and Transparency Act 88; joint service production 143; nonprofit organizations 90–91; performance-based contracting xviii, 64–65, 72; public management 21; Public Private Partnerships 109; social services 25; value for money analysis 101
acquisition/Acquisition, use of the term 180, 196n17
adverse selection 140, 141
Agnew, Spiro T. 197n19
ambiguity 32, 35n3
American Bar Association (ABA) 40, 41, 58n1, 58n2, 184, 197n20, 204; CPPC contracts 47; opening of bids 45–46; proposal evaluation 44, 58n3; terminology 42; unallowable costs 47; *see also* Model Procurement Code for State and Local Government
American Revolution (1775) 4, 8
Anderson, E. 26
Anheier, H. 76–77
animal welfare 82, 84
arts 82, 84
asset specificity 31–32, 34
Associated General Contractors of America (AGC) 212
audits 57, 110, 154, 155
Austin, J. 25, 26
Australia 99, 100, 101
availability payments (APs) 105, 106, 107–108, 110, 112
availability risk 108
award fee approaches 68–69
award term approaches 69

Bacon, Francis 4
Bel, G. 20, 26, 27, 229
benchmarking 28, 30, 69
Benefit/Cost (B/C) Analysis 19, 27, 35, 99–100, 111, 230
Benton, J.E. 89
best value 158, 197n22, 231; Federal Acquisition System 182; MPC 204; proposal evaluation 45, 51–52, 57, 166, 168–169, 232–233
bids 27, 31, 189, 197n22; loopholes 186; opening of 39, 45–46; use of the term 39, 41
Blom-Hansen, J. 25
Bloomberg, Michael R. 13
Boeing 155–156
bonuses 68–69
Booz Allen Hamilton, Inc. (BAH) 158
Boris, E. 83
Branch, Ted 161
bribery 149, 151, 153, 159–161, 164–165, 197n19
Brown, T.L. 19, 24, 26, 27, 28, 32–33
Brudney, Jeffrey L. xviii, 75–95, 231
Buchanan, James 7
budget deficit 228
Bureau of Labor Statistics 89–90
business case analysis 103, 111

capitalism 7, 9, 13
Carboni, Julia L. xix, 137–147, 232
center-led procurement (CLP) 198n34
Centers for Medicare & Medicaid Services (CMS) 158–159
centralization 204
certifications 163, 187, 199n40, 215–217
change orders 122, 123, 186
Chartered Institute of Purchasing & Supply 62
Chicago 13, 22, 204
city services 26
Civil War 148, 149–151, 184–185

clearance of contracts 55
Clinton, Bill 11
closeout 57
Coast Guard 166–169
codes of ethics 162–163, 215, 220–223
Cohen, S. 21, 176, 195n9
Collins, Jim 194
color rating schema 51, 52
commonality 119
communication management 39, 40, 50, 53, 177, 178
competition 3, 28–30, 205, 217–218, 226, 234; audits 57; cooperative procurement 207; cost savings 27, 35; Federal Acquisition System 182; Friedman's theories 7; impact of non-needs-related policies 188; local preference 210, 212; make or buy decision 34; market characteristics 142; mixed provision 24; privatization 17; Reagan era 11
competitive advantage 50, 53–54, 210
Competitive Dialogue 104–105, 111, 112
complaints 125, 129
complete contracts 31, 32, 33
complexity 104, 119, 139, 144
compliance 24, 56, 80, 185; monitoring 116, 117, 125, 141; Non Compliance Points 109; nonprofit organizations 92
concessions 96, 98, 105
conflict resolution 132, 134, 232
conflicts of interest 157, 163, 165, 177, 215, 220, 221, 222
contract administration 38–39, 56–57, 110, 131, 133, 161–162, 178
contract design 138, 141
Contract Management Maturity Model (CMMM) 198n35
contract planning 38–49, 57
contract types 39, 42, 47, 120
contractor status reports 129
contractors: acceptance considerations 121–122; certifications 163; communication management 40, 50; contract management 140–142; ethics 169–170, 171–172; favored 44; identification of 39; "kick-off" meetings with 130–132; local preference 39, 40–41, 189, 209–212, 218, 233; misleading of 55, 158–159; monitoring and evaluation 56, 116, 229, 232; motivations 144; negotiations 54–55; performance-based contracting 64, 69–70, 231; performance management 39, 49; preferences for certain demographic categories 189; presentations 39, 45; principal-agent theory 80, 140–141, 226–227;

relationships with 178, 196n14; response to solicitation 49–50; selection of 12, 38–39, 50–54, 57, 144, 165–169, 172, 231; substitutable 142, 144; termination of contract 56–57
convenience termination provisions 56–57
conversion costs 21–24, 27, 34, 35
cooperative procurement 207–208, 218, 233
corporations 12, 190
corrective action plans 132–133, 134, 232
corruption xix, 148–172, 184, 190, 195n2, 232–233; award of contracts 159–161; Civil War 149–151; contract administration 161–162; planning 155–156; preparation of proposals 157; Progressive Era 9; proposal evaluation 44, 158, 165–169, 172; recommendations to alleviate 162–169; requests for proposal 156–157; Teapot Dome scandal 152–153; World War II 10
cost-benefit analysis 19, 27, 35, 99–100, 111, 230
cost plus a percentage of costs (CPPC) contracts 39, 47, 149, 151–152
cost reimbursement contracts 42, 47, 56, 158
costs 229, 234; contract management 138, 140; controllability 195n6; cooperative procurement 208; deliverables tracking system 128; evidence on savings 21–27; Federal Acquisition System 182; inspection 124; life-cycle 100, 101, 111, 112, 212–213; mixed scanning model 20; monitoring and evaluation 116, 123, 144; nonprofit organizations 92; procurement cards 206; proposal evaluation 43, 44; Public Private Partnerships 106, 108; revenue sharing approaches 70; risk analysis 101; share-in-savings approaches 69; strategic contracting 178, 191; technology 194; total 196n10; unallowable 39, 47; unit cost/unit price approaches 70, 71; value for money analysis 100–101; *see also* transaction costs
Coventry, G. 25, 26
cryptic proposal evaluation results 165–169, 172
Cunningham, Marc Andre 161
Curry, William Sims xviii, xix, 38–58, 148–174, 228, 230–231, 232–233
Cyprus 130

Darwin, Charles 4–5
data, variable 39, 46
Davison, Bill xviii–xix, 116–134, 229, 232
"Deal Drift" 103, 112
debriefing 39, 48–49
debt 108
decentralization 204

decision-making 19–20, 21, 23–24; incomplete information 30–33; make or buy decision 27, 31, 34–35, 92, 178, 230; political influences 33, 34
default termination provisions 56–57
Defense Acquisition Regulation Supplement (DFARS) 182
deficit spending 10
Delaware 83
delays 122, 123, 185, 186
demand risk 106, 107, 112
Denmark 25
Departmental grants 84–86
Design-Build-Finance-Operate-Maintain (DBFOM) 96, 98, 102, 104, 105
design specifications 63, 231
Dillion Rule 211
direct monitoring 127, 131
discount rate (DR) 102, 112
discrepancy records 129
Dochia, S. 107
documents 12, 39, 41, 42–43, 45; deliverables tracking system 128; missing 154; performance 129; preparation of 55
Donahue, J. 92, 227
Druyun, Darlene 155–156
due diligence 103
Dulles Greenway 106
duration of contract 31–32, 91–92

economic conditions 228
economic theories 5–8
education 25, 79; higher 214–215; nonprofit organizations 82, 84
Edwards, Steven A. 12
Edwards, Vernon J. 196n18
efficiency 35, 64, 139, 180, 230; competition 17; performance specifications 63; Public Private Partnerships 105; scholarship 137–138; strategic contracting 178
Eimicke, W. 21, 176, 195n9
Eisenhower, Dwight 10–11
enterprise goals 176–177, 185, 188, 189, 193–194, 197n25
environmental sustainability 212–213, 214, 218, 233–234
equal treatment 49–50, 53, 55
equity 13, 17, 18, 218, 230
ethics xix, 148–174, 195n1, 215–216, 218–219, 220–223, 232–233; *see also* corruption
European Union (EU) 104
ex post markets 138, 142–144, 145

Fageda, X. 20, 26, 27, 229
failure to complete contract 116, 123
Fall, Albert 152, 153
False Claims Act (FCA, 1863) 9
Federal Acquisition Regulation (FAR) 40, 41, 154, 181–183, 196n18; contract types 42, 47; CPPC contracts 47; opening of bids 45–46; performance-based contracting 61, 62, 67; proposal evaluation 43–44, 51, 58n3; responsibility and responsiveness 48; terminology 41, 42; terms and conditions 47; unallowable costs 47
Federal Bureau of Investigations (FBI) 148, 153, 160, 164, 172
Federal Funding Accountability and Transparency Act (FFATA, 2006) 88
federal government: acquisition/Acquisition 180; certifications 216; contract planning 39–49; corruption 148–149; Hurricane Katrina 195n2; increase in contracting 79; market creation 213; nonprofit organizations 84–88, 89; officials 176; performance-based contracting 61, 66, 67, 68; selection of contractor 51–52, 53; service efforts and accomplishments 65; subcontracts 88, 89; withholding requirement 189
Federal Procurement Data System (FPDS) 86
fee-for-service arrangements 81, 82, 83
Fernandez, S. 88, 89, 90, 91–92
final proposal revisions (FPRs) 54, 55
financial disclosures 163, 165
first-mover advantage 32
Florida 214, 216
follow-up monitoring 127
Francis, Leonard 161–162
fraud 153, 159–160, 165–166, 171, 184–185, 231; Civil War 151; Federal False Claims Act 9; penalties for 164; preparation of proposals 157; proposal evaluation 57; testing 123; *see also* corruption
free market economics 5–6
Friedman, Milton 3, 6–7, 10, 11, 14

Gaebler, Ted 7, 227
gain sharing 69, 70
GAO *see* Government Accountability Office
Garvin, M. 108
Georgia 117, 193, 210, 214
gifts 163, 170, 171–172, 220, 221, 222–223, 233
Gilbert, D.L. 180–181
Ginter, Donna T. xix, 203–225, 229, 233–234
Girth, A. 26, 27

Glenn Defense Marine 161, 162
goal alignment 80, 90, 93, 109, 141, 231
Gordon, Stephen B. xix, 175–202, 233
Gore, Al 8, 11
governance 79–80, 92, 137–147, 232; contractor characteristics 140–142, 144; market-based 227; market characteristics 142–144, 145; networked 175, 176; Public Private Partnerships 109–110, 112; scholarship 137–138; service characteristics 139–140, 144
Government Accountability Office (GAO) 24, 25, 26, 27; Army Corps of Engineers case 156–157; competitive advantage 53–54; fraud 153; Hurricane Katrina 195n2; misleading of contractors 55; monitoring and evaluation 116–117; performance-based contracting 66; protests 48, 51, 158, 159; selection of contractor 53
Government Accounting Standards Board (GASB) 65
government intervention 5, 6, 8, 11, 227–228
Government Performance & Results Act (GPRA, 1993) 65
grants 82, 84–86, 90, 106
gratuity limitations 163, 165, 170–172, 233
Great Depression 3, 5, 6, 8, 9–10, 227
Greve, C. 33
Gronbjerg, K. 78–79
group purchasing 207–208
guarantees 106

"halo effect" 77–78
Hansmann, Henry 77, 78
health services 82, 84, 142
Hefetz, A. 21, 24
higher education 214–215
highways 25
Hobbes, Thomas 4, 5, 7
Hodge, G. 229
holdback approaches 70
Hopkins, Harry 10
human capital 13, 14, 230
human services 81, 82, 84, 90, 175, 180, 226
hurdles 69
Hurricane Katrina 195n2, 196n15

in-house provision 17, 18, 20, 21–23, 24, 29, 34–35
incentives 68, 80, 137, 138, 141, 194; market characteristics 144, 145; performance-based contracting 67; Public Private Partnerships 109, 110
incomplete information 28, 29, 30–33, 35

incrementalism 19–20, 23, 30, 34
Indiana Turnpike 106
individual ethics 170–171
inertia 20
information: asymmetries 80, 81, 140; decision-making theories 19; incomplete 28, 29, 30–33, 35; strategic intelligence 187; variable information table 46
information technology (IT) 54, 178, 180, 187
infrastructure 96, 99, 103, 111, 178, 180, 181, 186, 188
innovation 90, 103, 213, 217, 218
inputs 63, 72, 120
inspections 123, 124
interest group politics 190
intergovernmental contracts 28
internal rate of return (IRR) 102
international and public affairs 82
inverse preference 211–212, 218, 233
invitations for bids (IFBs) 41, 45, 49, 97, 207
Iowa 117
Iraq 154

Jefferson, Thomas 4
Jennings, Al 152
Johnson, J. 26, 27
Johnson, Lyndon 6
joint service production 143

Kado, Karl 160
Kelman, Steven 185, 190, 195n3, 197n26
Key Performance Indicators (KPIs) 107, 108–109
Keynes, John Maynard 3, 6, 8, 9–10, 11
Khan, Kerry F. 159–160
"kick-off" meetings 118, 130–132, 134
Kilpatrick, Bernard 160–161
Kilpatrick, Kwame 160–161
Kirby, John F. 161
Krugman, Paul 8

laissez-faire approach 4
Lawther, Wendell C. xviii, 96–115, 231–232
legislation 9, 65, 88, 188–189, 191; see also regulation
Leland, Suzanne xvii–xviii, 17–37, 229, 230
Lerner, A. 20, 24
Levin, J. 24
libertarianism 8
life-cycle cost analysis (LCCA) 101, 111, 112, 212–213
Lincoln, Abraham 8, 9, 197n22
Litton Systems, Inc. 157, 172

local government xix–xx, 23, 33, 203–225, 233; budget deficit 228; competition requirements 205; competitive bidding 197n22; contract planning 39–49; cooperative procurement 207–208; ethics 215–216; goals and objectives 204–205; growth in contracting 229; higher education 214–215; history 204; Hurricane Katrina 195n2; local preference 209–212; mandated services 34; market creation 213–214; non-needs-related policies 188; nonprofit organizations 83–84, 91–92; penalties for ethics violations 164; performance-based contracting 61, 66, 67–71; procurement cards 206; procurement policies 184; selection of contractor 51–52, 53; service efforts and accomplishments 65; small dollar procurements 205; sustainability 212–213, 214; terminology 180; withholding requirement 189; "yellow pages test" 18; *see also* Model Procurement Code for State and Local Government

local preference 39, 40–41, 189, 209–212, 218, 233

Locke, John 3, 4, 12–13

logic models 119–120

long-term contracts 31–32, 34

loopholes 186

Loveless, Bruce 161

Malta, J.V. 180–181

management xix, 137–147, 175–202, 232, 233; contractor characteristics 140–142, 144; market characteristics 142–144, 145; non-needs-related policies 187–189; problems and challenges 177, 185–187; scholarship 137–138; service characteristics 139–140, 144; strategic contracting 176–178, 179, 190–193, 194

market-based governance 227

markets 138, 142–144, 145, 213–214, 218, 226, 228, 234

Martin, Lawrence L. xviii, 61–74, 231

Maryland 184, 197n19

Massachusetts 216

materiel 178, 179, 180, 181, 186, 188

Matthews, Darin 194n1

McCue, Clifford xviii–xix, 116–134, 196n9, 196n16, 229, 232

mental health services 81, 143

Metropolitan Planning Organizations (MPOs) 99

milestone approaches 71

military-industrial complex 10

Milward, H.B. 79–80, 143

Milward, R. 26, 27

Miranda, R. 20, 24, 26

misleading of contractors 55, 158–159

mixed provision 24–25

mixed scanning model 20, 21, 24, 29, 30, 33, 34

model contracts 39, 45, 47, 54–55

Model Procurement Code for State and Local Government (MPC) 46, 47, 58n1, 184, 197n20, 204; basic principles 58n2; Maryland 197n19; price thresholds 40; proposal evaluation 44, 58n3; solicitations 41; terminology 41, 42

monitoring and evaluation xviii–xix, 12, 24, 27, 30–31, 56, 116–134, 229, 232; acceptance 121–122, 133; contract management 138; deliverables tracking system 128; evaluation methods 118, 123–126, 133; identification of deliverables 118, 119–122, 133; identification of problems 118, 122–123, 133; importance of 234; internal plan 118, 132–133; "kick-off" or post award meeting 118, 130–132, 134; level of surveillance 118, 129; monitoring and evaluation plans 117–118, 122, 124, 125, 133, 232; nonprofit organizations 92; principal-agent problem 80, 141, 227; progress reports 128; Public Private Partnerships 110; record keeping 129, 133; type and level of 118, 126–127, 133

monitoring by exception 126

monopoly 27, 29, 30

Moore, M. 88

moral hazard 80, 140, 141

Morgan, George D. 149–151

Morris, Robert 8–9

MPC *see* Model Procurement Code for State and Local Government

"multiple accountabilities disorder" 90–91

Nagin, Ray 198n31

National Aeronautics and Space Administration (NASA) 182

National Association of Chief Administrators (NASCO) 195n1, 197n20

National Association of Educational Procurement (NAEP) 163, 214

National Association of State Purchasing Officials (NASPO) 61–62, 163, 195n1, 197n20, 207, 212, 214, 216

National Audit Office 111

National Contract Management Association (NCMA) 163, 199n40

National Institute of Governmental Purchasing (NIGP) 122, 192, 197n20, 207; code of ethics

163, 215, 221; performance-based contracting 62, 63, 66; training 216
National Performance Review 209
natural selection 5
negotiations 54–55, 56, 105, 112; misleading 158–159; Public Private Partnerships 104, 232
network-based services 26, 27
Nevada 211–212
New Public Management (NPM) 7–8, 17, 32, 227, 230
New York City 13, 83
Newton, Isaac 4
NJ TRANSIT 222–223
non-distribution constraint 76, 77–78, 88
non-financial benefits (NFBs) 100
non-needs-related policies 187–189, 198n31
noncompliance 109, 117, 138
nonprofit organizations xviii, 28, 75–95, 175, 231; benefits of contracting with 88–90; characteristics of 75–77; drawbacks of contracting with 90–91; funding 82–88; postwar period 11; principal-agent problem 226; research 91–92; theoretical background 77–78; third-party government 78–80
North Carolina 210
numeric weighting 52, 166–169
Nye, J.S. Jr. 227

Obama, Barack 11, 12, 189, 199n40, 227–228
objective criteria 52–53
obligations 131
observation records 129
Office of Federal Procurement Policy (OFPP) 66
Office of Management and Budget (OMB) 79
offices of inspector generals (OIGs) 153–154
officials 196n9, 197n25, 198n29, 234; competencies 199n40; discretion 186, 195n3, 197n26; political environment 189; problems and challenges 185–187; procurement as a profession 216–217, 219; Public Private Partnerships 111–112; stereotyping of 176; strategic contracting 191–193, 233; top contracting officers 198n30, 199n41; transaction processors 196n12; *see also* management
Oklahoma 204
Operations and Maintenance (O&M) period 109–111
opportunism 28, 29, 31, 33, 34, 80; monitoring 141; nonprofit organizations 81, 91; relational contracts 140
Osborne, David 7, 227

outcomes: monitoring and evaluation 120, 121, 124–125, 126; performance-based contracting 63–64, 65, 69, 70–71, 72; review clauses 118
outputs: monitoring and evaluation 120, 121, 124, 126; performance-based contracting 63–64, 65, 69, 70–71, 72; review clauses 118

P3s *see* Public Private Partnerships
Pacific Telegraph Act (1860) 9
Page, Harry Robert 189
page limits 39, 45
Parker, M. 107
partial contracting 20, 29, 30
path-dependency 20, 34
payments: audits 57; contract administration 56; deliverables tracking system 128; "kick-off" meetings 131; performance-based contracting 62; Public Private Partnerships 105, 107–108, 112, 232
penalties 108, 109, 110, 164, 169, 170, 171
performance-based contracting (PBC) xviii, 61–74, 231; accountability and performance measurement 64–65; advantages of 64; approaches to 66–71; assessing the performance of 71–72; definitions of 61–62; design specifications 63; performance specifications 63–64; service efforts and accomplishments 65; use of 66
performance management 39, 49, 139–140, 232
performance measurement 56, 62, 64–65, 68, 69, 72; identification of deliverables 121; nonprofit organizations 92; Public Private Partnerships 105, 107, 108–109, 110, 111, 112
performance requirements 67, 68, 70, 105, 109, 131
performance specifications 63–64, 231
personality conflicts 123
Peters, Tom 7
Philadelphia 204
"piggybacking" 207
planning 38–49, 57, 178, 185, 231; corruption 155–156; monitoring and evaluation plans 117–118, 122, 124, 125, 133, 232; Public Private Partnerships 98, 99–103; strategic 192
political philosophy 3, 4–5, 234
politics 25, 189–190, 197n24, 203, 219; contracting out decision 33, 34, 35; local preference 209–212; strategic contracting 176
position 191
Potoski, M. 19, 24
preference policies 39, 40–41, 189, 209–212, 218, 233

Prentice, Christopher R. xviii, 75–95, 231
preparation of contract documents 55
presentations 39, 45, 170
price: cooperative procurement 208; local preference 210; performance-based contracting 61–62; price thresholds 40, 206, 218; unit cost/ unit price approaches 70, 71
Prier, Eric 196n16
principal-agent theory 80–81, 140–141, 226–227
prisons 12, 13–14, 25, 26
private sector 7, 13, 79, 203, 217–218; Public Private Partnerships xviii, 25, 96–115; Reagan era 11, 227
privatization 12, 14–15, 22–23, 79; efficiency 64; managers 195n9; New Public Management 17; Reagan era 11; water 229
processes 192, 194
procurement cards 206, 218, 233
program logic models 119–120
progress reports 128
Progressive Era 9
proposals: evaluation of 39, 43–45, 50–54, 57, 58n3, 158, 165–169, 172, 232–233; format of 39, 45; opening of 39, 45–46; use of the term 39, 41; *see also* requests for proposal
protests 39, 41, 48–49, 51, 198n28; ethics 156, 159; opportunity to file 56; selection of contractor 53
Provan, K. 79–80, 143
public choice theory 7
public entrepreneurship 7
public goods 78, 81, 90, 92
public interest 88, 96, 103, 106–107, 111–112, 234
public involvement 111
Public Private Partnerships (P3s) xviii, 25, 96–115, 231–232; definition of 97; planning 98, 99–103; post-contract award relationships 99, 109–111; pre-contract award steps 99, 103–109; role of procurement official 111–112; types of 97–98
public transit 22, 24, 26, 27, 35n2
punctuated equilibrium 19–20

quality 13–14, 18, 229, 230, 234; citizen sensitivity to 24; competition 17; compromises on 205; impact of non-needs-related policies 188; nonprofit organizations 92; performance-based contracting 62, 63–64, 67, 68, 69, 72; poor performance 123; review clauses 118; tacit knowledge 21; "three-failures theory" 77, 78
quality assurance (QA) plans 67, 68
qui tam lawsuits 169, 170

Rand, Ayn 8
random monitoring 127
rational-comprehensive model 19, 20, 23–24, 30
Reagan, Ronald 3, 5, 6–7, 11, 14, 83, 227, 228
rebidding 32
recycled products 214
refuse collection 26, 27, 97, 139, 229
regulation 5, 6, 181–185, 187, 195n3; *see also* legislation; Model Procurement Code for State and Local Government
Reinventing Government movement 7, 227
relational contracting 32, 81, 138, 139–140, 144
reliability 17, 18
Rendon, Rene 175, 198n35, 199n39
repeatability 119
reporting 65, 109, 128, 131
requests for proposal (RFPs) 12, 41, 49, 50, 97; cooperative procurement 207; corruption 156–157; opening of 45–46; Public Private Partnerships 104; testing requirements 123
requests for quotes (RFQs) 49
responsibility 39, 48
responsiveness 39, 48, 92, 197n22
revenue sharing approaches 70
review clauses 118
review of contracts 55
Richart, Mike 191–193
rights 9, 131
risk 97, 105, 139, 204–205; availability risk 108; monitoring and evaluation 117, 119; risk analysis 101–102, 111, 112; sharing demand risk 106, 107, 112; strategic contracting 178; systemic 138, 142, 143
Roosevelt, Franklin Delano 3, 5, 6, 9–10, 14
Roosevelt, Theodore 9
rules 3, 116, 185, 217
Rutherford, Jon 160

Salamon, L. 76–77, 79
salaries 187
sampling 126, 129
Savas, E.S. 11
savings 21–27, 219; cooperative procurement 207–208; make or buy decision 34–35; revenue sharing approaches 70; share-in-savings approaches 69; sustainable 190; value for money analysis 101
Schapper, P.R. 180–181
scheduled monitoring 127
science 10, 12
Sclar, E. 21, 28

scope of contract 130
Sea to Sky Highway 100
Sears, Michael 155–156
seat belts 213
Sebastian, R.J. 122
SeKON 159
selection of contractor 12, 38–39, 50–54, 57, 144, 165–169, 231
self-governance 76
self-interest 5–6, 7, 8, 80, 81, 140, 185
self-reporting 131
service efforts and accomplishments (SEA) 65
services 139–140, 144, 178, 180, 181, 186, 188
share-in-savings approaches 69
Shick, Robert A. xvii–xx, 12, 226–235
Signature Consulting Group 158–159
simple services 139, 144
Sinclair, Harry F. 152–153
skills 192–193, 216, 234
Skurski, Roger 13
small businesses 205, 208
small dollar procurements 205
"smart buyers" 18, 19
SMART principles 121
Smirnova, Olga Victorovna xvii–xviii, 17–37, 229, 230
Smith, Adam 3, 5–6
Smith, Steven S. 78–79, 83
Snider, K.F. 175
Soave, Tony 160
social capital networks 89
social contract 4
Social Darwinism 4–5
social services 25, 27, 79, 81; cost savings 26; federal expenditure on 83; nonprofit organizations 83, 90; performance-based contracting 61
socioeconomic policies 57, 187–188, 189, 209, 210; see also non-needs-related policies
sole source contracts 39, 40, 57
Solers, Inc. 158
solicitations 39, 41, 48; certifications 163; documents 45; ethics rules 165; issuance of 49–50; proposal evaluation criteria 43; protests 48–49
South Carolina 210
sovereign immunity 9
stakeholder involvement 111, 112
standards: employment 194; ethical 169, 216; performance-based contracting 62, 67, 68; Public Private Partnerships 97, 98, 105, 108, 109

state governments xix–xx, 203–225, 233; budget deficit 228; competition requirements 205; competitive bidding 197n22; contract planning 39–49; cooperative procurement 207–208; ethics 215–216; goals and objectives 204–205; growth in contracting 229; higher education 214–215; history 204; Hurricane Katrina 195n2; local preference 209–212; market creation 213–214; non-needs-related policies 188; nonprofit organizations 83–84; penalties for ethics violations 164; performance-based contracting 61, 66, 67–71; procurement cards 206; procurement codes or acts 184; selection of contractor 51–52, 53; service efforts and accomplishments 65; small dollar procurements 205; sustainability 212–213, 214; terminology 180; withholding requirement 189; see also Model Procurement Code for State and Local Government
statements of work (SOWs) 39, 45, 62, 123
stewardship theory 141
strategic contracting 176–178, 179, 190–193, 194, 217–218, 233
subcontracts 88, 89, 123
subjective criteria 52–53, 166–168
surveys 126, 129
sustainability 212–213, 214, 218, 233–234
systems 178, 179–180, 181, 186, 188

Tadelis, S. 24
Talley, W. 26
Tantus Technologies, Inc. 159
tax-exemptions 76, 88
Tax Increase Prevention and Reconciliation Act (2005) 188–189
Teapot Dome scandal 148, 152–153
technology 178, 193, 194, 213
Tennessee Valley Authority (TVA) 11
termination of contract 56–57
terminology 39, 41, 42–43, 180
terms and conditions 39, 47–48, 117, 131
testing 123–126
Texas 216
third-party government 78–80
"three-failures theory" 77, 78
time overruns 116
Tocqueville, Alexis de 75–76
trade associations 190
training 192, 199n42, 233; ethics 164–165, 171–172; local and state governments 216, 217; performance-based contracting 66

transaction costs 18, 24, 27, 34, 35, 139; complete contracts 33; contract management 138, 140; decision-making 19; procurement cards 206, 218
transparency 13, 180–181, 193, 217, 218, 230; competition requirements 205; Federal Funding Accountability and Transparency Act 88; proposal evaluation criteria 44; Public Private Partnerships 108, 109
Truman, Harry S. 10
trust 32, 33, 35, 215, 218; nonprofit organizations 91, 92; relational contracting 81, 139, 140
Tucker Act (1855) 9

unallowable costs 39, 47
uncertainty 32, 34–35, 91, 139, 140
unions 33, 177, 190
unit cost/unit price approaches 70, 71
United Kingdom 62, 111
Universal Public Procurement Certification Council (UPPCC) 199n40, 215, 220
unsatisfactory performance reports 129
U.S. Air Force 155–156
U.S. Army Corps of Engineers 50, 156–157, 159–160
U.S. Navy 149, 150–151, 161–162
user fees 105, 106–107, 112

"value-add" 206
value for money (VfM) analysis 100–101, 102, 103, 111, 112
values 12, 13–14, 15, 28, 227, 230, 234
Van Slyke, D. 19, 79
variable data 39, 46
Veterans Administration (VA) 14

Virginia 210–211, 214, 216
"Vision Map" 192
voluntarism 76–77, 89–90

wages 12, 13
Walker, Scott 227
Wallace, Henry 10
Warner, M. 21, 24, 25, 26, 27, 229
Washington, George 8
waste services 26, 139, 229; *see also* refuse collection
water services 26, 229
Waterman, Robert 7
websites 39, 40, 50, 53
Weikart, Lynne A. xvii, 3–16, 228, 230
Weisbrod, Burton 78
"Welfare State" 79
welfare systems 12
whistleblowers 9, 169
Williamson, O. 31
Witesman, E. 88, 89, 90, 91–92
withholding requirement 189
W.K. Kellogg Foundation 119
work breakdown structure (WBS) 120–121
workers 12, 13, 91, 177, 194, 199n41
working lunches 169
wrong products 123

"yellow pages test" 18, 226

Zeckhauser, R. 92
zero-tolerance approach 163, 165, 170–171, 172, 233
Zullo, R. 24–25, 26, 27